THE RENEWAL OF CHURCH
The Panel Reports
W. B. BLAKEMORE, General Editor

The Panel of Scholars Reports

VOLUME I

The Reformation of Tradition

R. E. OSBORN, Editor

VOLUME II

The Reconstruction of Theology

R. G. WILBURN, Editor

VOLUME III

The Revival of the Churches

W. B. BLAKEMORE, Editor

Volume II

THE RECONSTRUCTION OF THEOLOGY

THE

Reconstruction of Theology

Edited by

Ralph G. Wilburn

The Renewal of Church
The Panel Reports
W. B. Blakemore, Editor

THE BETHANY PRESS

St. Louis, Missouri

1963

Typography and design by David Homeier

Preface

THE main concern of this volume is the theological reconstruction actually taking place today, in relation to the great themes of the Christian faith. While most of the material in this volume is of significance for the ecumenical movement of Christian thought, one of the basic aims of the volume is to portray the theological reconstruction taking place among representative figures of the Christian Churches (Disciples of Christ).

The volume thus constitutes a serious attempt to analyze and clarify the fundamental theological lines along which contemporary Christian thought is moving. While there is nothing "official" in the denominational sense about the positions reflected in this volume, the chapters represent critical, scholarly work, the authority of which rests upon the quality and content of the work itself.

It should be borne in mind, however, that the authors of the various chapters are outstanding scholars in their respective fields. Their thought reflected in this book represents the distillation of years of careful thought and study. For this reason the book possesses a theological vigor and maturity which, it is hoped, will be stimulating and rewarding to the reader. For these reasons, these authors were chosen to make the contributions to this volume.

Although each author speaks for himself, it will be fairly clear to the reader that there is a general consensus which characterizes the volume as a whole. This is due partly to the fact that the authors have all shared fully in the theological renaissance of our day, and partly to the stimulating experience which these men had in sharing in the common task of the Panel over a period of some five years.

The editor wishes to take this means of expressing appreciation of the fine cooperation of all the authors, which has made the volume possible. Whatever value the book possesses is due to the many hours of careful thought and research so generously given by the authors.

The Editor
R. G. WILBURN

PANEL OF SCHOLARS' MEMBERSHIP
July 1956 to March 1962

CHAIRMEN

Howard E. Short: June 1956 to September 1958

W. B. Blakemore: October 1958 to March 1962

MEMBERS

WILLIAM R. BAIRD: November 1959 to March 1962
Professor of New Testament
The College of the Bible
Lexington, Kentucky

PAUL HUNTER BECKELHYMER: January 1957 to March 1962
Minister of Hiram Christian Church
Hiram, Ohio

W. B. BLAKEMORE: July 1956 to March 1962
Dean of Disciples Divinity House and
Associate Dean of Rockefeller Memorial Chapel
University of Chicago
Chicago, Illinois

JAMES A. CLAGUE: August 1956 to March 1962
Associate Professor of Systematic Theology
Christian Theological Seminary
Indianapolis, Indiana

STEPHEN J. ENGLAND: July 1956 to March 1962
Dean of The Graduate Seminary
Phillips University
Enid, Oklahoma

FRANK N. GARDNER: July 1956 to March 1962
Professor of Christian Thought
Drake University
Des Moines, Iowa

9

VIRGIL V. HINDS: October 1956 to March 1962
Associate Professor of Religion
Lynchburg College
Lynchburg, Virginia

J. PHILLIP HYATT: July 1956 to March 1962
Professor of Old Testament of the Divinity School and Chairman of the Department of Religion of the Graduate School
Vanderbilt University
Nashville, Tennessee

CLARENCE E. LEMMON: July 1956 to March 1962
Minister of First Christian Church
Columbia, Missouri

D. RAY LINDLEY: July 1956 to March 1962
President of Texas Christian University
Fort Worth, Texas

RONALD E. OSBORN: July 1956 to March 1962
Dean and Professor of Church History
Christian Theological Seminary
Indianapolis, Indiana

EUGENE H. PETERS: December 1959 to March 1962
Associate Professor of Theology
The Graduate Seminary
Phillips University
Enid, Oklahoma

GLENN C. ROUTT: July 1956 to March 1962
Associate Professor of Theology
Brite College of the Bible
Texas Christian University
Fort Worth, Texas

HOWARD E. SHORT: June 1956 to September 1958
Professor of Church History
The College of the Bible
Lexington, Kentucky (until September 1958)
Editor of *The Christian*

10

DWIGHT E. STEVENSON: June 1956 to October 1959
Professor of Homiletics
The College of the Bible
Lexington, Kentucky

WILLIAM G. WEST: July 1956 to March 1962
Minister of First Christian Church
Chattanooga, Tennessee

RALPH G. WILBURN: July 1956 to March 1962
Dean and Professor of Historical Theology
The College of the Bible
Lexington, Kentucky

THE EDITORIAL AND PUBLICATION COMMITTEE

W. B. Blakemore, Chairman, General Editor and Editor of
Volume III

R. E. Osborn, Editor of Volume I

R. G. Wilburn, Editor of Volume II

W. M. Wickizer for the sponsoring agencies

Contents

13

PART THREE

WORD AND SACRAMENTS

CONCLUSION

14

INTRODUCTION

❊ 1 ❊

The Place of Theology
in the Church

RALPH G. WILBURN

THIS introductory chapter is divided into two parts. Part
one deals with the decline and revival of theological concern
in the modern period of Western culture. Part two is concerned
with theology's role in the life of the church today. The assumption on which we proceed is that an effective exercise of theological responsibility presupposes an understanding of the present
situation of church and culture in historic perspective.

I

In American Christianity especially, there has been a long-
standing prejudice against theology. Only in recent years has
the American church begun to outgrow this prejudice.

Theology's Decline and the Popular
Prejudice Against It

One can understand the significance of this widespread decline of, and prejudice against, theology only if he perceives
the ecclesiastical and cultural influences which have brought
about both.

Spiritual inertia is such a ubiquitous and dominant factor in
religion that there has never been a time when the church was
not threatened by the lag of traditionalism. Since religion has

17

to do with man's ultimate concern, its modes of action and its verbal and liturgical symbols get closely bound to religious emotion. Once faith finds satisfying expression in a particular mode of action or belief, it is no easy matter for theology to separate the two and restructure the life of religion into patterns which are more meaningful and valid in relation to a changed situation in culture.

What has just been said points up the greatness and burden, the power and danger, inherent in religious symbolism. The power is the ability of these symbols to point to and inspire all-out commitment to that reality which is of supreme importance for human living. The danger is that religious symbols tend to become static, indeed often sacrosanct, breeding traditionalism with its complacent, but illusory, feeling of security—an idolatrous substitute for the certitude of faith.

Because of the false sense of security which traditionalism engenders, many church members have little or no desire to become theological in their religious thinking. They do not even want to face the question as to why the Word of God should be approached in any way other than with the simplest, nontheological faith. The peace that by-passes understanding leads them to feel that the simple gospel "was good enough for Paul and Silas and it's good enough for me."

This uncritical attitude of simple pietism is one of the major sources of the prejudice against theology. To more thoughtful minds it seems strange that so many church members stubbornly maintain such uncritical dogmatism. They maintain it in spite of the fact that the so-called "simple gospel" is not quite so simple as some conceive it to be. They maintain it despite the fact that historical facts puncture many of their pietistic balloons. Indeed, their emotional opposition to one who points this out would seem to indicate that they are not holding their religious beliefs with complete intellectual integrity.

The sources of prejudice against theology, however, are not to be found exclusively within the church. The church's mind is determined by its general cultural climate, as well as by the gospel. Other sources of the prejudice against theology lie in the cultural developments of the modern era.

First, in centuries past the church labored under the dominance of a bad kind of theology. For example, Albert the Great[1] felt that theology should deal with such questions as: Do the lost sin in hell? Is a smokey atmosphere a congenial element for demons? Can a number of angels be in the same place at the same time? Albert decided they couldn't, not because of the spatial inconvenience, but because of the confusion of activity which would result.

If *this* is what theology is, modern man wants no part of it. The empirical orientation in the modern quest for truth (since Francis Bacon and Immanuel Kant) eliminated the speculative type of theology as excess baggage in the quest for truth.

Second, the rationalism of the Enlightenment proved to be another powerful force in shaping the modern mind. Rationalism demanded that man assume personal responsibility for his own beliefs, religious and otherwise. It contended that a belief cannot be *truth for me* unless I perceive it to be true, and that a moral act can be *moral for me* only if I perceive it to be right.

This demand of rationalism for intellectual and moral integrity won a sweeping victory in the eighteenth century over the stodgy, lifeless orthodoxy that had developed not only in Catholicism but also in seventeenth-century Protestantism. The theology of the church became so lifeless that one could hear the rattling of the dry bones. All was fixed and frozen into a set of infallible doctrines "once for all delivered unto the saints." Little wonder that the theology of seventeenth-century Protestantism toppled before the powerful rational demand for integrity, and subsequently before the nineteenth-century discovery of historical relativism, which gave the lie to all forms of ecclesiastical authoritarianism.

Third, the fabulous success of the scientific enterprise cap-

19

tured the imagination of modern man and claimed a large amount of his intellectual energy. When Francis Bacon and his contemporaries inaugurated the new empirical philosophy, they set in motion a truth-seeking concern for *this* world which soon made the *otherworldly* concern of traditional theology and philosophy appear to be "old hat." The growth of science, with its visible tangible human benefits, generated a new "this-worldly" dream, which for the majority of modern men outmoded and replaced the "otherworldly" dream of classic philosophy and theology.

The shift in outlook from theology and/or religious metaphysics to naturalistic humanism came gradually, as the implications of empiricism slowly came to light. One can trace the uneven development of these implications in the writings of such influential figures as David Hume, Auguste Comte, John Stuart Mill, T. H. Huxley, Herbert Spencer, Fredrich Harrison, and A. Eustace Haydon.

During the gradual shift from theology to humanism, varying positions were adopted relative to the value of holding religious beliefs in the traditional sense. David Hume, "that prince of agnostics,"[2] was highly skeptical toward the value of any belief in "God." This skepticism was the result of Hume's effort to test this religious belief in the light of empirical evidence. He carefully examined the evidence only to conclude that it is "totally precarious and unsatisfactory" to warrant holding belief in God.[3]

John Stuart Mill reached a similar agnostic suspension of judgment, though he veered a bit to the right of Hume. The empirical evidence being inconclusive,[4] Mill felt that the reality of God remains an open possibility. It was his conviction that "this small and confined" human life "stands greatly in need of any wider range and greater height of aspiration" which religious imagination can generate "without running counter to the evidence of fact."[5] Theology should therefore be retained, for while it may not be "intellectually sustainable," it is nevertheless "morally useful."[6]

T. H. Huxley stands in the same empirical tradition, though he veered to the left of Hume. Huxley believed that one should be consistent in epistemological method. As he saw it, the ruling principle of empirical philosophy is that conclusions should be accepted *only when supported by adequate empirical evidence.* He repudiated as "immoral" the contrary doctrine "that there are propositions which men ought to believe, without logically satisfactory evidence."[7] Huxley declared that "the foundation of morality is to have done, once and for all, with lying; to give up pretending to believe that for which there is no evidence, and repeating unintelligible propositions about things beyond the possibility of knowledge."[8]

Some contemporary philosophers of the school of the Linguistic Analysts carry forward Huxley's agnosticism in an even more thoroughgoing way by arguing that if the term "God" is used as a metaphysical term, "then it cannot be probable that a god exists."[9] For to say that "God exists" is to make a metaphysical utterance, and by the ruling presuppositions of these philosophers, such an utterance can have no "literal significance" and must therefore be regarded as "nonsense."[10] The ruling assumption of this school is that "tautologies and empirical hypotheses form the entire class of significant propositions."[11] Hence all "metaphysical assertions are nonsensical."[12] All that remains of validity in man's knowledge is either the tautological propositions of formal logic or empirical hypotheses based on observation of sense data.

For a time it seemed that the new science of psychology might come to the rescue of theology in its struggle to survive in the battle with scientific empiricism. When William James came to the problem of religious beliefs, for example, he argued that *pragmatic* empiricism demands that one transcend the limits of immediate evidence. James held that one simply cannot avoid choosing to believe or disbelieve in God. Each man is, to be sure, free to choose, but he is not free to choose or not to choose: he must choose. One *must* make up his mind on such a crucial

21

issue as this. And by the "will to believe" one establishes his faith.

James proceeded to develop the conviction that although one cannot directly verify a religious hypothesis, psychological analysis can describe the difference which belief in God makes in the life of the believer. Theology is thus pragmatically justified, for it "exerts an influence, raises our centre of personal energy, and produces regenerative effects unattainable in other ways."[13]

The full abandonment of theology and metaphysics in America came with John Dewey, in whose thought pragmatism reached its climax. Dewey challenged James's argument that religious beliefs of the traditional variety are the most effective integrators in personality development. As James Ward Smith puts it, Dewey admitted that "metaphysical thinking *does* make a difference in human life—for the worse!"[14]

It was Dewey's belief that the traditional metaphysics of Pure Being was a "purely compensatory"[15] escape from the task of dealing creatively with the exciting possibilities inherent in the *real* world of change. The *ideal* world of classic philosophy is "a haven in which man finds rest from the storms of life"[16] and therefore diverts attention from the further application of scientific method to the practical problems of life. Such philosophical knowledge is tantamount to "a morally irresponsible estheticism."[17]

Dewey thus felt that classic philosophy with its "sterile metaphysics and sterile epistemology"[18] was just fifteen hundred years of intellectual lockjaw, and that by recovering from this sickness and adopting the "practical" for the "contemplative"[19] we can bring intelligence to bear upon "the observation and understanding of concrete social events and forces, can form ideals . . . which shall not be either illusions or mere emotional compensations."[20]

In varying degrees, the great peers of the Social Gospel shared in this negative orientation toward theology and metaphysics. A. Eustace Haydon bemoaned the fact that in most traditional religions the moral element "became a secondary thing when the gaze was on . . . the other world."[21] Though Shailer Mathews believed in God, he constantly warned his students not to wander off into the barren wastelands of metaphysics. The metaphysical aspects of Christianity were thus brushed aside; only the ethics of Jesus were retained. To the Social Gospelers, Jesus was not a metaphysician, but a moral, social reformer. It was their belief that the simple moral teaching of Jesus was later corrupted and obscured by the influence of Hellenistic philosophy with its passion for metaphysical system building.

It was thus the spirit of pragmatic empiricism that led the exponents of old liberalism to adopt a negative attitude toward theology and to set about to detheologize religion. The sneer of old liberalism toward "theology" is still not unseen in some quarters even today.

This was the lay of the land, so to speak, in the twenties of our century. Lord Bacon's "New Atlantis" was a much more exciting prospect than Saint John's "New Jerusalem." The hope of heavenly bliss seemed to be a blockage in the path to the good community, rather than a valid comfort for distraught souls. Hence the scientific mind regarded theology as bad, compensatory idealism. It resolved to make *this* world the good community which man has it in his own power to make it—if only he will get rid of his otherworldly opiates and dreams, which cut the nerve of moral effort.

Religious humanism carried through on the modern rejection of theology in a thorough way, yet it retained theology's idealistic fervor by giving a new definition to the term "religion." Eliminating reference to God, religion was now defined as "devotion to human values."[22] As Huxley put it, true religion is "simply the reverence and love for the ethical ideal, and the desire to realize that ideal in life."[23]

The Contemporary Theological Reawakening

To complete the story of what has happened in our modern period relative to theology, however, calls for an additional

23

word. After the initial excitement of the scientific enterprise and after scientism had its little day, an increasing number of sober minds began to feel that perhaps scientific empiricism abandoned too much when it tossed overboard the whole bagatelle of theology. The ship of science did not cruise as smoothly as was anticipated. And ethics cut free from its theological roots seemed to wither and die. Perhaps, many said, we have committed the fatal error of throwing out the baby with the bath.

In America, beginning in the midthirties, an increasing number of men began to feel the spiritual bankruptcy of humanistic liberalism—men like Rheinhold Niebuhr, H. Richard Niebuhr, Wilhelm Pauck, Paul Tillich, and Henry Nelson Wieman. In Europe, Karl Barth and Emil Brunner and others developed the conviction that to abandon theology is tantamount to abandoning the abiding essence of the Christian faith. The result of the critical work of these reformers has been called "a reawaken-of the metaphysical and theological tone in religion."[24]

A century earlier, Frederick Schleiermacher in Germany adjusted theology to the new spirit and method of science, thereby launching a new empirical method in theology. Yet he perceived that there is a unique place for theology, alongside the other sciences, for there is an ultimate dimension of experience with which theology alone can deal.

Whatever may be the just criticisms of the details of Schleiermacher's method,[25] must it not be conceded that in principle he was proceeding in a sound manner? If the fact that once upon a time alchemy was scientifically respectable does not justify the perpetuation of prejudice against the science of chemistry, perhaps modern man is not justified in continuing to nurture his prejudices against theology, merely because once upon a time a bad kind of theology was in vogue. What was called for was the formation of a more adequate and valid method rather than a hasty debunking of the entire theological enterprise.

A few decades prior to the theological reawakening in America, Peter Taylor Forsyth in Great Britain sensed the subjectivistic weakness in the empirical tradition. "Nothing produces more uncertainty," he wrote, "than a constant reference to subjective experience."[26] Forsyth attempted to break the tyranny of empiricism by recovering the idea of *evangelical* experience. He retained the empirical method in theology but distinguished between the human *seat* and the divine *source* of authority, between the "experience" and "the experienced." He insisted that in theology the primary emphasis must fall on "the experienced." Experience is certainly the only valid medium through which any revelation can be received. To this extent, Schleiermacher and the empiricists were correct. But the cause of theology is doomed if it permits this *experiential medium* to swallow up the *source* of revelation and if it proceeds thus to derive the *content* of faith from the medium instead of its evangelical source.

We called attention above to some of the cultural forces which caused theology to fall into disrepute in the modern period. Let us now note some of the historical forces which have contributed to the recent theological reawakening.

First, there is the modern crisis in Western social philosophy. The modern revolutionary faith in reason as an eternal principle of truth, humanity, and justice is inscribed in the cornerstone of American democracy. Its essence lay in its appeal to the mind of the common man, created in the image of God. It believed that liberating reason in every man would establish a universal humanity, that is, a harmony between the individual and society.

It is doubtless true that the founders of democracy failed to distinguish adequately between reason *as an eternal principle of justice and truth,* and reason *as it really is under the conditions of man's finitude and sinfulness.* Nevertheless, their faith in man's universal humanity represents a monumental achievement in history. It guided the social development in all areas: religious, philosophical, educational, economic, and political.

When, however, the revolutionary spirit of this faith in reason, which gave birth to modern democracy, was in time dropped aside, the character of the concern for reason underwent a change. As Paul Tillich reminds us,[27] modern man tended to lose sight of reason as a principle of truth and justice, and technical reason, reason as a tool in the service of technological scientific development, became predominant. This shift to scientific technology is perhaps the most significant development in Western social philosophy of the nineteenth century.

We are today witnessing both the good and evil fruit of this shift in concern to technology. The Frankenstein monster which it has produced provides us with a fabulous control over nature, eloquently confirming Francis Bacon's slogan that "knowledge is power." Yet it has resulted in a precarious situation, for the modern man has become less and less able to control this Frankenstein monster. As W. H. Pickering of the California Institute of Technology puts it,

This is the prospect we face: the decision to destroy an enemy nation, and by inference our own, will be made by a radar set, a telephone circuit, an electronic computer. It will be arrived at without the aid of human intelligence. If a human observer cries: "Stop, let me check the calculations," he is already too late, his launching site is destroyed and the war is lost.[28]

The tragic thing thus about our present situation is that human reason has lost control over human existence. Man has given himself so completely to the scientific task of harnessing the powers of nature, and has been so little concerned with the weightier matters of "wisdom and truth and the greatest improvement of the soul" (to quote Socrates)[29] that theologically speaking he is stumbling and blundering his way toward self-destruction.

Our fantastic knowledge of the atom and of the potential of this knowledge for evil is, however, steadily deepening man's concern to learn the truth about himself. The problem of man, the ultimate meaning of *human* existence, and the desperate need for an adequate social philosophy have generated a new theological mood today.

A second cause of the general theological reawakening in our day is a corollary of the first. It lies in the staggering social tragedies of the twentieth century. The vast amount of suffering, which is partly the result of the major wars of our century, partly the product of man's demonic will to power, and partly the outcome of poverty, ignorance, and disease, has stabbed us wide awake to the tragical, precarious character of human existence. It has also jarred and challenged the liberal faith in the goodness of man and demanded that we face up to the insidious evil of the human heart.

Since World War I, the widespread disillusionment and depression which followed, the holocaust of World War II, and the continuation of its inhumanity and tyranny by communism, it is hardly possible any longer to cling to the late nineteenth- and early twentieth-century faith in the progressive perfectibility of man and society. The problem for countless millions today is how to understand and live with persistent human selfishness and barbarity. What kind of faith is required to enable one to live victoriously as a victim of such evil forces, perhaps a victim until the day of his death? What does Christian hope mean in this tragic situation?

A third influence which has augmented the contemporary quest for the theological dimension of man's existence lies in the modern debunking of man and the decline of humanism. Ever since Sigmund Freud disclosed the emotional, or subrational, roots of human behavior, it has been a popular literary pastime to debunk the rationality of man.

Loss of faith in man's humanity has, of course, led some to a philosophy of pessimism. Anatole France holds that man is but a speck of dust on a ball of mud. Bertrand Russell speaks of this petty planet on which our bodies impotently crawl. Modern cosmic-centric philosophy tends toward the dissolution of man's faith in any ultimate significance of human life.

In this inconceivably vast universe of stars and galaxies, to some minds, human life seems to be a rather sordid and disgraceful episode upon one of the minor planets.

There is evidence on every hand that the Reniassance faith in man has been shaken to its foundations. The blithe confidence in man's ability to determine his own destiny has been seriously called into question. Human nature is more recalcitrant than had been believed. We cannot seem to educate man out of his idolatrous self-centeredness. The grand dream of scientific humanism was that we *could* thus educate man, and that basically all that was needed was just more education. This was the optimistic dream of Francis Bacon and René Descartes. It was the belief that every advance of knowledge *will bring* a corresponding advance in moral and social well-being. Despite the fact that there were protesting voices like Rousseau, Schopenhauer, and Santayana, which challenged the validity of this optimistic social hope, it continued to dominate the Western mind right down to our century. The stark naked truth, however, is that a biological, sociological, psychological understanding of human life has *not* enabled man to achieve the good life. In many instances, indeed, it has served only to increase man's potential for evil.

So humanism as a philosophy has declined. It now seems highly questionable whether we *can* believe in the human venture unless our faith in human values is more deeply rooted in the scheme of things entire. It seems highly doubtful that we can believe in *man* for long, unless we believe in *God,* the God in whose image man has been fashioned.

This breakdown in the philosophy of humanism has been a dominant force in the Western world, instigating a quest for the theological foundation of human values, reviving interest in religion, and generating a new cosmic concern in the general outlook of American culture.

A fourth cause of the theological reawakening is found in the impact of communism on our democratic faith. We now recognize that an adequate response to the Marxist challenge demands that we rethink the meaning of democracy, and reappraise its moral and spiritual foundations. In doing this, we have developed a new appreciation of the historic sources of democracy, with its belief in the inherent dignity of the individual and his inalienable right to life, liberty, and the pursuit of happiness, and with its desire to achieve the largest measure of freedom for the individual commensurate with the common good. All of these principles have historic roots in the teachings of Jesus and the New Testament about the dignity and worth of man as a child of God. Indeed, the very presuppositions of the democratic values that America holds dear came from the church.

One may say thus that even the political tensions of the past few decades have helped to generate the new theological mood of our present day.

II

We have indicated above some of the basic causes for the work of theological reconstruction taking place today. The urgency of the need for such reconstruction can hardly be overemphasized. Thoughtful church members cherish the gains of rational integrity, scientific knowledge, and the historical understanding of the Bible, which the modern period of culture has made the common possession of the Western world. They therefore find it impossible to return to the theology of prescientific dogmatism, biblicism, and ecclesiasticism. Thoughtful Christians are also equally appreciative of the ethical emphasis which modern liberalism brought to sharp focus. There must be no postliberal sacrifice of ethics for some new form of the old "otherworldly" fallacy. Granted, an eschatological corrective to the ethics of liberalism is now needed; yet it must be an eschatology which *includes* ethics, a transcendence that is "this-worldly."

The church of today rightly cherishes the gospel of God as

the answer to man's basic problem and therefore desires to attain the fulfillment of its historic mission under God. If it is to do so, the work of theological reconstruction must be regarded as absolutely imperative.

The chapters in this volume are to be understood as the effort of representative figures in Discipledom engaged in this vitally important work of theological reconstruction. Before we proceed, however, with the theological reconstruction in reference to specific central beliefs, it seems appropriate to outline briefly the role of theology in the church of today's world.

Theology as a Function of the Church

The word "theology" was used in a broad sense in the above analysis of the modern cultural situation. In this sense, any concern for the ultimate dimension of existence is "theological." There is also a stricter and more precise meaning of the word "theology" which is joined more closely to the life of the church. We turn our attention now to a consideration of the task of theology in this more precise sense.

As the word indicates, theology (*Theos*-God; *Logos*-word) in the strict sense of the term is language about God. The church speaks about God, first, through the life and daily conduct of each individual member,[30] and second, by its more formal proclamation in preaching, sacramental celebrations, teaching, and benevolent activity. In this comprehensive sense of the word, the entire action of the church is "theology."

Theology is not only the whole task of the church; it is equally the task of the whole church. It is erroneous to set theology and church over against each other, as if church, conceived as nontheological, were the really important thing, and theology, conceived as nonecclesiastical, a mere pastime to keep a few curiosity-seeking professors out of mischief. Strictly speaking, the task of theology is the task of the whole church. If the entire membership of the church is not interested in reaching an understanding of the meaning and truth of the

30

faith, something is seriously wrong with the church.

That theology is a function of the church implies that a person is first a member of a specific religious group (in this case the Christian community) and then *on this basis* he becomes theological by way of refining and interpreting the content of his faith. It would make for confusion for one to try to be a theologian first and then on the basis of his theology (derived from thin air so to speak) align himself with some religious group. In simple words, sharing in the life of the church precedes theological reflection on it and intellectual refinement of it.

This means that while theology is language about God, it is so in the perspective of faith. The language of theology thus differs from the language of philosophy, for example, even though some philosophers also speak about God. The term "God" does not mean quite the same thing in the two disciplines, though there are doubtless overlappings of meaning. Schleiermacher correctly reminds us that it might seem to be difficult to distinguish philosophical propositions about a Supreme Being from theological propositions about God. "But when they are considered in their connexions, these two indubitably show differences of the most definite kind."[31] Schleiermacher distinguished the two by saying that theological propositions "receive their impulse from religious moods of mind," while philosophical propositions about God "appear for the most part in purely logical . . . trains of thought."[32]

Since theology takes its rise out of, and finds expression in, the historical context of the church, the distinctive form of theological propositions is not dependent upon any particular school of philosophy. Theological fulfillment is not obliged to wait for the final word to be spoken in the enterprise of philosophy. Theological propositions derive their inward purity and distinctive form from the Christ-event, the primary source of the church's life.

We cannot here discuss at length the perennial question of

the relation between philosophy and theology. Our concern is mainly to show that the fact that theology is a function of the church provides theology with a different perspective than that of philosophy; or one might say that the two disciplines have different points of beginning. It is difficult to discuss this problem due to the fact that philosophers do not agree as to what philosophy is.

If the definition of philosophy used by some contemporary exponents of linguistic analysis be permitted to stand, the difference between theology and philosophy would be quite sharp. These verificational analysts[33] thoroughly abandon metaphysics, or any attempt to study "reality as a whole."[34] According to these thinkers, philosophy is merely a department of logic. The propositions of philosophy are linguistic in character; they "express definitions, or the formal consequences of definitions,"[35] but are in no way concerned with reality *as such*. Accordingly, exponents of this school regard theology as a futile and invalid attempt to deal with "a mystery which transcends the human understanding" and which they therefore regard as "unintelligible." That is, theology, like metaphysics, is regarded as "literal nonsense."

Theology might point out that the underlying point of view of the verificational analysts is, by their own basic criterion, "nonsense." For the basic criterion of these philosophers is the affirmation that "all statements which are not tautologies or empirical generalizations are literal nonsense." It is obvious, however, that this statement enclosed in quotation marks cannot be an "empirical generalization," for it is a universal, and by common agreement no empirical generalization can be a genuine universal; it can never get beyond the level of a high degree of probability, since empirical observation is never complete. Yet neither can the basic statement be tautological or analytical, since it is by no means self-evident or recognized by all that the idea of "literal nonsense" is an essential part of the subject of the sentence "all statements which are not tautologies or empirical generalizations." The statement "a triangle has three sides" is a genuine tautology, for the notion of three-sideness is clearly included in the idea of triangularity. But it is obvious, on examination, that the statement with which we are dealing is *not* this kind of statement. It is rather a dogmatic affirmation (that is, a presupposition) about the possible limits of human knowledge.

An increasing number of contemporary linguistic analysts have become aware of the dogmatic nature of the presuppositions of the verificational analysts, while yet maintaining with them that the proper area of philosophy is "the logical task of clarifying and illuminating the ends of language and the ways in which language is able to achieve these ends."[36] A more flexible approach is thus found in exponents of "functional analysis." As Frederick Ferré says, "if with verificational analysis, language is initially pictured as an instrument whose *essential* function is to make possible the communication of empirical facts, then conceptual shears are supplied to snip off those utterances which fail to further this function. But let language be approached, with functional analysis, as a natural phenomenon, and no *a priori* grounds are given for excluding any of the uses of language."[37]

This broader, more "empirical" (that is, factual) approach to the nature of what Ferré calls the "signification-situation"[38] rejects, as unwarranted arbitrariness, the hasty judgment that theological affirmations are noncognitive and merely "emotive" in significance. The prevailing mood in philosophy today is therefore one which promotes genuine concern to analyze the meaning of theological statements in the light of their rootage in human interests, activities, and purposes. Theology should welcome the critical, linguistic work of such philosophers with open arms, for such work holds promise of adding clarity to theology's own semantic self-understanding.

When one compares the concept of philosophy's task espoused by the linguistic analysts with that held by the metaphysical thinkers in the long tradition of philosophy, it becomes obvious that any definition of "philosophy" must be somewhat arbitrary. Paul Tillich represents the traditional point of view when he says that philosophy is "that cognitive approach to reality in which reality as such is the object."[39] This means that in philosophy there is no special place in reality to discern truth. The metaphysical philosopher believes that one can tap reality anywhere along the line, so to speak, and if he digs deeply enough he will be able to discover the fundamental nature of things.

The theologian, on the other hand, begins his task at a particular place, in a given historical situation. He begins where that reality which is life's ultimate concern has manifested itself in such a way as to grasp him and lay a claim upon him. Hence the *primary* source of theology is not the cosmic Logos of traditional philosophy, but the Logos manifested in the special historical event summed up by the phrase "Jesus Christ."

This difference between theology and philosophy also leads to a corollary difference in the manner of appropriation of truth in the two disciplines: in philosophy it is an attitude of contemplation and rational detachment; in theology it is an attitude of existential involvement and believing commitment. As the Apostle Paul put it, "no one can say 'Jesus is Lord' except by the Holy Spirit" (1 Corinthians 12:3). An attitude of completely objective detachment in theology would be tantamount to a denial of the essential truth perceived, a denial of the claim of Christ's lordship.

Ernst Fuchs puts the difference sharply, perhaps a bit too sharply, by saying that in philosophy the movement of thought *(Denkbewegungen)* represents a seeking *(Suche)* of truth; in theology the movement of thought represents a witness *(Bezeugung)* to the truth.[40] Philosophy clarifies what it conceives *(begreift),* theology what it believes *(glaubt).*[41] If, as we contend, these differences between theology and philosophy are valid, theology dare not permit any philosophical *a priori* to rob it of its own unique norm; though to be sure the conceptual

34

tools of philosophy are of substantial value to theology in its task of interpreting and rendering meaningful the content of the gospel. To this extent there is a valid place for "reason" in theological method. Hence revelation is not *utterly* discontinuous with reason, as Karl Barth seems to think. If the gospel is relevant, *really relevant* to our human situation, then *in some basic sense* it must be continuous with reason or the general structure of human existence.

It remains true, however, as Gustaf Aulén reminds us, that if it is the aim of theology to permit the content and significance of the Christian faith to be expressed fully and completely,

this can be accomplished only by letting the unique and vital viewpoints of faith itself be brought to light. But this cannot be accomplished if faith is examined and judged in accordance with perspectives which are external and foreign to it. . . . Faith must be understood from its own center. If it is forced into conformity with a system foreign to itself, it is misinterpreted and perverted.[42]

The Analytical Function of Theology

We are now ready to give a definition of Christian theology. Christian theology is a penetrating analysis, a critical clarification, and a systematic explication of the religious faith which is normatively determined by the special truth and power which came into the world through Jesus as the Christ, and of the relevance of this gospel for human existence. Putting it simply, theology is an earnest attempt to understand the meaning of faith. As Barth puts it, it is "the scientific test to which the church puts herself regarding the language about God which is peculiar to her."[43] Theology is the church taking her own measure against the given reality in faith: God's self-disclosure in Jesus Christ. To the extent that any Christian gives himself to this intellectual endeavor, he is a "theologian."

What, then, is the datum of the discipline of theology? The datum is the relation of faith, or the Christian experience of God, an experience determined by God's self-revelation in

Christ, and mediated by Scripture, tradition, and the church. This experience, of course, is exceedingly broad in historic sweep, and profound in personal depth. But in brief, the datum of theology is the concrete relation of faith, with all the historic structuring which this relation involves.

The theologian contends that the pious utterances of religious shibboleths in the sanctuary does not suffice if faith is to grasp and transform human existence. It is fine and proper for one to stand up and say, "Christ died for our sins," or "the Bible is the word of God," or "Jesus is the Christ, the Son of the Living God." Yet the mere utterance of these *can* be nothing more than pious platitudes. When they are such, they do not suffice to redeem human life.

The underlying meanings of confessional statements must be made explicit and clear if one is to appropriate the saving truth of God in a way in which this truth will exercise a transfiguring influence on his being; if, that is, he is really to *become* what God has made it possible for him to *be*. This means that the church must recognize that the function of theology stands alongside the function of corporate worship and is of equal importance with it. When the church neglects either of these functions, either the theological or the doxological, its existence as church is to this extent placed in jeopardy and its mission is to this extent distorted and ineffectual.

The Prophetic Role of Theology

We said that critical self-analysis is one of the basic functions of theology. Theology is the church engaged in an effort to understand itself as determined by God's grace. This is the depth dimension of the theological task. It represents the church penetrating to the inmost center of its being and grasping the ultimate significance of its life in and with God.

A second dimension of theology might be called the breadth dimension. In the breadth dimension theology's concern is with the church's mission in the world. If the former function represents the inward movement of the church's life and thought, the latter concerns the church's outreach in the world.

One aspect of this outreach might be called the "prophetic" role of theology. The feeling is widespread that there is urgent need in our day for the church to come alive in its prophetic role. Perhaps these two functions—the analytic and prophetic—support each other mutually. Perhaps if the church comes alive in theological self-understanding, it will also take on new life in redemptive outreach. Perhaps *only* if it attains depth of theological self-understanding *can* it attain a true vision of its mission in the world. As one of my colleagues says, the best way for the church to combat communism is to study Christianity.

It may well be that the church of our day is so secularized and so comfortably integrated with the general moral life of the community that there is now need for the church to exercise this prophetic role in relation to its own members. As James Sellars reminds us, "It is one of the commonplaces of our church life that people who call themselves Christians very often know next to nothing about the Christian religion."[44] The church today is perhaps filled with so many who are in substance really not "insiders," but "outsiders," that we must now come to grips with the fact that there are two kinds of "outsiders": (1) those who are in no formal sense "insiders" (though to be sure they have, in varying degrees, been influenced by Christianity), and (2) those who are formally "insiders" but materially "outsiders."

In a recent book, Gerhard Lenski argues that although the primary concern of Protestantism originally was the attainment of spiritual values, it "has become so identified with economic success, respectability, and middle-class virtues, that large numbers of the clergy and laity alike have lost sight of basic spiritual goals."[45] Is this true? Has the church in our time been conquered and rendered harmless by the pervasive secular spirit of modern culture—conquered so thoroughly that it no longer has the ability to exercise even a Socratic gadfly function in the social order?

37

The gospel of God stands in judgment not only on many aspects of modern man, but on the organized churches themselves when they fail to exercise their theological responsibility. It stands in judgment on churches who lapse into liturgical complacency, pietistic obscurantism, or cultural respectability.

In the latter half of the twentieth century the time has come for the church to come alive in faith, and confront and challenge modern culture with the judging, healing power of the gospel. There are signs that the church is beginning to become theologically responsible in this redemptive sense. It has become sufficiently aware of the impotence of a culture-bound religion that its conscience is disturbed, at points deeply disturbed. Correlated with this disturbed conscience is the fact that the nineteenth-century view of the church as a mere human contrivance growing out of the natural need for fellowship has steadily lost ground during the past quarter century, due mainly to developments in theology and in biblical studies.

The combination of this disturbed conscience and these theological developments is leading the church to a rediscovery of the religious source of its own inner integrity. It holds promise of liberating the church from its culture-bound predicament, from the pathetic tendency to become a culture-vulture, to capitulate to cultural and intellectual movements merely because they happen to be popular at the moment.

The main task in the outward reach of the church, then, is not so much to cultivate prevailing cultural norms and values, which fluctuate with the winds of ideological and social change, but to *challenge* the social *status quo,* to serve as an instrument in the hands of God whereby the gospel of love can be brought to impinge on human existence, in judgment and with healing power.

Theology in Dialogue with Church and World

The prophetic aspect of the world outreach of the church centers in theology's role as a critic of culture. This critical role must be balanced, however, by yet another function in the church's outreach. This other function, we call the dialogical role. Theology attains its most effective influence only when it also enters into dialogue with culture, indeed only when it shares deeply the problems and ambiguities of human existence.

When the church is as it should be, it sustains a sort of paradoxical relation to the ongoing life of man in the world. It must sustain both "distinction from" and "identity with" the world. Whenever the church preserves "distinction from" the world, and construes this distinctness in a way that forfeits "identity with" the world, the church succumbs to a bad kind of otherworldliness. The history of religion, including that of the Christian church, is marked by paths of otherworldly withdrawal of this kind. For example, the eightfold path of Buddhism leading to the otherworldly bliss of Nirvana; the Hindu quest for immediate union with the Infinite (Brahman) by way of a renunciation of the entire phenomenal world as illusion *(maya)*; and in Christianity, early Christian Gnosticism, medieval monasticism, and twentieth-century fundamentalism are all guilty of misinterpreting the distinctness of the faith as otherworldly withdrawal.

On the other hand, whenever the church secures itself in its "identity with" the world and interprets this identity in a way which forfeits its "distinction from" the world, Christianity loses its inner *raison d'etre* and becomes nothing but another aspect of the life of the world *per se.*

This unique stance which the church occupies in relation to the world means that, in a way, theology straddles both church and world. Theology must carry on a two-way dialogue: with the church and with the world. Theology is the discipline in which church and world meet in this creative encounter.

For these reasons, it is not a healthy kind of theology that maintains its distinction by restricting itself to the biblical and ecclesiastical traditions. Theology must come to grips with the concrete human situation. The church of course must not cut itself wholly loose from its historic roots. By doing this it would cease to be the church, for the church is a community which not only has its beginning in a particular time and place in history, but which also finds in this beginning point an indispensable part of its ultimate norm. Yet neither must theology permit itself to be *restricted* to the biblical witness to the living stream of church tradition, but must be an active participant in the present human situation.

The way in which theology participates in the situation is, of course, vitally important. It will sadly err if such participation is motivated by the desire to derive the *essential content* of faith from the human situation, or if it simply subordinates faith to some rational system among the disciplines of culture. Because of the persistent sinfulness of man and the transcendent nature of the kingdom of God, tension and conflict will always be present in the exercise of theology's dialogical role.

The creative tension involved in theology's dialogue with culture, however, can and should have two major results. First, such conversation can and should effect a redemptive correction of culture and a co-ordination of its systems of truth into a wider system of coherence, thereby saving cultural authorities from what Rheinhold Niebuhr calls "idolatrous aberrations."[46] Second, such mutually interpenetrating dialogue between theology and culture can and should enrich and deepen the Christian faith by the particular insights of the intelletcual disciplines of culture.

It is our contention that only by such mutually interpenetrating dialogue can we *relate* faith meaningfully to the ongoing historic process. Only thus can religious thought achieve genuine contemporaneity. Only thus can theology rescue traditional religious faith from the museum of yesterday's relics and enable it to come alive in the traffic of human living today.

Say then that this second aspect of the church's world outreach is that theology stands at the growing edge of this outreach. Christian theology stands where the church's message meets the spirit of the times in which the church's being is realized and fulfilled. It is part of the task of theology to see to it that this meeting *takes place,* and that it takes place at the deepest level of honest intellectual searching for life's meaning and destiny.

The Formative Function of Theology

There is yet a third phase of theology's work in relation to the church's mission. Theology must not only engage in vigorous dialogue with the other intellectual disciplines, but also exercise a formative function by helping the church develop new symbols and structures in the contemporary situation, thereby enabling faith to achieve cultural integrity.

The vital need for, and validity of, this formative work of theology rests upon the fact that the *inner spirit* of the Christian faith is not identical with but must be distinguished from the *outer forms* through which it is realized. This means that the Christian faith is bound to a reality which transcends all of its changing historical forms of expression, though to be sure it finds concrete realization in and through these forms. And only because Christianity is such a faith, only because in its abiding truth it transcends *any* situation can it be vitally relevant to *every* situation whatever the shifting structures of human existence.

It is now obvious what this dynamic relation between faith and the changing forms of historic process means for theology. It places a demand on theology to seek new forms of expression in order to release the healing power of the gospel of love in the historical actualities of today's world. Vital religious faith refuses to be entombed in the dead forms of yesterday. It cannot live today in the forms it assumed on the American frontier, in medieval Europe, at Nicea, or even the forms of Apostolic Christianity. It is imperative that theologians learn *how to say again* what the ancient gospel of love means, in terms of human existence today. As A. N. Whitehead aptly says, "You may preserve the life in a flux of form, or preserve the form amid an ebb of life. But you cannot permanently enclose the same life in the same mould."[47]

There are numerous new insights and developments in man's contemporary understanding of himself and the world: in psychology, cosmology, history, sociology, ethics, art, and the problematical complex of world interrelatedness. We cannot here enter into a discussion of these. It must suffice to say that theology must rethink and restate its understanding of man and the world in the light of this growing body of scientific knowledge, if it is to develop new forms of expression so that the relevance of the gospel to the present situation can find redemptive expression.

The situation calls for theological imagination that can develop new methods of procedure, new strategies for peace, new forms of Christian service, by which the ancient gospel of love can be brought to bear on the new situation in effective ways. It calls for bold and sacrificial action in seizing the opportunity for constructive work in the struggle of world growth. What modern man needs, and needs desperately, is a religious leadership inspired by a divine discontent, endowed with creative imagination, and blessed with pioneering attitudes.

The following chapters represent serious theological effort toward the goal of helping the church to fulfill its theological responsibility, as outlined in this introductory chapter. The hope of the authors is that this volume will be both stimulating and of substantial value in the educational program of the church for our day.

NOTES

1. Famed teacher of Thomas Aquinas in the Middle Ages.
2. Thomas H. Huxley, *Science and Christian Tradition* (London: Macmillan and Company, Ltd., 1909), p. 249.
3. David Hume, *Dialogues Concerning Natural Religion* (New York: Hafner Publishing Company, 1951), p. 42.
4. Though Mill felt that "the adaptations in Nature afford a large balance of probability in favour of creation by intelligence." *Three Essays on Religion* (New York: Henry Holt and Company, 1884), p. 174.

5. *Ibid.*, p. 245.
6. *Ibid.*, p. 74.
7. Huxley, *op. cit.*, p. 310.
8. From *Essays upon Controversial Questions*, p. 183.
9. Alfred Jules Ayer, *Language, Truth, and Logic* (New York: Dover Publications, Inc., 1946), p. 115.
10. *Ibid.*, p. 34.
11. *Ibid.*, p. 41.
12. *Ibid.*
13. William James, *Varieties of Religious Experience* (New York: The Modern Library, 1902), p. 513.
14. *Religion in America*, edts. James Ward Smith & A. Leland Jamison (Princeton: Princeton University Press, 1961), I, 427.
15. John Dewey, *Reconstruction in Philosophy* (New York: Henry Holt and Company, 1920), p. 117.
16. *Ibid.*, p. 118.
17. *Ibid.*, p. 117.
18. *Ibid.*, p. 126.
19. *Ibid.*, p. 116.
20. *Ibid.*, p. 131.
21. A. Eustace Haydon, *The Quest of the Ages* (New York: Harper & Brothers Publishers, 1929), pp. 11-12.
22. *Ibid.*, p. 219.
23. Huxley, *op. cit.*, p. 249.
24. Smith, *op. cit.*, p. 432.
25. Such as: (1) too great a reliance on his own philosophy of religion ("feeling of absolute dependence") as an *a priori* for his method; (2) making the corporate Christian self-consciousness the datum of theology, instead of the actual relation of faith, thereby tending toward subjectivism and psychologism in theology; (3) a tendency to equate Christ with culture, thereby losing the prophetic power of Christianity; (4) an inadequate grasp of the historical dimension of the Christian faith, so that the ellipse of religious psychology and history tends to be resolved into a circle. On this last criticism see Karl Barth's illuminating essay on Schleiermacher in his book *Protestant Thought from Rousseau to Ritschl* (New York: Harper & Row, Publishers, Inc., 1959), pp. 306-354.
26. Peter Taylor Forsyth, *The Principle of Authority* (London: Independent Press, Ltd., 1913), p. 347.
27. In *The Christian Answer*, ed. Henry P. Van Dusen (New York: Charles Scribner's Sons, 1945), pp. 4-5.
28. *New York Herald Tribune*, January 22, 1958. Used by permission.
29. In Plato's *Apology*.
30. Cf. Matthew 5:16.
31. Friedrich Schleiermacher, *The Christian Faith*, trans. by H. R. Mackintosh & J. S. Stewart (Edinburgh: T&T. Clark, 1928), p. 82.
32. *Ibid.*
33. Frederick Ferré labels this branch of the modern linguistic approach to philosophy "verificational analysis." *Language, Logic, and God* (London: Eyre & Spottiswoode, Ltd., 1962, and New York: Harper & Row, Publishers, Inc.), p. 8. Used by permission.
34. Ayer, *op. cit.*, p. 47.
35. *Ibid.*, p. 57.
36. Ferré, *op. cit.*, p. 3.
37. *Ibid.*, p. 59.
38. *Ibid.*, p. 146.
39. Paul Tillich, *Systematic Theology* (Chicago: University of Chicago Press, 1951), I, 18.

40. Ernst Fuchs, *Was ist Theologie?* (Tübingen: J. C. B. Mohr, 1953), p. 7.

41. *Ibid.*, p. 8.

42. Gustaf Aulén, *The Faith of the Christian Church,* trans. Eric H. Wahlstrom & G. Everett Arden (Philadelphia: The Muhlenberg Press, 1948), pp. 9-10. Used by permission.

43. Karl Barth, *Church Dogmatics,* trans. G. T. Thomson (New York: Charles Scribner's Sons, 1955), I., 1. p. 1.

44. James E. Sellers, *The Outsider and the Word of God* (Nashville: Abingdon Press, 1961), p. 27.

45. Gerhard Lenski, *The Religious Factor* (New York: Doubleday & Company, Inc., 1961), p. 317.

46. Rheinhold Niebuhr, *Faith and History* (New York: Charles Scribner's Sons, 1949), p. 167.

47. Alfred North Whitehead, *Science and the Modern World* (New York: The New American Library of World Literature, Inc., 1958), p. 187.

PART ONE
BIBLE AND TRADITION
FOR THE FAITH TODAY

❊ 2 ❊

The Place of the Old Testament
in the Christian Faith

J. Philip Hyatt

THE attitude which many Christians have regarding the Old
Testament was expressed in a letter which I received once from
a layman in which he was recommending a prospective graduate student. This layman wished to give a high recommendation
to the prospective student, who had already done a considerable
amount of teaching. He said that he had heard the young man
lecture on several occasions, and that he had the ability to make
the Old Testament live. Then he added: "To one who has
always regarded the Old Testament as a dry and somewhat unnecessary prelude to the New Testament, this is quite a feat."

It is well known that Marcion was one of the first heretics of
the Christian Church, living in the first half of the second century. Marcion said that the Bible presents us with two deities:
the Creator God of the Old Testament who is just but harsh,
and the Redeemer God of the New Testament who is a God of
love. He thought that a Christian should reject completely the
Old Testament and its God, and incidentally he did a good deal
toward promoting the formation of a canon of the New Testament. Marcion was considered a heretic, and the Christian
church has always officially considered the Old Testament as
an important part of Scripture, though there have been debates
on the extent of the canon. Unfortunately there is a widespread

47

unofficial and ambiguous Marcionism in many quarters of the Christian church today.

Perhaps the strongest attack which has ever been made upon the Old Testament as Christian Scripture was made by the late Professor Friedrich Delitzsch, who published a book with the title, *The Great Deception*.[1] Delitzsch was a scholar at the University of Berlin who made important contributions particularly in the field of Assyriology. He was the author of the famous book, *Babel and Bible,* 1903. His father Franz Delitzsch, professor at Leipzig, was an outstanding Old Testament scholar with a strong conservative bent.

Friedrich Delitzsch in this book said that he wished to approach the Old Testament from the standpoint of an intelligent layman reading the book as a connected narrative but with a critical mind. He considered in some detail three sets of Old Testament narratives: the account of the conquest of Palestine, the revelation on Mount Sinai, and the stories of the early prophets. It was not difficult for him to show that there are many inconsistencies and difficulties, both of a historical and of an ethical nature in the conquest of Palestine. In speaking of the revelation on Mount Sinai, he says it is a great deception for the Old Testament to claim that there is any relationship between the God revealed on Mount Sinai and the Christian deity. He goes on to point out many of the things that are often said about the Old Testament—its fanatical racialism, the low moral standards found in many places, and so on and on. He summarizes his point of view as follows:

The Old Testament is full of deceptions of all kinds: a veritable hodge-podge of erroneous, incredible, undependable figures, including those of Biblical chronology; a veritable labyrinth of false portrayals, misleading reworkings, revisions and transpositions, and therefore of anachronisms; a constant intermixture of contradictory particulars and of whole stories, of unhistorical free compositions, legends and folktales—in short, a book full of intentional and unintentional deceptions, in part self-deceptions, a very dangerous book, in the use of which the greatest care is necessary. I repeat the Old Testament is in all its books full of linguistic beauties and of archaeological information, and it retains its value as a historical document in spite of its defects, but it is in all directions a relatively late and very cloudy source, a tendentious document from the first chapter of Genesis to the last of Chronicles.[2]

I have cited Delitzsch only as the most extreme example of modern Marcionism. It may be that this work and its author can be understood by psychological analysis, but at any rate it shows an attitude of rejection of the Old Testament in extreme form.

The problem of the place which the Old Testament ought to have in our Christian faith is, of course, a part of the larger problem of the authority of Scripture—that is, the question as to what authority the written book has for us as Christians, the relationship between the written words and the Word of God, and so on. The Old Testament has always presented certain special difficulties which are not encountered in the New Testament. To achieve my objective I wish to assume that the New Testament has authority for the Christian, and I want to treat the question of the authority or the place which the Old Testament ought to have for Christians today both in its relationship to the New Testament and in its own right.

Before proceeding to discuss the problem in a positive manner, it will be helpful to summarize some of the erroneous ways of treating the Old Testament, because it is certain that the Old Testament has often been treated in wrong ways by Christians. The great problem has always been to assess properly both the continuity and the discontinuity existing between the Old and New Testaments. Sometimes errors have arisen from overemphasizing the continuity between the Testaments, and at other times the discontinuity has been overemphasized.

Views Overemphasizing Continuity Between the Testaments

Let me first consider the error of emphasizing too much the continuity between the Old and New Testaments, or the error of over-Christianizing the Old Testament. There are several different ways in which this has been done.

(1) One way in which the Old Testament has often been over-Christianized has been that of viewing it as a collection almost exclusively of predictions of the coming Messiah. This has taken place all through the centuries and in many individuals and churches. For example, Martin Luther saw the Old Testament as being to a great extent a collection of messianic prophecies; he could speak of it as being "the swaddling clothes and crib in which the Christ lies."[3] He often read into the text messianic predictions in cases where they are rather farfetched. Many theologians of the present time look upon the Old Testament in the same way. Perhaps an extreme example is to be found in a book by a Barthian, Wilhelm Vischer; in *The Witness of the Old Testament to Christ,* of which Volume I has been translated into English, he insists that the Old Testament tells us *what* the Christ is, and the New tells us *who* he is. He finds witness to Christ in many parts of the Old Testament. For example, he can say, since he takes the pre-existence of Christ very seriously, that when Jacob wrestled with the angel at the River Jabbok, the name of the one with whom he wrestled was Jesus Christ.[4]

It must be admitted that the New Testament itself has drawn upon the Old Testament for messianic prophecies, and indeed it has sometimes taken verses out of context and used them as messianic predictions when they were not such originally. Perhaps the most striking example is the use in Matthew 2:15 of the sentence in Hosea 11:1, "out of Egypt have I called my Son." The New Testament writers used the Old Testament in an atomistic way as a source of messianic predictions; in this they largely followed the lead of Jewish interpretation of the time.

There are many things that must be said against this attempt to see messianic predictions throughout the Old Testament. The first is that the Old Testament, studied historically, contains very little concerning a personal Messiah, and the Hebrews apparently had very little interest in the person of the Messiah. There is in the Old Testament a great deal of eschatology, and of messianism in a very broad sense, but to see messianic predictions throughout the Old Testament looking forward to the coming of Jesus Christ is simply to practice eisegesis. Many of the passages which came to be interpreted messianically, such as the Royal Psalms and Isaiah 9:1-7 and 11:1-9, were probably used originally in connection with events in the lives of Israelite kings.

The second thing to say is that Jesus of Nazareth was not simply a Jewish Messiah, nor simply a fulfillment of Old Testament predictions and of Hebrew-Jewish hopes. Jesus is the Christ of the Christians and not simply the Messiah of the Jews. This comes, I believe, largely because of the reinterpretation of the Servant of the Lord in Second Isaiah in the direction of messianism.

One who views the Old Testament as largely a collection of proof texts for the Messiah is guilty of what Richard Niebuhr calls Christism—that is, the error which reduces theology to Christology, and sees the Old Testament as only a collection of predictions fulfilled in the New Testament.[5]

(2) A second method in which the Old Testament has been sometimes over-Christianized is by taking over much of the Old Testament law, including even the civil law or the ceremonial law, along with the ethical commandments. The Christian church has ordinarily taken the point of view expressed in the XXXIX Articles, that the Christian is under the moral law of the Old Testament but not under the ceremonial or ritual law. John Calvin took over a good deal of the law of the Old Testament, and through Puritanism this passed into early America. Calvin was concerned to show that there was but one covenant and one people in the whole of the Bible, and among other things he wished to show that even in the Old Testament there was throughout the promise of immortality. E. G. Kraeling in speaking of Calvin says that he Christianized the Old Testament

and Judaized the New Testament in his effort to make the two appear as one.[6]

(3) The Old Testament is sometimes over-Christianized in a third way by those who put the theology or the religious ideas of the Old Testament on a level plane with those of the New Testament, and deny the progressive development or the progressive revelation which is to be found in that book. For example, many of the Protestant reformers were very much interested in showing that the hope of immortality is found throughout the Old Testament, and some modern scholars have been very much concerned to show that Moses was a monotheist. When we study the Old Testament historically, we must allow for the possibility of progressive or historical development in the theology of the Old Testament, and this does not necessarily mean a uni-linear evolutionary development.

(4) It remains to be pointed out that the Old Testament has sometimes been used by various sects who have chosen to emphasize one or another of the aspects of Old Testament religious practice, such as the observance of certain dietary laws, the wearing of certain types of clothes, rigid observance of the Sabbath, or the like.

Views Overemphasizing Discontinuity Between the Testaments

The other great error that has been committed has been that of seeing too great a discontinuity between the Old and the New Testaments, and thus denying the close relationship that exists between the two. This is to be seen especially in those who emphasize the great contrast between the Testaments as being the contrast between law in the Old Testament and gospel or grace in the New Testament. It also usually occurs in those writers or thinkers who divide human history up into very neat dispensations.

Martin Luther said that the Old Testament contains commands and the New Testament promises, and he and other

Protestant reformers spoke of the difference between the two as being the difference between law and grace.[7]

Alexander Campbell apparently belongs in this general category. His Sermon on the Law of 1816 was one of the principal grounds of his separation from the Baptists. In it he said: "There is an essential difference between law and gospel—the Old Testament and the New."[8]

He believed that history could be divided into three dispensations. The first was that of the patriarchal age extending from Adam to Moses, which he called that of starlight. The second dispensation was that of the Jewish Age, from Moses to Christ, which he called moonlight. The third dispensation is the Christian Age, that is the time of Christ to the present, which he called that of sunlight. Campbell believed that the Jewish Age terminated with the burial of Jesus. The forty days from the resurrection to the ascension constituted a period between the Jewish and Christian Ages when Christ allowed no one to speak to the unbelieving; thus the Christian Age begins with the ascension and the outpouring of the Spirit at Pentecost. In this scheme the life and teachings of Jesus are at the end of the Jewish Age, and it appears that Campbell gave relatively little attention to the Four Gospels but greatly emphasized the Book of Acts. As to his specific view of the Old Testament he said: "As to divine authority, I have at all times viewed it and represented it as equal to the New. But that Christians are not under it, but under the New, I have contended, and must still contend."[9] In the Sermon on the Law he seems to say that the Christian is not obliged to observe even the Ten Commandments; yet he has much to say about the law of nature, or conscience, under which even the pagan lives.

In the Declaration and Address of Thomas Campbell, Proposition 4 expresses the following view of the relationship of the testaments:

That although the Scriptures of the Old and New Testaments are inseparably connected, making together but one perfect and

53

entire revelation of the Divine will, for the edification and salvation of the Church, and therefore in that respect cannot be separated; yet as to what directly and properly belongs to their immediate object, the New Testament is as perfect a constitution for the worship, discipline, and government of the New Testament Church, and as perfect a rule for the particular duties of its members.

The early Disciple leaders were apparently so intent upon restoring the principles of the New Testament that they did not really give profound thought to the Old Testament and its relationship to the New, and to its part in the Bible as a whole.

It must not be denied that to some extent this contrast between the Old and New Testaments is a valid one—that is, the contrast between the two covenants or dispensations, and the contrast between law and gospel. However, this contrast can easily be exaggerated.

In the Old Testament itself the priestly writer does apparently have a scheme of successive dispensations. Furthermore, the difference between the Old and New Testaments do include the difference between the old covenant and the new covenant; this distinction lies within the usage of the New Testament itself. It is very significant, however, that the Old Testament passage which predicts a New Covenant (Jeremiah 31:31-34) speaks of a new *covenant* but not of a new *law*. The law is to be written on the hearts of men rather than on something external, like tablets of stone.

The difficulty with this view is that it is entirely too neat and overlooks the fact that each of the Testaments contains both law and grace. I shall have more to say about this later. Also, this view often overlooks the necessity of law in the life of the Christian and the need for considering God as the ultimate source of the order in our lives and in our world. Still further, the distinction between what is usually called ethical law and ritual or ceremonial law is one which is sometimes quite difficult to make. One might ask, for example, whether the Sabbath laws are ethical laws or ritual laws. Furthermore, some of the so-called ethical laws have been superseded, as, for example, those laws regarding slavery in the Old Testament.

Suggestions Toward a Balanced View

If we may proceed now to the positive side of our topic, we must insist that any adequate view of the place of the Old Testament in the Christian faith must do justice to both the continuity and the discontinuity between the Old and New Testaments, and it must not obscure the rich variety which exists in both Testaments. It is quite impossible to treat this subject comprehensively in a single paper, but I wish to suggest some of the lines along which a positive view of the place of the Old Testament might be considered.

(1) First of all, we must insist that the Christian church has always taken the point of view that the *whole Bible* constitutes our canon of Scripture. This does not mean that we must accept the whole of the Bible from cover to cover. It does not mean that the whole of the Bible is equally authoritative or that it is all equally inspired; nor does it mean that we must accept every part of both Old and New Testaments.

What this does mean from a positive point of view is that we must seek to do justice to the many varying points of view in the Bible, and we must seek to determine those points of view and those ideas which represent the highest, and are normative in the Bible as a whole. This will furnish us a corrective against fanaticism and against an overemphasis upon any one aspect of either of the two Testaments.

It is quite true that we find in the Old Testament some things that represent a very low level of religious or ethical development. For such things we need not apologize, because when we consider the whole of the Bible as our scripture, we can see that it is self-criticizing, and therefore self-correcting. It was part of Jesus' own use of the Bible that he sometimes used one part of his scripture to correct another part. We may quite properly do the same thing ourselves.

(2) It must be admitted by all that in some measure the Old Testament is necessary for the understanding of the New Testament. The Old Testament provides the intellectual and religious background against which the New Testament is to be understood. It is simply a matter of historical fact that Jesus himself, his disciples, and perhaps the majority of the early Christians were in the first instance Jews. They were nurtured in the Jewish faith in the synagogue and schools, and their religious experiences and their religious ideas were largely based upon first-century Judaism.

In writing on this point R. H. Kennett has said that, although Jerusalem crucified Jesus, "Athens, far worse, would have smothered His preaching in ridicule."[10] The Jews in Palestine of the first century could understand Jesus well enough to know that he should be crucified; in Athens or in any other Hellenistic culture he would not even have been understood, and thus would have been ignored.

Godfrey E. Phillips has written a book, *The Old Testament in the World Church with Special Reference to the Younger Churches.*[11] He points out that missionaries have often had the experience of discovering that, though they seemed to have immediate success in acceptance of their message, their new converts did not really understand the words they were using. He insists that the Old Testament is indispensable for the understanding of many of the central Christian concepts such as sin, atonement, sacrifice, salvation, Christ, and so forth.

All of this is only a way of saying that for us to try to understand the New Testament without the Old Testament is like entering upon the fifth act of a drama without knowing anything about the preceding four acts.

This is the real sense in which the New Testament is the fulfillment of the Old Testament. We should not find that fulfillment simply in terms of the fulfillment of specific messianic predictions. It is in the New Testament, and more particularly in the life of Jesus Christ, that we see the fulfillment of the drama of salvation which began with Abraham.

It is very significant that a strong antagonist of the Old Testament like Friedrich Delitzsch finds that he must deny that Jesus was a Jew. This, however, goes contrary to the historical record.

(3) The Old Testament is, from one point of view, a long record of the dealings in history of God with the Hebrew-Jewish people. It tells the story of how God, out of his love, chose for himself a nation through whom he might reveal himself as through no other people. It is always important in speaking of the Old Testament to emphasize the history which it contains, because both Christianity and Judaism are religions that place great emphasis upon history. Both of these religions have a history, and both look upon the revelation of God in the acts of history as being important.

It has become customary to speak of the history which is contained in the Bible as being *Heilsgeschichte*. This word has a double meaning: it is a saving history, that is, a history through which salvation came to mankind; and it is also a history of salvation.

History is the stage on which God has revealed himself to men. In the biblical sense, revelation is not primarily the communication of knowledge, or of theoretical truths from and about God. Secondarily, it does involve that, since there must be intellectual apprehension of revelation. When we say that God has revealed himself, we mean that he has given himself in the creative deeds of history, culminating in the incarnation in Christ.

In this revelation the Old Testament plays a special role, since it was through Israel's history that God was revealed in a special way, according to the faith of both the Jew and the Christian. This is a fact that even the secular historian should recognize. We need not deny that to some degree he was revealed in the history of other nations—for example, of Greece and of Rome—but the main line of revelation leads through the

57

Old Testament. There was a once-for-all-ness—an *Einmaligkeit* —about the history of Israel that was important for the totality of Christian revelation.[12]

Some writers on the Old Testament have stressed the "mighty acts" of God in history, but it seems to me they have limited the acts of God too narrowly to a few events. For example, G. E. Wright in various writings, most recently in *The Book of the Acts of God*,[13] speaks of the rootage of the faith of Israel as being in five significant events: (1) the Israelite patriarchs, who received certain promises; (2) the exodus from Egypt which was interpreted as God's freeing of a people from slavery; (3) the revelation on Mount Sinai, where the understanding of society and of community obligation was obtained in the law or teaching regarding community duty; (4) the conquest of Canaan which was interpreted as God's gift of an inheritance; and (5) the conquests of David which were regarded as the final fulfillment of the promise of land, and the Davidic government which was regarded as the final fulfillment of the promise of security from enemies and from slavery. Wright is correct in viewing the Old Testament as a history of the acts of God and he is correct in saying that a biblical event is both a happening in history and the interpretation which was given to that happening. However, he has restricted much too narrowly the number of the mighty acts of God in history. Those which he names belong to the very early part of the history of the Hebrew-Jewish people, and for some of them we can hardly speak of "history." Some very significant events are left out, such as the exile into Babylonia and its interpretation by Second Isaiah. It would be far better to consider the whole history of Israel as comprising the revelatory event, or at least a long series of historical happenings. It is a history that to some extent represents progressive development, and it is a history of the patience of God with the people, and of both their faithfulness and their unfaithfulness.

When we speak of the New Testament as being the fulfillment of the Old Testament, we should speak of it as being the culmination of the history which is found in the Bible. It is a culmination of the drama of salvation for which many of the early acts are to be found in the Old Testament.

(4) The Old Testament is also a record of the lives of many inspired individuals. The Christian will find these inspired individuals especially among the prophets of the Old Testament. The prophets should not, of course, be looked upon primarily as prognosticators of the future. They were inspired proclaimers of God's will to the people of their own time. If we look upon them as having a message for their own times, we can find that we, too, often have a need of the same message in our time. From the human side, the prophets were religious geniuses. It is not heretical to assert that in prophets such as Hosea, Isaiah, and Jeremiah "the Word became flesh"—only in part, to be sure, but in reality.

The Old Testament does not contain anything that may be called in the strict sense mysticism, or a record of mystical experiences. The Hebrew prophet was never one who became completely absorbed in the divine, because he always was conscious of the difference between himself and God. And yet the Old Testament does provide us with the messages and the examples of many individuals who in their own time had unusual experiences with the divine.

(5) In some respects we must speak of the Old Testament as supplementing the New Testament and, as we shall see, in some respects it serves to correct the New Testament.

In the Old Testament we have in the Book of Psalms a literature of devotion which has always been recognized as peculiarly useful to Christians. As a deposit of the piety of the ancient Israelites as they sought to worship God, these hymns and prayers are still of great value and usefulness to us. To some extent we may reinterpret them, and we may feel the need of rejecting some of them; yet no literature of the world can quite match them.

Another point at which the Old Testament is a very valuable supplement to the New Testament is the emphasis which it places upon the concept of God as Creator and the world as his creation. This is, of course, generally taken for granted in the New Testament. It is brought out specifically in the Old Testament not only in the first chapters of Genesis, but also in some of the Psalms and in passages such as Job 38ff.

(6) There are some points on which we can actually speak of the Old Testament as furnishing a valuable corrective to the New Testament. Among these we may mention the following:

(a) The New Testament is very largely an individualistic book in that it treats largely the salvation of the individual. It is possible to find some social ethics in the New Testament and it is true that the Christian church was considered as the new Israel. Yet the Old Testament is far more concerned with the salvation of society and of the people and nation, and we may use the Old Testament to correct the somewhat exaggerated individualism of the New Testament.

(b) Very closely related to this is the fact that the New Testament was largely written by, and also for, a people who lived under the Roman government. There are, therefore, some statements in the New Testament regarding the attitudes toward government, such as those of Paul, that were suitable to such a situation, but are hardly suitable to a people living today under a government of their own choice. The Old Testament, on the other hand, was composed by and for a people who for a long time lived under their own rulers. Therefore, our situation parallels more closely that of Israel in the ninth to the sixth centuries B.C., than the situation of the Christian church in the first century A.D.

(c) The Old Testament also provides a correction for, or protection against, a false asceticism which has sometimes derived from the New Testament. In the Old Testament there is generally the point of view that God's creation is good, and that life in this world is potentially good. The New Testament is in some of its parts afflicted by a dualism which looks upon this present world as entirely evil. This is to some extent involved in the eschatological framework of much of the New Testament. At this point we may believe, in the light of subsequent history, that the Old Testament can protect the Christian against a false asceticism.

(d) Another somewhat practical point is that a modern institutional church in which people grow up and become Christians without violent religious experiences is much more like that of the ancient Jewish "church" than it is like the earliest Christian church of the New Testament times, in which membership was based upon personal decision and involved conversion from one religion to another. The situation is, of course, different on the mission field, but in countries which are at least superficially Christian the situation is closer to that of the ancient Jewish "church" than to that of the New Testament church.

(e) The Old Testament can give us an appreciation of nature and also of the revelation of God in nature which is almost lacking in the New Testament. We can hardly do justice to many of the Psalms (19, 29, 104, etc.) and to some other parts of the Old Testament without believing that God does reveal himself in nature as well as in history; and since this world is good, we should have an appreciation of the world of nature.

(7) Finally, it must be emphasized in the interest of objectivity that the Old Testament contains a very large element of the gospel, with its emphasis upon grace, as well as law. It is quite erroneous to speak of the Old Testament as containing only law and the New Testament as containing only grace. This is emphasized by many writers on the subject. We may take as a good example Rudolf Bultmann, a New Testament scholar who is of the opinion that the Old Testament, though it is not entirely essential for the Christian, is nevertheless very valuable for him.[14] He says that in the Old Testament existence under the law is understood also as existence under grace. As examples of God's grace he cites the call of the people of Israel to be

a people of God, the giving of the law to them, and the constant offering to man of the forgiveness of God. He believes that forgiveness is not always offered freely and graciously, but it often is, in the Old Testament.

It cannot be emphasized too strongly that the God of the Old Testament is the same as the God of the New Testament, a God both of love and of justice, a God who makes both promises and demands, giving to man both the gospel and the law.[15] Sigmund Mowinckel has expressed this in the following manner:

That with which both the Old Testament and the New Testament are ultimately concerned is the righteousness of God . . . Righteousness is at the same time the actuating principle of the being and work of God and the demands he presents on the basis of these. It is also the principle of "salvation," the acknowledgment of and the fellowship with himself and the quality of life that he gives those who will accept it. It contains at the same time both the demand, the law—and the grace, the gospel.[16]

The point at which we often misunderstand the Old Testament is in not realizing that much of the law which it contains is what in modern times we would call secular law. Indeed, many of the things that are presented as the commands of God should be looked upon as no more than custom or habit—for example, regulations regarding what one should eat and one should wear. These latter illustrate the desire of the people of Old Testament times to present themselves as a holy people before God. We may rightfully question, however, whether some of the things which are represented in the Old Testament as law ever were really a part of the will of God for man. All of this does not mean that we may dispense with the concept of law as originating in God, because he is the source of all the order in our lives.

I would close by emphasizing the fact that our understanding of the Old Testament should always be, or at least it should begin with, a historical understanding. That means that we must understand the Old Testament in its historical setting and in its own context. Only that which is clearly allegory should be interpreted as allegory (e.g., Isaiah 5:1-7); and only that which is clearly typological should be interpreted as typology (e.g., many of the "types" in Daniel). With much truth Bultmann says that allegorizing of the Old Testament is *"Spielerei oder Unfug* [trifling or mischief]."[17] We should not impose Christian standards upon the Old Testament, and we should not read into it that which came later. The Bible is always properly read forward and not backward. The Old Testament is an introduction to the New Testament; we should not turn that proposition around, as some have tried to do, and say that the New Testament is the proper introduction to the Old Testament.

When we understand the Old Testament historically and on its own terms, then we have no need to defend the whole of the Old Testament, any more than we should defend literally and completely the whole of the New Testament.

When we read it historically, and as a part of the whole canon of Scripture, the Old Testament is far from being a "dry and somewhat unnecessary prelude to the New Testament." It is a fascinating and dynamic book, and a wholly *necessary* prelude to the New Testament. More than that, it is Scripture in its own right, indispensable as a vehicle of the Word of God for the Christian of today.

NOTES

1. *Die Grosse Täuschung* (Stuttgart and Berlin: Deutsche Verlag-Anstalt), 2 vols. 1921. This has not been translated into English.
2. *Ibid.*, II, pp. 52-53.
3. *Vorrede auf das Alte Testament*, Abs. 3, quoted by Wilhelm Vischer, *The Witness of the Old Testament to Christ*, Vol. I, Transl. by A. B. Crabtree (London: Lutterworth Press, 1949), p. 15.
4. *Ibid.*, p. 153.
5. *The Purpose of the Church and Its Ministry* (New York: Harper & Bros., 1956), pp. 44-46.
6. Emil G. Kraeling, *The Old Testament Since the Reformation* (London: Lutterworth Press, 1955), p. 32.
7. See, e.g., Luther's *Treatise on Christian Liberty* and *Introduction to the Old Testament*.
8. See the reprint of the sermon in *Historical Documents Advocating Christian Union*, ed. by C. O. Young (Chicago, 1904), p. 250.
9. *The Christian Baptist*, 1826, p. 231. For Campbell's views on Scripture, inspiration, and principles of interpretation, see Cecil K. Thomas, *Alexander Campbell and His New Version* (St. Louis: Bethany Press,

1958), pp. 113-169; on the Old Testament, see espec. pp. 163-66. That Campbell did not continue to hold all the views expressed in the Sermon on the Law is suggested by the fact that he later (1831) referred to his "most juvenile essay in a Sermon on the Law" (*ibid.*, p. 164).

10. In the essay, "The Contribution of the Old Testament to the Religious Development of Mankind," in *The People and the Book,* ed. by Arthur S. Peake (Oxford: Clarendon Press, 1925), p. 396.

11. (London and Redhill: Lutterworth Press, 1942.)

12. See, on this point, Sigmund Mowinckel, *The Old Testament as Word of God,* transl. by Reider B. Bjornard (Nashville: Abingdon Press, 1959), pp. 35-59.

13. G. Ernest Wright and Reginald H. Fuller, *The Book of the Acts of God* (Garden City: Doubleday & Co., 1957), pp. 19-21.

14. "Die Bedeutung des Alten Testaments für den christlichen Glauben," *Glauben und Verstehen* (Tübingen: J. C. B. Mohr, 1933), pp. 313-336.

15. See my article, "The God of Love in the Old Testament," in *To Do and To Teach, Essays in Honor of Charles Lynn Pyatt,* ed. by Roscoe M. Pierson (Lexington: College of the Bible, 1953), pp. 15-26.

16. Mowinckel, *op. cit.,* p. 56. Used by permission.

17. *Loc. cit.,* p. 335.

3

The Place of the New Testament in the Church

William R. Baird, Jr.

T HE New Testament has long held a place of importance in the life of the church. Ever since the canonization of the twenty-seven books which compose this document, the New Testament has been used with reverence in worship, preaching, and instruction. This is particularly true in the Protestant tradition wherein the Reformation of the sixteenth century is usually viewed as a return to biblical religion. Whereas a Roman Catholic theologian of the fifteenth century could say, "Whatever is done by the authority of the Pope is done by the authority of God," John Calvin could write, "God has been pleased to write down his truth for all eternity." Focus on this writing of God was even more sharply drawn in the seventeenth century when theologians of both the Lutheran and Reformed traditions pointed out that in their view every jot and tittle of the biblical text was an accurate representation of the mind of the Almighty.

The rise of modern historical criticism of the Bible ended all of that. It was now obvious that God had not dictated the vowel points of the Hebrew original and that hundreds of New Testament manuscripts made a completely accurate text impossible. For the modern man, the Bible had lost its authority. There were those, of course, who did not accept the results of the new criticism; these held to the Bible as their only sure anchor within the raging storms of the science-religion controversies. They advocated biblical authority, but largely relegated it to the much reduced realm of religion. In the church, the sacraments should be regulated by reference to chapter and verse; in the world, it seemed more fitting to live by Mr. Darwin's doctrine of the survival of the fittest.

By freer spirits, the new criticism was hailed as the herald of a "brave new world." Gone was the outmoded authority of the Bible, and so let it be! To be sure, the Scriptures should be held in high esteem, for they contained inspiring literature, noble ideals. As records of man's progressive quest for higher values, the writings of the prophets of Israel and the teachings of Jesus of Nazareth were worthy of serious consideration, even though much that was in the Bible fell far below these lofty achievements. But to a century which experienced two world wars and the terror of totalitarian states, even the Book of Judges seemed relevant.

Some preachers, too, felt with Karl Barth that the critics had robbed them of a vital message. What the world needed was a word from God. In search of that word, the Swiss theologian led men back to a concern for the message of the Bible. But was this new orthodoxy another passing fancy—another tenuous theological system rooted in the chaotic soil of the times? Should one embrace its loyalty to the Scriptures simply because every one was doing it? Would this loyalty, so couched in the complex jargon of the theologians, allow a view of the authority of the Bible which could genuinely guide the total life of today's church? These are the questions which now confront us. In what sense is the New Testament authoritative for the life and faith of the people of God?

I

At the outset, it needs to be acknowledged that any view of the Bible's authority is inevitably based on extrabiblical grounds. This assertion comes immediately into conflict with the common notion that somehow the Bible establishes its own authority. Yet to cite 2 Timothy 3:16 to prove that "All scripture is inspired by God" is at best to fall into the fallacy of circular argument. The arguer, of course, may insist that his basic assumption is deeper than human reason and is grounded in the word of God. But one wonders how he then justifies using reason, as he usually does, for interpreting a document whose authority is established on nonreasonable grounds.

Moreover, the texts which he quotes seem to be open to more than one interpretation. What is meant by "all scripture?" What is the meaning of the Greek term *theopneustos* which is usually translated "inspired of God"? The text at least allows the rendering that all scripture [*which*] is inspired by God . . . is profitable for teaching," and who would not agree to this? In short, the theory that the Bible establishes its own authority rests on assumptions derived from theological sources and principles of interpretation which are found outside the Scriptures. "Thus," writes C. H. Dodd, "our quarrel with the traditional way of reading the Bible is that actually it does less than justice to the Bible itself, in the interests of a theory about the Bible."[1]

More serious is the view of some theologians that the Bible has an intrinsic authority—"the authority of truth itself, compelling and subduing."[2] Thus Calvin writes:

As to the question, How shall we be persuaded that it came from God without recurring to a decree of the Church? It is just the same as if it were asked, How shall we learn to distinguish light from darkness, white from black, sweet from bitter? Scripture bears upon the face of it as clear evidence of its truth, as white and black do of their colour, sweet and bitter of their taste.[3]

Similar is Barth's dictum that "the Bible is the canon just because it is so."[4] There is an obvious degree of truth here, for Berdyaev is no doubt correct when he asserts that truth has no criteria outside itself; otherwise the criteria by which truth is judged must be acknowledged as in reality the truth.[5]

However, the Bible is not, as we shall see, this kind of truth;

it is a body of objective data about which some criteria of judgment are necessary. Besides, the notion that "the Bible is the word of God because it is the Word of God" presupposes an ear which can hear and a mind which can accept what is heard as the voice of the Almighty. On what grounds is that decision to hear and accept to be made? Why are we to decide that in this book and not that, in this Hebrew-Christian document and not in the Koran, God is speaking to us? Is it merely the subjective decision of the hearer? But even a subjective decision is made on some basis. And this is simply to say that the authority of the Bible is always based on extrabiblical grounds. The question which concerns us here is, How valid are those grounds? The answer can be found only by serious investigation of the problem of revelation.

II

The idea of revelation is complex, and to suppose that one brief chapter could solve a problem which has baffled the best theologians would be presumptuous. Moreover, it is apparent that any solution offered will be conditioned by the basic presuppositions of one's whole theological perspective. These presuppositions must be stated at the outset.

It is assumed here that revelation has to do with the making known of the Ultimate. In theological terms, this Ultimate is called God. He is the absolute Truth, the Truth which can be judged by no other criteria. He is the transcendent One, Maker of heaven and earth, Ruler of mankind. If this is true, it is clear that man in his finitude can never possess complete knowledge of God. As C. H. Dodd says, "God in His full essence cannot be known by a finite being."[6]

God, therefore, cannot be known as an ordinary object; God cannot be investigated in the way one observes chemical elements in a test tube. Man cannot wrap his mind around the transcendent Lord, since man is too small and God too "big" for that. Also, from a religious perspective, this attempt to objectify God has serious moral implications; in it, man tries to make God into his own image, and conversely, to make himself into the image of God. The sin of idolatry is persistent, whether men make idols with their hands or speculative systems with their minds. Yet to worship the creature rather than the Creator is always folly, never wisdom.

These presuppositions have some obvious implications. For one thing, it is evident that revelation is not the communication of a body of data and doctrine no matter how accurate that data and doctrine might be. What is revealed is God. To be sure, the knowledge of God may be communicated through data and doctrine, but these are at best media of revelation rather than the content of revelation itself. John Baillie is correct when he says,

what is revealed to us is not a body of information concerning various things of which we might otherwise be ignorant. If it is information at all, it is information concerning the nature and mind and purpose of God—that and nothing else. Yet in the last resort it is not information about God that is revealed, but very God Himself incarnate in Jesus Christ our Lord.[7]

Another implication of our presuppositions is the belief that revelation is primarily an act of God. Since man cannot know God by ordinary means of knowledge, since God is not an object to be discovered by man's intellectual endeavor, it appears that God is known as he makes himself known. As MacKinnon observes, "the primary thing about religion is not man's search for God, but God's search for man. The initiative lies with God."[8] This conclusion, however, is not derived rationally from some doctrine of God or some preconceived notion of revelation; it results from the fact of revelation. We believe that revelation is an act of God because God has in reality so acted that men may know him.

Participants in the Hebrew-Christian tradition believe that God acts in history. But what is meant by this currently popular theological shibboleth? It certainly does not mean that God acts in history only, so that no revelation is possible through his work of creation; nor that only *God* acts in history so that man's freedom to act is thereby denied. Nor does it mean that the theologian is enabled to point to certain events of his own time and say, "Lo here, lo there." Rather it means that God who is the Creator of heaven and earth and the Ruler of all men is working in and through the processes of history for the accomplishment of his purposes. It means that history has meaning. Thus for the idea of revelation, history as the realm where God works involves both happening and meaning, both event and interpretation.

The confession of the Christian theologian, however, is that the meaning of all history is given through a particular event of history. This is the scandal of Christianity—that in the midst of history's relativities is revealed the end, the *telos,* the goal, the meaning of the whole process of history. Of necessity, this assertion is an act of faith. Man has no knowledge of the end whereby he can judge the validity of the historical revelation which confronts him. Yet this revelation is no mere body of objective data about which he can make some intellectual decision, it is an event in the midst of his own historical existence which makes an absolute claim upon him.

When one confesses that Jesus Christ is Lord, then he comes to know that in this revelation is fulfilled all the requirements of an event which can convey ultimate meaning, a history in which God is acting. This revelation is historical—concrete and real in the midst of our very own history. We can know him, for the Word became flesh and dwelt among us. This revelation is personal, known on the highest level of human perception, the level of personal encounter, so that God is known as 'Thou,' not as 'it.' This revelation is transparent, open to a clear unveiling of the transcendent God. "The acceptance of the cross, both during his life and at the end of it," writes Tillich, "is the decisive test of his unity with God, of his complete transparency to the ground of being."[9]

Although the revelation of God in Jesus Christ is primarily an act of God, it also involves the response of man. This response is called faith. By faith we do not mean intellectual assent to the validity of certain propositions, but personal commitment to a personal revelation. Since the revelation of God is through a person, the response to that revelation must be likewise personal. God has entrusted himself to us; we are called upon to entrust ourselves to him. Moreover, this faithful response of man participates in the event of revelation. It is false to assume that revelation is an act of God occurring *in vacuo* to be simply received or rejected by men. No, response is necessary before revelation actually occurs. Not until men have faith can they confess that Jesus Christ is Lord.

Now this view that response is an essential element of the revelatory event has led to confusion. If human response is necessary before revelation can take place, it seems that the occurrence of revelation is determined by men, and that revelation is not, as we have previously affirmed, primarily an act of God. Similarly, if faith is necessary for revelation, one wonders how man can respond unless something has first been revealed. Which comes first, faith or revelation?

Objections of this sort indicate that revelation is inadequately understood. It is not a mechanical transaction which can be subjected to objective analysis. It is an act of God in which man participates; God acts with man in Christ to make himself known. There are no "firsts" or "seconds," but one event which opens the eyes of faith to see "the glory of God in the face of Christ" (2 Corinthians 4:6). It is only by the grace of God that we can see at all, and to the man of faith, even his own free response seems to be an act of God. This is perhaps what Paul means by the "gift of faith." In the divine human relationship it is difficult, it is impossible, to know precisely what is of God and what is of man. "Work out your own salvation with fear and trembling; for God is at work in you" (Philippians 2:12).

71

It has been implied that this revelation of God in Jesus Christ is somehow final, or better, "once for all." This many find difficult to accept. How can it be that one event of revelation occurring two thousand years ago through a Jew from Nazareth is valid for all men in every time? This objection often indicates misunderstanding of the revelation concept also. What is communicated through the revelatory event is not primarily new information, but new life. Jesus Christ is not the once-for-all revelation because he has the last word on atomic physics, but because he is the saving Word from God. He is the solidly historical, fully personal, totally transparent revelation; he evokes a response of total personal commitment; he grants a salvation which is full and complete.

The fullness of this revelation, of course, no man can know, nor can he presume upon what God may yet make manifest. Yet one thing is clear: God's revelatory act in its very essence makes an absolute claim which demands an absolute response. Since it is in the cross of Christ that this revelation is most clearly seen, it is evident that man must make this claim in absolute humility. Yet for the eyes of faith, a revelation which would transcend that given through Jesus Christ is in this world inconceivable.

Yet "the form of this world is passing away" (1 Corinthians 7:31). Although the revelation in Jesus Christ is final for this historical existence, it is apparent that a fuller revelation is yet to come. Even the Christ had to empty himself in order to come into history, and because of the mists and vapors of existence, man sees through a glass darkly. Man's response is never really absolute, and the salvation received is never fully realized in this world. Yet the revelation at the end of history will be nothing radically new, but only the consummation of what has been revealed. This is why the early church expected the *eschaton* as the *parousia*—the coming of Jesus Christ as Lord. The revelation of God in Christ is the revelation at one point in history of the way in which God deals with man in the beginning, in the midst, and at the end of history. There is not a kind of progressive revelation whereby God makes himself known on the installment plan,[10] but the varying response of men to the One God, who is Creator, Revealer, Redeemer.

III

The Bible, particularly the New Testament, gains its authority as witness to the revelation of God in Jesus Christ. The New Testament is our primary historical record of what God has done in the revelatory event. As John Baillie says, "We know nothing of Christ except what comes to us through the Bible, all later communication of Christian knowledge being dependent upon this original record."[11]

However, the New Testament is more than a mere record of what happened in history. As we have seen, revelation in history involves both event and interpretation, both act of God and response of men. The New Testament not only tells what Jesus said and did, it also relates the significance of Jesus as the Christ. Actually, a clear distinction between what happened and what it means cannot be sharply drawn in the New Testament or in any historical document, for that matter. The New Testament is throughout an inextricable intertwining of event and meaning, divine action and human response. Since revelation is not complete without response, it is evident that the New Testament is a witness to the "complete circuit"[12] of the revelatory event. We are dependent, then, not only on the New Testament as a prior witness to historical events, but also on the New Testament as a unique medium of divine revelation. Without both God's act in Christ and the faithful response of the apostles, it would not be possible for us to receive revelation. God's revelatory action is one, and our response must be one with those who first called him Christ and Lord. Thus the New Testament has a priority and normative function in our understanding of the will and purposes of God.

Although the New Testament is a unique medium of the

revelation of God, it participates in the relativities of history. Revelation is not the transmission of an objective body of data and doctrine even though that data and doctrine may be found in the Bible. The New Testament is obviously something less than *the* revelation of God in Christ; and if even Christ emptied himself, it is evident that the Bible does not fully contain a final manifestation of God. The New Testament is historical, but, unlike the revelation in Christ, it is not fully personal or completely transparent to God. Indeed, to interpret the biblical canon as the "perfect" thing which is to come (1 Corinthians 13:10) is to disregard the human imperfections of the Bible as well as to distort the biblical concept of revelation. For the Bible, the Word of God is a person, Jesus Christ (John 1:1, 14); the words of Scripture are words which men use to describe and confess faith in that Word.

Further illustration of the thoroughgoing historical character of the New Testament is seen in the development of the canon. As any serious student of the Bible knows, the twenty-seven books of the New Testament did not fall from heaven on the day of Pentecost bound into one morocco-leather volume. The canon of the New Testament developed in history. Out of the mass of early Christian writings, these twenty-seven documents were selected as representing the true faith of the early church. The principle of selection was apostolicity; those books which seemed to come from an apostle or represented valid apostolic tradition were accepted. The accepting was done in accordance with usage, and final approval was given by the hierarchy individually and meeting in council. Not until the fourth century was a New Testament containing precisely our twenty-seven books generally accepted. Some valuable Christian books were omitted and some debatable books included; we must agree with Reid that "much less than what we have in the New Testament . . . would suffice; and on the other hand there is no reason why we should not have had much more."[13] This means that the canon is relative and not absolute as a witness to divine revelation. To posit an absolute canon, is to posit an absolute church.

However, the canon of the New Testament does have a high degree of authority. It is our exclusive witness to the event of revelation which involves both God's act and man's response; we are ever dependent on the sight and faith of the apostles; apart from these we do not receive the revelation of God in Christ. The books selected by the early church do in the main represent historical priority and theological continuity with the faith of the apostles. It may be that men of the second and third centuries could judge better what was apostolic than men of the sixteenth or twentieth. "But it remains true," as Reid says, "that in the Bible we have a group of works manifesting a combination of qualities which together distinguish them from other works: qualities of integrity, authenticity, and proximity to the subject of their writing, together with at their centre the hard core of eye-witness record."[14]

This discussion of the formation of the New Testament canon gives rise to a further question in regard to biblical authority: What is the relation of the authority of the Bible to the authority of the church? Although it is theoretically true in the Roman tradition that Scripture and church have equal authority, in actual practice the dogma that the church is the sole interpreter of Scripture gives the church an authority above the Scripture.[15] One must agree with the Roman Catholics that the church antedates the New Testament and that the New Testament canon was formulated by the church—even a church which already was beginning to bear the marks of the church of Rome.

One must insist however, that the church is secondary to the event of revelation of which the New Testament is a unique witness. The essential error of the Roman doctrine of revelation is its tendency to understand revelation as propositional, as the transmission of revealed truths which can be written down in Scripture and interpreted in the dogmas of the church. Rather, the dynamic event of revelation is an act of God, received in faith, and witnessed in the work of the apostles. This witness is proclamation, *kerygma*, and response to the *kerygma* creates the church. The essential function of the church is proclamation, witness to what God has done in Jesus Christ. If the church is to remain the church, it must ever be loyal to and judged by that historical revelation, and the primary witness to that revelation is found in Scripture.

This is not to assert a rigid doctrine of *sola scriptura*. Obviously the tradition of the church has been essential in the formation and transmission of the New Testament. Not only the selection of the canonical books, but even the writing of the New Testament documents took place within the ongoing life of the early church. Perhaps the latest book, probably 2 Peter, was not written until about A.D. 150. But why should a line be drawn in the middle of the second century; why should not the spirit which was working in this vital tradition be allowed to guide men into all truth?

Yet a line was drawn, indeed, had to be drawn. The essential reason for drawing the line was to make clear the important distinction between scripture and tradition—a distinction which was firmly grounded in the conviction that revelation is historical.[16] Failure to draw the line would have been to deny the essential historical nature of Christianity. The documents on one side of the line had priority due to their proximity to the revelatory events and to their faithfulness to the apostolic confession. It is interesting that those who in the second century wanted the line drawn some other place were also those most eager to deny the real historicity of the divine revelation. It is also interesting that the line which separated tradition from scripture was drawn by the tradition itself. To acknowledge the validity of tradition is to recognize the priority of Scripture.

One must not hasten to easy conclusions. If it is tradition which establishes scriptural authority, then tradition seems to have authority over Scripture. Actually the authority of both Scripture and tradition is grounded elsewhere—in the revelation of God in history. Scripture gains priority as the primary witness to the revelatory events, but Scripture must be interpreted in the tradition of the church. Thus both Scripture and church have a secondary authority through their witness to revelation. Scripture is only a witness to the event, and tradition's interpretation must be true to the event as witnessed in the Scriptures. The Scripture is proclamation of the word of God, but only when that *kerygma* is proclaimed in the living church does the gospel become the power of God to salvation. Thus Scripture and tradition stand in a tension of mutual correction—a tension, which maintained, witnesses to the revelation of God. The church must ever be "built upon the foundation of the apostles and prophets, Christ Jesus himself being the chief cornerstone" (Ephesians 2:20).

In all this discussion of revelation and the Bible, something seems notably lacking: the doctrine of inspiration. Is not the New Testament an inspired document? The concept of inspiration has heretofore been avoided partly because of its variety of uses and meanings. The term "inspiration" is used to mean anything from the rigid doctrine of verbally inerrant dictation, to the vapid notion that "what is inspiring is inspired." Basically the doctrine of inspiration means that the Holy Spirit has performed a unique function in the formation of the biblical witness. Just what this function is remains a matter of debate. Some suggest that not the writing, but the writer was inspired, thus avoiding such problems as minor textual inaccuracies. Others insist that writing as well as writer are inspired, although allowance is usually made for the humanity of both language and author. Some reserve the term "inspiration" exclusively for the communication of revelation, while others employ it freely to refer to the illumination which comes with the receiving of revealed truth.[17]

The confusion in regard to the doctrine of inspiration results in the main from a failure to understand the meaning of revelation correctly. For most inspirationists, as for most Roman Catholics, revelation is understood as propositional. The Bible is a collection of revealed truths, spoken by God to his chosen messengers and, therefore, without error. Unless man can build his faith on such sure doctrines, all other ground is sinking sand. This view confuses the words of Scripture with the Word of God, the word of witness with the Word made flesh.

At any rate, a valid doctrine of inspiration ought to avoid identification with the ideas of infallibility and inerrancy. As C. H. Dodd says, "Inspiration therefore does not imply moral perfection or intellectual infallibility."[18] To suppose that man can prove the truth of inspiration by citing inerrancy is to subject the activities of the Holy Spirit to the empirical and rational judgments of men. Or to quote the conservative theologian Geoffrey W. Bromiley, "To try to defend inspiration in terms of inerrancy is thus to commit it to inevitable relativization."[19] Indeed, Protestant theologians who have been inclined to relegate the activity of the Spirit to the scriptorium need to be reminded that the spirit blows where it wills. No doubt it was at work in the writers and writings of Scripture, and no doubt these witnesses were faithful and true, for these are the valid and vital witness to the revelation of God. Yet what the spirit gives to them is not primarily accuracy, but power. The God who is Revealer and Redeemer is also the One present in his Word to do his work.

IV

If it is true that the New Testament is our primary witness to the proclamation which gave birth to the church and in which the church finds its essential function, it is obvious that the New Testament ought to have an important place in the life of the church. We have already seen that the church ever stands under the judgment of the historical revelation to which the New Testament bears witness, and that the church is the interpreter of that scriptural witness. Now we turn to practical concerns. How is the New Testament to be used in the ongoing life of the Christian community?

We may begin by raising the question: How is the Bible to be interpreted? Since the New Testament witnesses to a historical revelation and since it is itself a phenomenon of history, the answer is clear: The Bible must be interpreted by the best methods of historical research. This indicates that the modern approach of scientific historical criticism is essential to a valid understanding of the New Testament. The methods of lower criticism whereby a relatively accurate text is established, and the methods of higher criticism in which the authorship, date, and historical backgrounds of the writing are investigated, must be employed; i.e., the Bible must be studied by essentially the same methods as any other document of ancient history. Unless this principal is observed, the conviction that God's revelation actually occurred in history is undermined, and the possibility of an intelligible, universal witness to that revelation is endangered. Revelation-history must remain real history—a history which can be related through historical media to historical men.

This is not to suggest that historical method guarantees absolute results or that it has achieved perfection as a method of research. No one knows better than the historian the relativity of his results. Yet, for all its failings, this is the best method we have. Of late, there have been some significant attempts on the part of philosophers of history to refine the method. They have observed that the older emphasis on cold objectivity in the analysis of historical sources may have been somewhat misplaced. Since history involves both event and meaning, it seems that ability to share the meaning of historical records aids in their interpretation. Indeed, the historian is inevitably a participant in history, and his participation may help rather than hinder his understanding of the history he seeks to interpret. Only the man who has an ear for music can understand Beethoven; only the man who shares to some degree the faith of the New Testament can fully understand New Testament history. This is why the Bible can best be interpreted within the church; not because the church has some esoteric gift of interpretation but because it allows more effective employment of historical criticism.

Nevertheless, the theological value of historical criticism seems to have come into question through the writings of two of our most respected practitioners of the critic's art—Rudolf Bultmann and John Knox. These theologians insist that the faith of the Christian is in no essential way determined by the results of historical criticism. Their motives in this assertion differ slightly. Bultmann, taking up a thoroughly Protestant view of faith, insists correctly that faith is never grounded in objective data, and thus, never dependent on the results of biblical research.[20] Knox, on the other hand, is anxious to show that the results of historical criticism are not entirely negative; despite the common notion to the contrary, the biblical critics are on the side of the "good guys" and not the "bad guys" after all. In defending this thesis, he insists that the essential elements of the faith remain unassailable to the historian's assaults. He even goes so far as to say that "our knowledge of Christ is not dependent upon what can be reliably known about the historical life of Jesus."[21]

Bultmann's view of faith seems, at least to this observer, to be sound. Moreover, the implication of his idea of faith—that the content of revelation is nonobjective—is in essential agreement with the view expressed above. But the media through which this revelation comes and by which this faith is evoked have a genuine historicity. Indeed, the historical media shape any understanding which may be given to the revelation and any form of confession which may be given to the faith. When we say that God's way of dealing with men is revealed in history in Jesus Christ, we acknowledge that our understanding of that way is determined by what we see Jesus saying and doing.

In his assertion that knowledge of Christ is not dependent upon what can be reliably known about the historical life of Jesus, Knox intends to stress the word *reliably*. That is, he quite correctly wants to show that our faith does not rest on the security of the details of Jesus' career. However, his tendency to draw a distinction between the memory of the church and the history of Jesus fails to take the concept of historical revelation with adequate seriousness. The early church remembered *what happened,* and through those happenings God is revealed. No doubt, many of the details of the Galilean's career remain obscure, but certain events like the crucifixion have fundamental significance for faith. Knox is on much surer ground when he writes, "Over and over again in these pages it has been affirmed that the revelation of God in Christ was God's action in and through a historical event. . . . On the other hand if the affirmation is true, the value of historical method is established, for only by this method can any historical event be recovered."[22]

What Knox apparently intends to point out is that the ordinary believer is not at the mercy of the whims of scholarly minutiae. It is obvious that there were Christians before the science of historical criticism was invented, and to picture the faith-seeking souls of the laity as sitting down with gaping mouths awaiting the latest discovery from the Judaean desert is preposterous. Knox points out that the essential elements of our faith—that the event of revelation really occurred and that it has a significance for the life of the believer—are known in the life of the Christian community. But what he fails to observe is that when the church knows these things, it in effect becomes an historian. To assert that an event occurred is to speak as an historian. Whenever an illiterate Christian even tells "the old, old story of Jesus and his love," he relates history; and our understanding of the quality and character of that love is determined by our picture of Jesus. Some elements in that portrait, such as the length of his beard and the color of his hair, are of obvious insignificance; this is why the New Testament never mentions such things. But every new insight we can gain into the character and conduct of Jesus will enrich our understanding of the Christ who is the revelation of God. Such new insights will come through the study of history by historians trained and untrained.[23]

What we need in the church, of course, is more trained historians in the pew—not more professional biblical critics, but more ordinary men of faith who can and will study the primary witness to the event of revelation in which their faith is grounded. But as H. Cunliffe-Jones observes, "The Bible has become too much a book for specialists; a book on the serious discussion of which men are hesitant to embark lest they trespass on some technical preserve, and be condemned out of hand for some highly technical errors."[24] The Bible has become the captive of a new brand of scribes, who tithe verb conjugations and text criticism but neglect the weightier matters of the gospel. These matters would include serious instruction of the laity in the study of the Bible. Here is the source for the very life and faith of our people, and to offer them less is to give them serpent for fish, stone for bread.

There may be some truth, for instance, in the charge that our church school material is lacking in biblical teaching. No doubt there are some stories in the Bible which are too harsh for tender ears, but after the violence of much of contemporary television melodrama, even the conquest of Canaan seems mild. The important thing, of course, is not the telling of "Bible stories," but the relating of the story of the Bible. This is the history of salvation, the record of God's dealing with men. Perhaps even the children are tired of lessons which only urge them to "see God's beautiful trees"; it may be that they, too, are bored with the notion that all ethical problems can be solved by "sharing with brother" and "helping mommy."

The Bible must be at the very heart of the whole life of the church. The worship of the church is the praise and adoration of the God who has revealed himself in Jesus Christ, a revelation whose primary witness is found in the New Testament. The preaching of the church must always be biblical, for the church's proclamation is the declaration of the Word of God, the Word made flesh, witnessed in the New Testament, re-presented in the words of the preacher. The sacraments of the church are grounded in the historical revelation of God as witnessed in the Bible and dramatically re-enacted in the ongoing life of the people of God. The ethical life of the Christians is a response to the redemption which God has freely revealed in Jesus Christ so that the New Testament is not a set of moral principles to be literally applied to today's problems but a witness to the kind of response in faith which men must make in their own ethical situations, always responsible to the love of God revealed in Christ. The church is the body of Christ and its essential function is to carry on the work of God; the form of that body has been revealed in Jesus Christ, and the character of that work is manifest in the life of those who first called him Lord.

We have seen that the New Testament occupies a unique place of authority in the life of the church. That authority is not established by the Bible itself, but is grounded in a theology of revelation. The view of revelation taken here is that God has acted in history in Jesus Christ; the New Testament gains its authority as primary witness to that historical revelation. The Bible, therefore, must be interpreted by the best insights of modern historical method and made relevant to the whole life of the church. But can it yet be affirmed that the Bible is the word of God? If we mean by this that the words of Scripture are the precise words of the Almighty, then the answer is, No. Or if we suggest instead that the Bible contains the word of God, the answer is still 'No,' since the Scriptures should not be understood as a container nor the revelation of God as some object which can be carried around. But if we mean that the Bible is the message of God—a living witness to his revelation in Christ who is the Word, then the Bible may be called the word of God.

NOTES

1. C. H. Dodd, *The Authority of the Bible* (2d ed. New York: Harper and Row, Publishers, Inc., 1938), p. 12.
2. *Ibid.*, p. 21.
3. Jean Calvin, *Institutes,* I, vii, 2.
4. Karl Barth, *The Doctrine of the Word of God,* trans. G. T. Thomson (Edinburgh: T. and T. Clark, 1936), p. 120.

5. Nicolas Berdyaev, *Truth and Revelation,* trans. R. M. French (London: Geoffrey Bles, 1953), p. 39.

6. Dodd, *op. cit.,* p. 274.

7. John Baillie, *The Idea of Revelation in Recent Thought* (New York: Columbia University Press, 1956), p. 28.

8. John Y. MacKinnon, *The Protestant Doctrine of Revelation* (Toronto: Ryerson Press, 1946), p. 9.

9. Paul Tillich, *Systematic Theology* (Chicago: University of Chicago Press, 1951), I, 136.

10. This terminology is suggested and well refuted by J. K. S. Reid in *The Authority of Scripture* (London: Methuen and Co., Ltd., 1957), p. 184.

11. Baillie, *op. cit.,* p. 117.

12. Cf. Emil Brunner, *Revelation and Reason,* trans. Olive Wyon (Philadelphia: Westminster, 1946), p. 122.

13. Reid, *op. cit.,* p. 139.

14. *Ibid.,* p. 237.

15. Cf. *Ibid.,* p. 103.

16. John Knox, *Criticism and Faith* (Nashville: Abingdon Press, 1952), p. 62: "To say that the event has this normative value is to say that the earliest period of the church's life has an importance which no subsequent period can have." Cf. also, p. 82.

17. For a discussion of definitions, cf. R. A. Finlayson, "Contemporary Ideas of Inspiration," in Carl F. H. Henry (ed.), *Revelation and the Bible* (Grand Rapids: Baker Book House, 1958), pp. 221ff.

18. Dodd, *op. cit.,* p. 128.

19. "The Church Doctrine of Inspiration," in Henry, *op. cit.,* p. 215.

20. Cf., for example, Hans Werner Bartsch (ed.), *Kerygma and Myth,* trans. Reginald H. Fuller (London, S.P.C.K., 1953), p. 35; Rudolf Bultmann, *Jesus Christ and Mythology* (New York: Charles Scribner's Sons, 1958), p. 54.

21. Knox, *op. cit.,* p. 47.

22. *Ibid.,* pp. 78f.

23. The significance of historical study for faith is made clear by James M. Robinson, *A New Quest for the Historical Jesus,* "Studies in Biblical Theology No. 25" (London: SCM Press, 1959), pp. 85ff.

24. H. Cunliffe-Jones, *The Authority of the Biblical Revelation* (Boston: Pilgrim Press, 1948), p. 34.

⚛ 4 ⚛

The Tradition of the Life
and Teachings of Jesus in the *Kerygma*

Stephen J. England

THE scholarly discovery of the *kerygma,* a feature of New Testament study in our time, has been associated conspicuously with the scholarly labors of C. H. Dodd. Many other scholars have enlarged on the concept. The basic concept is that we can now discern in the literary remains coming down from the earliest church two strata of material. It is widely held that the earliest mission preachers proclaimed the mighty acts of God for human redemption and that the response to this proclamation or *kerygma* led to the formation of Christian communities, or congregations, in which the teaching *(didache)* was developed in order to meet the various needs of personal Christian life and communal living.

The present paper deals with the question of the content of material in the *kerygma* and specifically, the extent to which it included the tradition of the life and teachings of Jesus. The question is relevant to the teaching of New Testament in the theological seminary and whether this department should include a course in the Life and Teachings of Jesus. A casual survey of catalogues of theological seminaries indicates that this particular area has declined in popularity to a remarkable degree in recent years. In part, the decline may be traced to an understandable reaction to some of the findings of the Form Criticism.

Investigation of the oral tradition which is believed to lie behind our present gospels has led in some quarters to the belief that we can know little reliably about anything that Jesus either said or did. Recent theological studies, based in part upon the Form Criticism, have raised the additional question whether, even if we can know many of the facts and teachings, the information would be significant material for the preacher. At basis, we deal here with the relation of the knowledge of presumed fact to the religious experience of the person who studies the historical record. As Dibelius pointed out,[1] history and faith are not identical. What may be called "the assured results" of scientific historical study are not the same as "saving truths." It is at least theoretically possible to accept the literal accuracy of the records in our gospels concerning the deeds and teachings of Jesus without undergoing a mystical type of conversion experience or without being "existentially involved" in that which is accepted as accurate. It is equally possible for one to become a Christian, in some sense of the term, without knowing very much about any supposed facts from the life of Jesus. Most of us have known devout laymen and effective ministers who have grown up in Christian homes, who breathed the generally Christian atmophere of Western culture, who have fallen under the influence of a Christian congregation and who as a result display "the fruit of the Spirit" (Galatians 5:21) but who have only the haziest idea, critical or otherwise, about anything that is reported to have happened in the career of the historical Jesus.

The rather widely held opinion that the study of the life and teachings of Jesus is, if not futile, at any rate without practical value is doubtless in part a reaction to this observed situation. Investigation of the content of the *kerygma* might serve to restore the study of the Life and Teachings of Jesus to a position of importance; or alternatively to ease our consciences at its elimination.

The topic is especially relevant to preaching and theology

among Disciples of Christ. In 1826 Walter Scott launched an evangelistic movement among the churches acknowledging the leadership of Alexander Campbell which eventuated in consequences of the most remarkable kind. It has been said by historians of Disciples of Christ that the success of his evangelism made the separation of Disciples from the Baptists inevitable. Because his evangelism was so enormously successful (at least in point of numbers reached) evangelism became a central emphasis among Disciples from the time of Scott down to the fairly recent past. The success of his evangelism, based upon certain theological ideas, fixed a number of characteristic theological positions of Disciples. Among these were the concept of faith as based on the acceptance of evidence; conversion as a rational, nonemotional procedure based upon normative Scripture; and baptism for remission of sins.

A brief review of Walter Scott's evangelistic preaching and procedure will indicate the relevance of our study to his positions. The literal authority of the words of Scripture was widely, if not universally, accepted by Scott and his contemporaries. It was therefore an immense enhancement to the power of his preaching when he came to believe and persuaded others to agree that he was preaching the gospel as it had been preached at the first. In the scholarly context of our time, we might say that Walter Scott had discovered the *kerygma*. Although he was innocent of the scholarly and critical presuppositions of our time, his studies led him to a position which, in certain interesting ways, is similar to the scholarly development with which we are now dealing. Referring respectively to Thomas Campbell, to Alexander Campbell and to himself Scott said,

First the Bible was adopted as the sole authority in our assemblies, to the exclusion of all other books. Next the Apostolic order was proposed. Finally the True Gospel was restored.[2]

He called the last item "the original arrangement of the elements of the gospel." In an interesting anticipation of modern scholarship, Scott analyzed "the things of Christianity" as consisting of "Faith," "Order," and "Morality."

In such a division, . . . "The Faith" would include all the parts of our religion which are strictly evangelical. . . . "The Order" would embrace whatever . . . belongs to the public order of the church. . . . "The Morality" . . . would comprise the public and private morality and manners and customs enjoined upon its professors. The first part is intended to . . . make men Christians; the second is to keep them such; and the third is intended to show what christians are, or must become . . . if they would honor their profession and please God.[3]

A century before C. H. Dodd, Scott distinguished between proclamation in the earliest church, response to which made men Christians, and teaching in the earliest church, which proceeded from that point. Scott, much like Dodd, used the sermons in the first half of Acts as normative for the "gospel" which he believed he was restoring.

In his preaching, Scott's method was very simple. Accepting the gospel records as literally accurate and as being intended in the wisdom of God for the sole purpose of presenting the evidence that Jesus was the Messiah, Scott would make the presentation from the Gospels concerning the deeds, the words, and the character of Jesus. He urged his hearers to accept the literal truth of this record, which acceptance would, he believed, lead them to faith. When his hearers believed that Jesus is the Messiah, they would raise the question, "What shall we do?" At this point, Scott would reply with the famous five-finger exercise, outlining the steps of obedience to the *kerygma*.

It is a commonplace observation that Disciples of Christ are now rethinking their position. One current and urgent question is the reason why evangelism seems to be declining. It seems evident enough that the difficulty is not entirely methodological, but is basically theological. To reproduce the evangelistic victories of Walter Scott in our day, we cannot simply parrot his preaching, for most ministers now do not share the precritical attitude toward the Scriptures which he held. It may, however, be the case that the evangelistic application of the concept of the *kerygma,* based upon intelligent scholarship, may serve the needs of our churches. The present study seems relevant to this issue. In the attempt of Disciples to define their theology, the related questions of the nature of Christian faith and the character of the experience of conversion are paramount. In Scott's thinking, history and faith were inextricably related and conversion ultimately rested on acceptance of facts. The topic of this paper is a preliminary step to the reassessment of theological thinking among Disciples in this area.

Certain theological issues of our time are related to the topic of our study. One of these is the relation of faith and history. In a special way, the question of the possibility of knowing much, if anything, about the life of Jesus bears on this problem. The emergence of an existentialist philosophy and theology, combined with the Form Criticism of the gospels, has led in some quarters to a deep skepticism about our knowledge of the career of Jesus. It may be questioned whether the depth of the skepticism is entirely dependent on the Form Criticism. Bultmann, one of the most skeptical of the Form Critics, is also a dedicated existentialist; and it is probable that his philosophy, minimizing the importance of the record of the life of Jesus, has inclined him to dismiss the record as in fact inconsequential. Other Form Critics (such as Vincent Taylor and Martin Dibelius) have not been so skeptical as Bultmann.

The tendencies toward dismissal of the importance of the records of the life of Jesus are clearly stated by Bultmann in his *New Testament Theology:*

The personality of Jesus has no importance for the kerygma either of Paul or of John or for the New Testament in general. . . .

It was not as the one who was the living embodiment of the religion, the obedience, which he demanded nor as the one who filled those open to his influence with fascination and enthusiasm, kindling them to "imitation" of himself that he was esteemed

. . . nor was it *the mystery of his nature* as if the "numinous" had there taken form.[4]

Bultmann affirms that Paul held that "Jesus was a definite concrete man. . . . But beyond that, Jesus' manner of life, his ministry, his personality, his character play no role at all; neither does Jesus' message."[5]

Some recent scholars feel that this leads us in the direction of a new Docetism. For example, Colwell and Titus in *The Gospel of the Spirit* say,

There is a contemporary tendency in some quarters to emphasize the living Christ of faith to the virtual exclusion of the Jesus who lived in history. . . .

This emphasis on the divine Christ to the virtual exclusion of the historical Jesus constitutes a modern equivalent of the ancient docetic heresy. From the point of view of the Christian church it is a dangerous emphasis, for it is a denial of the historic roots of the revelation. Furthermore, it fails to recognize that the Christ concept if it is to be true to the historic roots of the Christian religion must maintain some kind of continuity with the attitude and spirit which characterized Jesus of Nazareth. How easy it is to depart from that attitude and spirit has been demonstrated repeatedly and tragically in Church history.[6]

In similar vein, C. H. Dodd in *History and the Gospel* said,
We may describe the story of the Gospels as a narrative of events . . . in which is to be discerned the mighty act of the transcendent God which brings history to its fulfillment. . . . If we lose hold upon that historical actuality, the Gospels are betrayed into the hands of the Gnostics, and we stand upon the verge of a new Docetism. Moreover, the denial of the importance of historical facts would carry with it a denial of what is the essence of the Gospel, namely, that the historical order . . . has received a specific character from the entrance into it of the eternal Word of God.[7]

This paper is not presented as an attempt to solve the complex theological problems involved in the concept of a revelation of God within history. It is, however, an approach to a phase of that problem which seems basic to the whole. It presents a brief survey of the extent to which the tradition of the words and deeds of the human Jesus was employed in the *kerygma* of the early church. On this basis, the preaching of Walter Scott, as a part of the heritage of Disciples of Christ, is then evaluated.

In making a survey of the *kerygmatic* preaching in the early church, certain erroneous presuppositions held by some modern writers must be avoided. In the first place, it is unrealistic to suppose that the early church rigidly distinguished between *"kerygma"* and *"didache,"* as modern scholars do. The *kerygmatic* announcement blended into the *didactic* admonition in the words of the missionaries, as is the case in the epistles of the New Testament.

In the second place, even though it seems clear that the ancient *kerygma* included the tradition, certainly no complete biographical account of the life of Jesus from its beginning to its close, or even a complete account of everything he did and said during his public ministry, was the basis of the call to repentance and obedience. This appears clearly in the nature of the material left to us in the presently existing gospels.

In the third place, however, even though the ancient preachers might have been willing to restrict their *kerygmatic* announcement to mention only of the death and resurrection of Jesus, or of the resurrection as preceded by the death, their audiences would scarcely have permitted them to do so.

The initial question we are considering, then, is largely factual. How much of the tradition concerning what Jesus did and said was actually used in the mission preaching of the early church? Was the offer of forgiveness and salvation based upon a revelation of God found exclusively in the death and resurrection of Jesus, or was it based upon a revelation which, climaxed by death and resurrection, included the deeds, attitudes, words, and character of the historic Jesus? A related question is the extent to which Disciples, in their heritage, were committed to an existentialist interpretation of the New Testament, especially the Gospels.

The Gospels as Kerygmatic

We may begin our investigation where Walter Scott started his typical preaching: with the gospels. While it is evident enough that he was unconcerned about (because unacquainted with) the complexities of the Synoptic problem, that is not the point of interest. He, like his contemporaries, would never have raised the question whether the records in the gospels were factually accurate. They were unaware of the critical problem presented by the fact that the gospels, in their present form, arose long after the original preaching which led to formation of the Christian communities. The basic point, however, is not whether Scott was abreast of modern critical scholarship, but his concept of the purpose which led to the writing of the gospels.

Modern discussions in general discover one of three purposes behind the books. First, the gospels were biographical, intended to record the history of the life and ministry of Jesus. Or second, they were *didactic,* preserving materials developed to help congregations in meeting practical problems of the Christian life. Or third, they were *kerygmatic,* that which was to be preached in order to win adherents. The division is, of course, oversimplified; the lines overlap. But in such a classification, Scott would agree with the third position. He held that God inspired certain men to produce the gospels in order to present the evidence that would generate faith on the part of the hearers that Jesus was the Messiah of God. Although he did not use the technical term, he held that the *kerygma* of the earliest church rested upon recital of the deeds and words of Jesus. The position upheld in this paper agrees in general terms with Scott.

At the time of their collection into a canon of gospels the church believed that this material was a record of the *kerygma.* The character of the material itself supports the same position.

When the canon of gospels was formed, perhaps about A.D. 120, the title given to the fourfold document was "The Gospel," with subtitles "According to Matthew," etc., appended to the respective books. The title of the canon of gospels seems to have been equivalent to "the missionary message of the church." By the time the gospels were combined into a canon, it was the belief of the canon makers that the material in these books was itself the church's missionary message. By this time, the account of what Jesus did in his life prior to the passion, no less than the passion itself, was the content of the *kerygma,* or "gospel." A similar usage of the word "gospel" as in general equivalent to *"kerygma"* occurs in Romans 2:16, 1 Thessalonians 1:5; and especially 1 Corinthians 15:1.

The Gospel according to Mark opens with the statement "the beginning of the gospel of Jesus Christ," which Grant paraphrases as "the good news about Jesus Christ."[8] Whether the words originated with the author or were appended at the time the book was put into circulation, the conclusion is the same. Either the author or someone very near his time believed that the church's mission preaching really began when Jesus entered his ministry, a beginning joined to the coming of John the Baptist. A similar use of the word "gospel" occurs in Mark 14:9, "wherever the gospel is preached in the whole world." Grant remarks that the word "gospel" here "includes incidents from the life of Jesus which presumably the apostolic preaching included from the beginning."[9]

In general, the use of the word "gospel" in relation to the first four books of our New Testament canon indicates that, from an early time dating back to the origin of our second Gospel, it was believed that the ministry of Jesus, climaxed of course by his death and resurrection, was to be included in the *kerygma.* We may not here digress into detailed study of the complexities of the purposes of the authors who wrote the books. There is general agreement that the books had a didactic purpose, including the affirmation of the faith of the respective authors and that of the churches in the areas where they wrote. A further didactic purpose was doubtless to support the faithful in the difficulties and persecutions which were the lot of Christian communities in the late first and early second centuries. Thus Matthew may be understood as a support of Christians amid an unfriendly Jewish environment; Mark, the putting of iron into the souls of those facing Roman persecution and martyrdom; and Luke, the adding of certainty to the nebulous Theophilus addressed in its prologue (1:1-4).

Beyond this didactic purpose, we must agree with G. Ernest Wright and Reginald Fuller that "the primary purpose of the gospels is . . . to evoke faith."[10] The earliest church was not merely on the defensive, attempting to sustain its members physically and spiritually in an unfriendly social situation. The church was intensely evangelistic, and was devoted to winning adherents while persecution was going on. The announced purpose of the Fourth Gospel applies to all (John 20:31): "these things are written that you might believe that Jesus is the Christ, the Son of God, and that believing you may have life in his name." The conviction of the author was that recital of what Jesus did would lead to belief and to life. In the terms of that Gospel, the reality of the incarnation (John 1:14) was demonstrated by what Jesus did; and the deeds, brought to a climactic conclusion by his death and resurrection, reached back through the entire ministry. The other authors, thinking in other christological terms, yet use their materials in the same way as did John. Recital of what Jesus did and said will lead to belief that he is the redeemer of men. That is, our Gospels, as we have them, are *kerygmatic* in character. It is no new observation to say that the material in the Gospels is heavily weighted with the story of the Passion. This indicates not only that the account of Jesus' death was climactic to his life, but also that his death was the point at which the ministry was most distinctively redemptive. Further, the passion was definitive of all else that was recorded. Everything that the earliest disciples remembered of the career of Jesus had to be interpreted in the light of the death and resurrection of the Lord. The insights of the earliest followers were carried over into the church, and rightly color the accounts of the life of Jesus found in the Gospels.

The interpretation may be illustrated by the theme of "fulfillment." The exact expression "that it might be fulfilled" occurs three times in Mark; twelve times in Matthew; four times in Luke; and six times in John. In Mark, the references are to the ministry, linked to John's coming (1:2); to the hardened hearts of the hearers (4:12); and to the arrest in the garden (14:49). Nine of the occurrences in Matthew are peculiar to that Gospel. The incidents thus interpreted run from the birth to a virgin mother (1:22) through the ministry and to the death of Judas (27:9). In addition to the exact expression, Matthew employs similar terms in an additional seven instances. The emphasis is strongly on the demonstration of Jesus as the hoped-for Jewish Messiah. Luke's usage begins with the promised birth of John the Baptist (1:13) and ends with the giving of the Great Commission (24:44), including the ministry in Galilee (4:21) as a "fulfillment." The Johannine material revolves around the rejection of Jesus by his people (15:25); the treachery of Judas (13:18; 17:12); and the manner of his death (19:24; 19:36). It is of the utmost importance to note that fulfillment of Old Testament predictions and hopes was seen not only in the circumstances of the death, but also in the total scope of the ministry. Emphasis on that ministry as fulfilling the Servant passages of Isaiah is also striking and significant.

Each of the authors of our Gospels employed a selection of materials, and an arrangement of order, different from the others. Each made his own emphasis, looking to the specific purpose in his mind. These obvious facts make it clear that no author considered it necessary for his readers to know everything that the historic Jesus did, in order that they might come to the conclusion he desired for them; or that the sequence of the events was essential to faith. In each case, however, the assumption of the author is that the readers must know enough of what Jesus did to establish his character as the bearer of God's self-revelation. The presumption in all the Gospels is that the complete record, if available, would not essentially change the picture of Jesus. In modern terms, the authors used typical events; complete knowledge would not invalidate the arguments.

The relatively late dates of our Gospels, while not allowing us to use them as direct evidence for the original *kerygma,* will not operate to prevent us from penetrating to the earlier practice. The literary criticism of the Gospels leads us to a considerably earlier time. Grant estimates Mark as "the Christian message of salvation believed and preached among Gentiles in the middle of the first century," while the Q-material (non-Markan material common to Matthew and Luke) is generally believed to be equally early.[11] As early as twenty years after the death of Jesus, written material, calculated to establish faith on the basis that God had redemptively revealed himself in the entire ministry of Jesus, was circulated. Further investigation of the practice of the earliest church leads to consideration of the Book of Acts and the Epistles.

The Early Kerygma in Acts and Epistles

I. THE EARLY CHURCH IN PALESTINE

Evidence for the content of the *kerygma* as used in the pre-Pauline church in Palestine may be found in the early chapters of the Book of Acts and in certain references in Paul's epistles. To date the production of the Book of Acts in the ninth decade of the first century does not invalidate its use for our purpose. Since the monumental researches of Harnack issued more than a half-century ago it has been customary to find sources in the first half of Acts. The sermons in the early chapters, in particular, are useful for our investigation. There is sufficient evidence to support the conclusion that these sermons are not simply free compositions of the author, but that his work depended upon his use of Greek translations of Aramaic originals. While the sermons are not exact transcripts of Peter's words, they represent the type of proclamation Peter and his associates made in the earliest church.

These "highly schematic sermons" (as Bultmann characterizes them) are "variations upon a common theme which occurs in almost stereotyped form," to use a phrase of C. H. Dodd. As Dodd outlines them, the general pattern of the sermons is as follows:

1. The age of fulfillment has dawned.
2. This has taken place through the ministry, death and resurrection of Jesus. His Davidic descent is claimed; his ministry of power is briefly detailed; his death by crucifixion is set forth; and his resurrection by the power of God is proclaimed.
3. By his resurrection, Jesus is now exalted to the right hand of God.
4. The Holy Spirit in the Church is the sign of his present power and authority.
5. He will return to usher in the Messianic Age.
6. Forgiveness and the gift of the Holy Spirit are offered to those who repent and are baptized.[12]

In these sermons, the theme of fulfillment, already noted as occurring in our Gospels, is traced to the very beginning of the church. It could scarcely have been otherwise. Mission preaching in Palestine must have faced handicaps which bare and unsupported assertions that Jesus rose from the dead could hardly have dissipated. It was obvious that he had died as a condemned criminal. As Paul remarked a quarter-century later (1 Corinthians 1:23f), a crucified Messiah was a stumbling block to Jews; and we may be sure the difficulties were evident to Jewish hearers from the very start. The charge would require the preachers to produce evidence of his innocence of the charges laid against him. Further, the mission preachers called their hearers to a religion whose ethical demands were even more rigorous than those of the Judaism from which it sprang. The call could be supported only by evidence of the ethical character of the chief figure in the new faith, as seen in his own life. Perhaps most important of all, he was proclaimed as the hoped-for Messiah of the Jews. They had some ideas about what this figure would do and be; and the preachers must have been under compulsion to show what he did, in his life and ministry, to support the claim.

In the light of the situation, the outlines of the sermons in Acts make it clear enough that the preachers referred to the deeds of Jesus as part of the *kerygma;* and that the theme of fulfillment, while not elaborated in the surviving materials, was emphasized. Such fulfillment must have included not only citation of Old Testament proof-texts but also the actual deeds which were believed to match the predictions. The story of the conversion of the Ethiopian (Acts 8:26-38) gives us exactly this picture.

II. THE PRE-PAULINE CHURCH OUTSIDE PALESTINE

The materials dealing with the pre-Pauline church in Hellenistic areas is even more scanty than that referring to Palestine. Ostensibly some of the material beginning in Acts 13 refers to these communities. We may use some of the materials in Paul, employing the criteria proposed by Bultmann: where Paul seems to imply that which his readers already know; or general statements of the nature of a formula; or assertions made without the apparent attempt to establish them.[13] The Thessalonian correspondence is very useful, as are also Romans, where Paul desires to commend himself to a Gentile church he had not founded, and Galatians, another letter to a Gentile community where the apostle seems to refer to a common fund of tradition.

The *kerygma* in non-Jewish communities must, as Bultmann has pointed out,[14] have started with the attempt to overthrow idolatry and establish faith in the one God; in this, it did not differ widely from the non-Christian Jewish missions. Assertion that there is one God occurs in Paul's sermons reported in Acts (14:15; 17:23), as well as in his letters (1 Thessalonians 1:9; Galatians 4:8). The moral degradation of idolatry appears in Romans 1:24-32; and the warning that God will judge the world appears in Acts 17:31 and 1 Thessalonians 1:10. The ethical demands of the gospel must have been reinforced in the

Gentile communities by appeal to the manner of life of Jesus, the redeemer, as, indeed, Paul makes clear (1 Thessalonians 1:5).

The distinctively Christian *kerygma* among the Gentiles proclaimed its Christology, different from that used among the Jews. Jewish Messiahship seems little emphasized; although the Roman Christians knew that Jesus was descended from David (Romans 1:3) and was himself a Jew (9:5). He was more distinctively the deliverer from the coming wrath (1 Thessalonians 1:10) and the judge who sits beside God (Romans 2:16; Acts 17:31). The strongly eschatological emphasis stands out; and it is implied (1 Thessalonians 1:5) that the criterion of judgment is conformity to the manner of life which the Lord himself displayed. This would involve a necessary reference to the deeds and character of Jesus in the *kerygma*.

The scantiness of the remains from the pre-Pauline period and communities must not be allowed to argue decisively and negatively that the *kerygma* did not include material from the tradition of the life of Jesus. The reporters were not concerned to expound the *kerygma,* as did the authors of our Gospels. It is significant that the slight remains agree in general with the Gospels.

III. THE KERYGMA OF PAUL

The issue here is clearly stated by Bultmann in a passage already cited; to Paul "Jesus was a definite concrete man; but beyond that, Jesus' manner of life, his ministry, his personality, his character play no role at all . . . neither does Jesus' message." Bultmann's statement, which makes a slight concession to antidocetism, can be supported only by heavy reliance upon the silences of Paul—a precarious argument. We must beware of conclusions drawn from what Paul does not say in his extant writings. Should we rely solely, for example, upon Romans, we would conclude that Paul knew nothing of the Lord's Supper or the resurrection, mentioned specifically only in 1 Corinthians.

99

If Paul does not expound his *kerygma,* we must remember that he had little occasion to do so, except when some special problem in one of the churches demanded a reference to what must have been well known. If we should rely on isolated statements taken from Paul, we would come to contradictory conclusions as to his *kerygma.* His *"kerygma"* (using the actual Greek word) was simply that Jesus was crucified. So he reminded the Corinthians (1 Corinthians 1:23f; 2:2) and the Galatians (Galatians 3:1). It was evidently the manner of Jesus' death, by crucifixion, that was the essential item; thus "the word of the cross" was God's power (1 Corinthians 1:18) and it was the *crucified* one who is God's power and wisdom (1 Corinthians 1:24).

Contradicting this, the apostle asserted that "if you believe in your heart that God raised him from the dead, you shall be saved" (Romans 10:9). Here it is not the manner of death, but the fact of resurrection which is the one essential. Yet in 1 Corinthians 15:1-11, the "gospel" by which the believers are saved is described as the death, the burial, and the resurrection; the fact that this was "according to the Scriptures," the fulfillment of prophecy; and that the evidence for the resurrection was the unanimous tradition. So important is this that to reject the resurrection is to remain unforgiven (1 Corinthians 15:17).

These isolated statements should warn us against taking any one statement of Paul as defining the sole content of his *kerygma.* The question before us is not whether his *kerygma* included the death and resurrection, or whether the resurrection was so central to him that apart from it there was no "gospel."

The question is whether he proclaimed only the death and the resurrection, or whether he proclaimed some part of the tradition of deeds and words of Jesus so that the response he demanded was a response to the tradition because Jesus' manner of life determined his saviorhood.

According to Paul's own statement (Galatians 1:18), he had an opportunity to know something about the life of Jesus, reaching back to a point not later than three years following his conversion experience. There is no hint that Paul believed he disagreed with the earlier apostles in regard to the tradition of the life of Jesus. Whatever their disagreements may have been, they did not deal with this particular matter.

The extent of his knowledge of details concerning the life, the teachings, and the character of Jesus may be briefly set before us. Paul knew that Jesus was born a Jew (Romans 9:5; Galatians 4:4). He was descended from David (Romans 1:3). He had brothers (1 Corinthians 9:5) with one of whom, James, Paul was closely acquainted (Galatians 1:19). The ministry of Jesus was carried on among Jews, not Gentiles (Romans 15:8). He ate a last meal, after which he was betrayed (1 Corinthians 11:23), and Paul knew some details about the meal and what went on at the time. He was put to death by crucifixion (1 Corinthians 1:23; 2:2, 3; 3:1; 2:8). Therefore, his death was the result of a Roman execution, although the Jews were responsible for it (1 Thessalonians 2:15). It is interesting to note how Paul here agrees with the tradition stated in our Gospels. Jesus was buried, and was raised the third day (1 Corinthians 15:4-11), and the evidence for the resurrection is cited.

Paul knew specifically of a teaching of Jesus (1 Corinthians 9:14) which authorized the support of the ministry and which can be identified with Luke 10:7. He knew statements of Jesus concerning divorce (1 Corinthians 7:10f) which were similar to if not identical with Mark 10:11. The interesting point here is that Paul distinguished between his words and those of the Lord, and asserted the identity of the Lord who spoke with the Jesus who lived. He knew, also, of the character of Jesus. Paul speaks of the gentleness and forbearance of Jesus (1 Corinthians 10:1) and of his humility (Philippians 2:7f), to cite specific instances. As we shall remark below, it was the ethical character of Jesus that was to be imitated by his converts. This in itself would imply that Paul had a considerable knowledge both of the individual actions and the total character of Jesus.

For our purpose, the question of the extent of Paul's knowledge about what Jesus did and said is less significant than the use he made of these items. It is quite clear that it was the humanity of Jesus which was redemptively significant in Paul's system of thought. This stands out distinctly in Galatians 4:4. The atmosphere here is that of controversy between Paul and the Judaizing opponents in Galatia. Paul assumes that the Galatians who were non-Jews know that the Son of God had been sent forth (a reference to his human life) and that he had been born "under the law" which was the significant point in the immediate controversy. Both these items, the fact of human birth and the fact of being born subject to Jewish law, were evidently a part of what had been "proclaimed" to the Galatians. It is against this background that J. Weiss asserts: "The life and work of the earthly Jesus was of the highest importance to Paul. . . . The essential thing is that the heavenly Lord . . . is the same as the one who died on the cross."[15] It was for this reason that Paul attributed salvation to the fact that Jesus became flesh, endured the suffering of a human life, became obedient to the will of God, and suffered a bitter death. Two highly significant redemptive statements from Paul support this idea. In Romans 8:3, Paul says, "God . . . , sending his own Son in the likeness of sinful flesh and for sin, condemned sin in the flesh." In 2 Corinthians 5:20f, the appeal for reconciliation to God is followed by Paul's assertion "[God] made him to be sin who knew no sin." So significant are these statements that Sabatier can say, "The Redeemer must be really man, for he could save humanity . . . only by partaking of its nature. On the other hand, the human sinlessness of Jesus is the primary basis of Pauline Christology."[16] Paul must have proclaimed enough of the tradition of the life of Jesus to sustain his christological argument. It could not have been sufficient merely to make the bold, unsupported statement that Jesus was truly human and truly sinless. It is in the highest degree important to note that we are dealing here not with a sustained argument and the defense of that which is assailed, but that which is assumed as known on the part of his readers.

That Paul made ethical demands upon his converts is universally agreed. It is not so generally recognized that these ethical demands were a part of the *kerygma* and that they were based upon the manner of life which Jesus displayed.

The ethical life of the Christian, Paul says, is to be an imitation of Christ. Thus, "as the Lord has forgiven you," so you are to forgive (Colossians 3:13); as "Christ has welcomed you," so you are to welcome others (Romans 15:7). The Corinthians were urged to imitate Paul, as he imitated Christ (1 Corinthians 11:1). Most significant for our purpose is his reminder to the Thessalonians that in the beginning of the gospel, they had become imitators of Paul and of the Lord (1 Thessalonians 1:6), linking the ethic specifically with the *kerygma*. Paul must have proclaimed the manner of life of Jesus at the same time he was calling on them to respond with repentance and obedience to that proclamation.

Of equal interest is Paul's emphasis on the example of the human Jesus. While the reference in 2 Corinthians 8:9 is ultimately a comparison of the voluntary poverty of the human Jesus with the riches of the pre-incarnate Christ, yet the evidence for the poverty was in the human life of the man Jesus, and this was to be imitated in Corinth. Similarly, Paul admonishes the Philippians (Philippians 2:5-8) to imitate the mind of Christ by their humility and obedience, traits which he displayed by voluntary humbling of himself in his human life. These traits are assumed as well known to the readers.

The same conclusion follows from consideration of the general structure of Paul's epistles. The long, carefully argued Christology and soteriology of Romans is followed (chs. 12-15) by an appeal to ethical living based upon the saviorhood of Christ, and culminating in the admonition, "put on the Lord Jesus" (13:14). The ethical demands of the gospel are inseparable from the saviorhood of Christ; and it seems impossible to divorce Paul's assertion of the ethical manner of the life of Jesus from his proclamation of redemption by faith in Jesus. This conclusion is supported by the observation, made by many students of the early church, of the remarkable agreement between the ethic proposed by Paul, and the ethic standing before us in the Gospels. The story of redemption could hardly have arisen apart from this ethical impact; and Paul could hardly have avoided using the tradition in his *kerygma,* if the evidence before us is to be taken seriously.

The evidence from Acts and the Epistles, scanty though it is, supports that from the Gospels. The *kerygma* of the earliest church proclaimed Jesus as the promised Messiah, playing upon the theme, "that it might be fulfilled," and employing the tradition of his life and words to support the claim. The death and resurrection were climactic; all took its meaning from these facts; but the tradition itself was also essential. The *kerygma,* that is, was an *interpretation* of history; on the other hand, what was interpreted was real *history,* comprising deeds and sayings of a real person.

The conclusions of this brief study support Walter Scott's claim that he had "restored the gospel"; that is, in proclaiming the facts of the ministry of Jesus climaxed by his death and resurrection and by the offer of forgiveness and the gift of the Holy Spirit consequent upon faith, repentance, and baptism, Scott had returned to the manner of proclaiming the gospel that had prevailed in the earliest days of the church. Typical of the founding fathers of the movement, his "critical position" (to employ the terminology of the present) avoided equally the extreme emphasis of "realized eschatology," which would nullify what has been called "the cruciality of the cross"; and the opposite extreme of the existentialist, who would nullify the redemptive significance of the life of Jesus.

NOTES

1. M. Dibelius, *Jesus,* trans. Chas. B. Hedrick and Frederick C. Grant (Philadelphia: Westminster Press, 1949), Chap. I.
2. Walter Scott, *The Gospel Restored* (Cincinnati: O. N. Donogh, 1836), pp. v f.
3. *Ibid.,* p. 129.

4. Rudolf Karl Bultmann, *Theology of the New Testament,* trans. Kendrick Grobel (New York: Charles Scribner's Sons, 1951), I, 35. Used by permission.

5. *Ibid.,* p. 294.

6. E. C. Colwell and E. L. Titus, *The Gospel of the Spirit* (New York: Harper & Row, Publishers, Inc., 1953), pp. 12f. Used by permission.

7. C. H. Dodd, *History and the Gospel* (New York: Charles Scribner's Sons, 1938), pp. 36f. Used by permission.

8. *Interpreter's Bible* (Nashville: Abingdon Press, 1951), VII, 648.

9. *Ibid.*

10. Wright and Fuller, *The Book of the Acts of God* (Garden City, N. Y.: Doubleday and Company, Inc., 1957), p. 237.

11. Dibelius, *op. cit.,* p. 632.

12. C. H. Dodd, *The Apostolic Preaching and Its Developments* (London: Hodder & Stoughton, Ltd.), pp. 21-23. Used by permission.

13. Bultmann, *op. cit.,* p. 64.

14. *Ibid.,* p. 65.

15. J. Weiss, *The History of Primitive Christianity,* Frederick C. Grant, ed. (New York: Wilson-Erickson, 1937), II, 454.

16. A. Sabatier, *The Apostle Paul; a Sketch of the Development of His Doctrine,* trans. A. M. Hellier, 5th ed. (London: Hodder and Stoughton, 1903), p. 327.

5

The Role of Tradition in the Church's Experience of Jesus as Christ

Ralph G. Wilburn

THE word "tradition" stems from the latin *traditio* (*paradosis* in Greek), which means a surrender or delivery. Thus the dictionary definition follows: "the delivery of opinions, doctrines, practices, rites, and customs from father to son, or from ancestor to posterity; the transmission of any opinions, practices, from forefathers to descendants by oral communication, without written memorials."

The Christian tradition, however, is a bit more complex than the simplicity of the dictionary definition suggests. In the early period of the church's life, *paradosis* meant that content of apostolic teaching (later to be put in written form, and still later to be made into a canon of scripture), handed on orally especially by the ancient presbyter who had heard the preaching of one or more of the apostles. This tradition, which preserved the purity of the original message, was coupled with the scripture of the Old Testament, and in time became the Christian Bible.

Clement of Rome writes of "the glorious and venerable rule of our tradition,"[1] by which Clement meant something broader than apostolic teaching. He seems to have used the term *"paradosis"* to mean the entire complex of beliefs and behavior which constitute the church's unique way of life.

The word *"paradosis"* took on another dimension still, as a result of the church's encounter with Marcionism, Montanism, and Gnosticism. In distinction from these "heretical" teachings, *paradosis* came to mean "transmitted *authoritative* Christian teaching." Here tradition took on the added dimension of being joined with the living voice of the episcopate, as the threefold norm of canon, creed, and episcopate was crystallized in ancient Catholic Christianity. The word "tradition" now took on new, doctrinaire meanings.

Gradually also, the term "tradition" came to include established liturgical patterns, a definite episcopal order, and finally the great creeds, especially Nicea and Chalcedon. Subsequent to Nicea, it came to include also the teachings and interpretations of the church fathers.

In a later development still, the term came to mean the organic development of the church's dogma, tradition in the sense of equating development with gradual transformation. And perhaps one of the most significant of later meanings was articulated by Vincent of Lerins: tradition as the unanimous voice of the church, in all periods.

The word "tradition" has thus meant different things in different periods of the church's thought. This complexity must constantly be borne in mind.

However, it is not my intention in this chapter to give a critique of any one of these multiple meanings. My aim rather is to offer a critique of the broad perspectives on tradition which have dominated Christian thought, and to suggest a few fundamental principles which may be of some help in the development of a more adequate understanding of the role of tradition in the experience of Jesus as Christ. We shall therefore proceed with our theme under the broad definition of tradition as "the living stream of the church's life." The specific meanings of the term will come in for consideration as our exposition proceeds.

The Present Situation in Protestantism

Four factors have determined the present situation in Protestantism in such a way that Protestants are now called upon to rethink the problem of tradition.

First, classical Protestantism so emphasized the principle of *sola Scriptura* as its authority, together with the persistent accusation that much of the church's tradition represents a corruption effected by the papacy, that a strongly negative attitude toward tradition has characterized much of subsequent Protestant thought. By way of silence, such negativity seems to be implied by Chillingworth's famous saying, "the Bible and the Bible alone is the religion of Protestants."

This Protestant tendency to relegate tradition to "the babylonian captivity" of the church was partially the result of an uncritical acceptance of the Catholic definition of tradition as a deposit of infallible dogmas, handed down, and infallibly interpreted, by Pope and church councils. The prophetic power of the Reformation shattered this idol of church authority and directed the Christian conscience to scripture as its only external norm.

Second, the ecumenical movement has generated a truly catholic impulse throughout Protestantism, reviving interest in the tradition of other groups than their own and in the total historic continuum of the church. This renewed interest is expressed in a vivid way by the definition given to the term "tradition" by the report of the Edinburgh Conference on Faith and Order in 1937, which has been adopted for this chapter, namely, "the living stream of the church's life."

This broad definition of tradition reflects the modern "historic sense" and its significance for an understanding of Christianity; it reflects an awareness of how deeply all human life and thought are embedded in historic process. And it suggests a new understanding of the past which has conditioned us and which is an organic part of us, and of scripture (itself a part of our past), which Protestants must think through anew. Perhaps indeed, our traditional "protest" has been too uncritical; perhaps we have too naïvely accepted the Catholic definition of tradition and thrown out the baby with the bath. In any case, we *have* become aware of the fact that one does not experience the revelation of God in Christ in separation from the historic people of God. This revelation comes to one only as he stands within "the living stream of the church's life," and it releases him for active membership in Christ's body.

Third, the "impregnable rock of scripture," upon which classical Protestantism planted its feet, is not so impregnable any more, thanks to the science of biblical criticism. The infallible book of old Protestantism is gone forever for critical, thoughtful minds. We can no longer fight the battle against an infallible church with the weapon of an infallible book. Our tents of battle must now be pitched on surer ground; but the question is: where?

And *fourth,* critical study has disclosed the fact that the biblical writings are closely interwoven with, and determined by, tradition. We have learned that these books were compiled and edited by later generations, and that their witness of God's mighty acts in history was given *in terms of a concrete cultural situation,* that one generation's interpretation of God's acts in Israel conditioned the future of Israel's history itself, etc. We have learned, that is, that scripture itself is an organic part of tradition so that the old Protestant dichotomy: "scripture or tradition" will no longer hold. Scripture and tradition are not self-sufficient entities. As Daniel Jenkins says, "The old frontiers between them are down and they must find new landmarks by which to distinguish themselves from each other."[2]

Four Inadequate Perspectives on Tradition

I. The flight from tradition into subjectivity

This flight into subjectivity represents a way of thinking about the work of the Holy Spirit which crops up again and again in history. It represents an effort to soft-pedal, or forth-rightly to eliminate, any *controlling* function of tradition in the work of the Spirit. The Spirit is, so to speak, abstract and detached more or less completely from history and from scripture. One thinks of such movements as Montanism, Gnosticism, and the sixteenth-century Anabaptist mystics. In such movements redemption is thought of as taking place not by the original revelation in Christ, mediated by traditional forms, but by a second inward revelation, which does not so much *fulfill* or *complete* the historic revelation, but rather supersedes and supplements it. These groups who care little or nothing for history seem to have another comforter than the Jesus who promised: "I will not leave you desolate; I will come to you" (John 14:18).

The question is in order, whether that which such groups call "the Spirit" is in reality the *Holy Spirit*. One's theology is not very highly developed if he is unable to distinguish between "participating in the Holy Spirit," and any sort of religious feeling called "spirituality."

In his treatise *Against the Heavenly Prophets* (the Anabaptist mystics) Luther aptly wrote, "These wise birds, the new spirits, contend that faith alone saves us, and that works and external things add nothing of value. We reply that of course nothing works *inwardly* but faith. . . . But these leaders of the blind will not see that faith must have something *in which* it believes, *to which* it clings, and *on which* it can *firmly plant its feet*."[3]

Again, Luther said that we have the apostle Paul to thank that Christianity long ago was delivered from such factious spirits as these fanatics. "Otherwise we would be sitting quietly throughout the Sabbath day, gazing blankly into empty space, like they do, holding our heads in our hands, waiting for the heavenly voice of the spirit."[4]

For the mystics, then, it is not the case of meeting God through the historic Christ, *made present* by the influence of the Spirit, but rather, as P. T. Forsyth says, in a spirit "once symbolized by the historic Christ. The only focus of revelation is the *individual experience* (Christ being but a particular case of it)."[5]

The basic error of this flight into subjectivity is that, in principle, it tears the faith loose from its historic anchorage to Jesus Christ. What the mystic really wants is to brush aside all historical media, indeed the whole realm of finitude, and enter directly into the infinite.

But as Paul Tillich has written,

. . . the Messiah always remained related to history, i.e., to a historical group, its past and its future. The Messiah does not save individuals in a path leading out of historical existence; he is to transform historical existence. The individual enters a new reality which embraces society and nature. In messianic thought, the New Being does not demand the sacrifice of finite being; instead, it fulfills all finite being by conquering its estrangement.[6]

II. The Roman Catholic distortion of tradition

The Reformation emphasis on the Bible as the "only rule of faith and practice," combined with the embarrassing fact that Catholic leaders found themselves hard put to produce any concrete traditional authority for many of their doctrines and practices which had grown up through the centuries, led to two results in Catholic thought: (a) the tendency more and more to subordinate scripture to tradition; and (b) the tendency to exploit, to the advantage of papal authority, the pseudo concept of tradition which the Council of Trent hit upon.[7] In contrast to the *traditio Christi* (the words of Christ handed down through the apostles and the church), this pseudo concept, called the *traditio apostolorum,* is the idea of a secret, inaccessible tradition, made known by the Holy Spirit, in the final analysis only to the Pope. This means that the Pope turns out *himself to be* the "apostolic tradition"; his voice *is* the voice of "apostolic" authority. This idea of tradition proved to be such a delightfully uncontrollable polemical instrument that it was exploited more and more to support the idea of papal authority.

111

This pseudo idea of tradition won a complete victory in Catholic theology. It enables the Roman church to adopt an attitude of indifference toward history and even toward the church fathers. The church is hereby liberated from her dependence upon Christian antiquity and is blessed with a unique progressive inspiration, bound forever to the See of the fisherman. To be sure, this progressivism is not bluntly stated. One does not say that through the voice of the Pope the church enjoys *new revelations*. Rather, one says more simply (and more ambiguously) that *the ecclesiastical tradition simply* is what the church (i.e., the Pope) has formulated, as dogmas of faith. As Heinrich Holtzmann says, Tradition here means

the perpetual stream of ecclesiastical formation of doctrines and morals is no purer in its beginning than in the middle or the end of the stream, regardless of the extent to which this stream was enriched by manifold, apocryphal subsidiary sources in the various ages. This flow of tradition has not been qualitatively but only quantitatively altered.[8]

Since Rome operates with this pseudo idea of tradition, she cannot be bothered about traditional proofs and authentications of new dogmas. Indeed, *original* and *certain* doctrines of the church are those for which no external proofs can be cited. For to use such external tradition *as proof* of the truth of papal dogmas would be tantamount to a weakening or even nullification of the "apostolic" authority of the church. Hence traditional references are added only as academic adornments to enhance the glow of church dogmas.

Now several things are wrong here. (1) This Catholic view leads to an intellectually dishonest handling of history; our Catholic brethren have yet to learn the lesson of taking historical facts seriously. (2) Cutting the faith loose from its anchorage in history has actually led to a de-Christianizing and secularizing of Christianity. (3) This Catholic view resurrects from the dead and establishes the church upon two heresies, which in the patristic period the church regarded as mortal enemies of the faith:

112

(a) the Gnostic idea of a secret apostolic tradition, and (b) the spiritualist notion that the total authority of the Holy Spirit becomes incarnate in one single church leader. According to ancient Catholic Christianity, Roman Catholicism is today the most heretical sect of all.

III. THE PETRIFICATION OF TRADITION IN EASTERN ORTHODOXY

If the Vatican distortion of tradition and the mystics' flight from tradition into subjectivity are erroneous, Orthodoxy has erred in yet another direction. If the mystics *pulverize* tradition, Orthodoxy *petrifies* it, transforming Christianity into an authoritarian objectivism which tends to stifle the spirit of man and imprison the Spirit of God. This petrification of tradition, which distorts the *historic means* of God's act of revelation into *idolatrous ends,* is equally destructive of revelation.

Our Orthodox brethren claim that their basic idea of *sobornost* protects them against the fallacy of the excessive selectivity which is so dominant in Western Christianity. And to be sure, this emphasis on the mind of the total Christian community does make possible "a more diffused and long-range form of *magesterium*"[9] than the *papal* form of church authority. The question, however, is whether *sobornost* really amounts to anything more than a less effective, if more charitable, version of the Vatican view. It requires more patience and intellectual labor to determine just what the mind of Orthodoxy is; but once this has been determined, is not the result an external authority just about as absolute as papal dogmas? The *method* of establishing church dogmas differs, yes; but is not *the end product* an equally rigid dogmatism, which henceforth admits of no critical reformatory correction and advance?

The major error of the Orthodox view lies in a blind spot which makes Orthodoxy unaware of the *essentially mutable* character of history, an unawareness of the unrepeatable and irreversible character of every event. This blindness generates the grand illusion of an immutable tradition.

Who can read history, with his eyes open, and fail to see that there is not much in common between a bishop in Asia Minor A.D. 140, a Catholic bishop of the seventh century, a medieval prelate of an extensive diocese, and a contemporary bishop of the American Methodist Church? The same historic stamp of mutability marks the sacraments, both in terms of form and content. Change and development seem to be the very law of history. And we demand of our Orthodox brethren *that they take history seriously,* and abandon theological presuppositions which oblige them to be intellectually blind in the reading of history.

One would think that modern man, especially, could no longer resist this truth about the changing character of history, for it presses in upon him from every nook and cranny. We are conditioned by these changing historical forces, and we live in an age of fantastic revolutionary change. The scientific and industrial development of the past 100 years has changed the pattern of human society so radically that our great-grandparents would be totally lost should they suddenly return to life on our planet, to say nothing of how flabbergasted the apostle Paul or Confucius would be.

The church is set in *this kind* of world, a world of change. Does not this mean that growth and development *in the church itself,* in history, is part of the will of God, for which God endowed his church with the gift of the Holy Spirit? Does it not mean that change in the structure of church order and thought is inevitable, if the church remains a vital part of world life? How is it possible for her to remain *in history* and be *relevant* to historical existence otherwise? The question to our Orthodox brethren therefore is: have they taken the *order of creation* and the *character of history seriously?* Are they not still operating on the unwarranted assumption that the mutability of the church is due wholly to its sinfulness? If the church refuses to participate in the mutability of history, will she not inevitably become stereotyped and irrelevant to life in the modern world?

There are several fallacious aspects which Roman Catholicism and Orthodoxy share in common, in regard to their understanding of tradition.

(1) Their traditional*ism* idolatrizes Christ. That is, it distorts the referent in Christian experience into an objective datum. By so doing, Catholicism blurs the *transcendental character* of God's word of revelation which always stands above us, in judgment and in mercy, and should therefore never be equated with any finite form of its expression. And it blurs and distorts this transcendental character of revelation because it is operating on the erroneous presupposition that religious truth is an infallible objective datum, correlated with infallible life-giving sacraments, "preserved by a majestic sacramental society."[10]

(2) Catholic traditionalism loses sight of the fact that, in the final analysis, when the chips are down, it is *living personal faith in God* which really matters. Catholicism leads its devotees to put their trust too much in things, in the institutions of the church, her sacraments and her priestly power; and she thereby actually interposes the church as a barrier between man and God. The important thing, however, is not whether one is, or is not, able to secure the sacrament of extreme unction, but whether through the revealed will of God in Christ one has come to participate in the new being in Christ with a faith which says, "in all these things we are more than conquerors through him who loved us. . . . For I am sure that . . . [nothing] . . . in all creation will be able to separate us from the love of God in Christ Jesus our Lord" (Romans 8:37-39).

As D. E. W. Harrison says, "the true tradition is to be found wherever this meaning is actualized in life."[11] Such men of *faith* are able to face up to the fact that no human schemes and programs, including those of the church, *can* possess *unbroken* continuity, any more than they can possess infallibility.

(3) What I have been saying has a significant bearing on the problem of ethical decision. For the Catholic, the mind of the church (*equated* with the wisdom of the Spirit's leading)

has already been given in infallible canonical law. The ethical problem is merely one of learning what these church pronouncements are, and then moving logically to an application of these dogmatic principles to concrete situations. Here again, we find Catholic absolutism coupled with a strange kind of blindness. This authoritarian morality refuses to "supplicate and discuss terms with conscience"; it makes a totalitarian demand on conscience "and requires that it surrender itself to the Word of God *as proclaimed by the church.*"[12] This totalitarian morality is coupled with an ethical blind spot. The fact is not appreciated that changing circumstances alter the entire framework within which ethical decisions have to be made; nor are we wise enough to predict just what these altered circumstances will be. Such situations cannot be adequately faced ethically, in authentic personal decision, except by those who are involved existentially in the situation in which the decision must be made. The rule of thumb ethics in Catholic traditionalism thus fails to nurture the freedom of spirit, and it fails to transmute the individual into a responsible subject, in the ethically ambiguous situation.

Furthermore, when we do come upon ethical situations in which the proper thing to do, morally, is *not* specifically prescribed by the moral canons of the church, Jesuitistic casuistry corrupts ethical integrity by condoning the ethical theory of probabilism,[13] a theory which, after long and bitter struggle against Cornelius Jansen and Blaise Pascal, has finally triumphed in Catholic ethics.

IV. The Puritan[14] neglect of tradition

Puritanism differs widely from the former three in that it clings firmly to the Bible as its sole authority. It is however positively related to the flight from tradition into subjectivity, in that it too tends to neglect tradition; it regards the authority of scripture as *independent* of tradition. The Protestant principle of *sola Scriptura,* combined with the doctrine of the right of private judgment, tended to generate an attitude of neglect of tradition.

116

There is a vital truth in this Puritan perspective, namely the supremacy of the voice of scripture. It *was* the power of scripture which, in the Reformation, rescued the Christian conscience from the absolutism of Catholic traditionalism.

This truth about scripture became distorted, however, and was twisted into a principle which has much to do with the rampant sectarianism and fragmented individualism which Protestantism has spawned. Many Protestants came to believe that they could ignore the bulk of tradition entirely and derive their life exclusively from scripture.

Many Protestants were thus misled to develop a warped view of Christian history as restricted mainly to scripture, plus the traditions of their own particular group. Hence the fantastic tunnel concept of history found in numerous "restorationist" groups,[15] who lost the vision of the *total sweep of Christian* history, tended to set tradition too sharply *over against* the Bible, and mistakenly fancied *themselves* to be determined solely by the Bible, and free from the "shackles" of tradition. Such Christians have not infrequently been the most tradition-bound of all.

However, this unrealistic attempt to put on a pair of seven-league boots and leap back to Jerusalem, to use another metaphor, letting the intervening centuries drop into oblivion, was doomed to failure. For Christianity is a historic continuum; it persists in continuity in history, by the presence in power of the Holy Spirit. And historical time is irreversible.

In a real historic sense, the new life in Christ is always given "in, with and under"[16] tradition. The indispensable conditions for Christian experience are *handed down* from one generation to another. If, therefore, we are to talk about religion in any realistic way, that is, in terms of its concrete forms, "the historical claims of religion cannot be avoided and its historical symbols cannot be overlooked."[17] This "historic sense" can help, immeasurably, to correct the warped view of Christian history in Puritanism. It can help us recover the Catholic concept of the total historic sweep of tradition as a great school of Christian discipleship.

117

As James Martineau says,

To insist that religion shall owe nothing to the past, and be the same as if there were no history; to demand that each shall find it for himself, *de novo,* as if he were the first man and the only man . . . is to require terms which the nature of man forbids and the providence of God will disappoint. Transmitted influence from soul to soul, whether among contemporaries, or down the course of time, is not only as natural but as spiritual as the direct relation of each worshipper with God.[18]

In our critique of these four inadequate perspectives on tradition, we have already suggested several positive principles which may be useful in our task of theological reconstruction. However, it might be helpful to attempt more explicitly to lay a foundation for a more adequate perspective on tradition, in our post-Protestant era.

A Synthesis through Revelation Understood as Eschatological Event

From our analysis of the perspectives which have prevailed in Christian thought, it would seem that the basic problem of tradition has not been adequately resolved due to the fallacy of constant oscillation between subjectivism and objectivism. We have here a kind of Hegelian problem, which calls for a higher synthesis.

We suggest that the positive values in subjectivism and objectivism *can* be preserved, while the distortions of each can be avoided if we work out a synthesis through understanding the character of the revelation of God in Jesus Christ as eschatological event. The two dimensions of history and subjectivity can and should be held together in the traditioning of the experience of Jesus as Christ, in the ongoing life of the Christian community.

The word "eschatological" is here used not in the sense of a temporally terminal end *(eschaton)* of history, but in the more philosophically defensible sense of the term as the ultimate goal

118

(telos) and meaning of human existence, or the transcendent purpose of human life. So understood, eschatology is concerned with eternity *in* the *now* of time; it has to do with the reality of God *in* the world; it deals with the ultimate concern of religion, not merely as a temporal terminus, but as the ultimate transhistorical dimension of human existence. It is this understanding of the term which must be borne in mind in speaking of revelation as eschatological event. Revelation is no ordinary historical event, but an event which involves one, at the same time, in the ultimate dimension of human existence.

The central symbol of the Christian revelation binds the historical and the subjective dimensions together securely, from the very beginning, the symbol "Jesus Christ." This phrase implies that history and faith are somehow bound together, for *Jesus as the Christ,* is both an objective historical fact *and* a subjective grasp of the meaning of this fact in faith, a meaning summed up in the word "Christ." To bind the two words together, therefore, is to unite the historical and subjective dimensions in the experience of faith.

Precisely how faith and history are interrelated is still a bit of a problem. Granted, if God so willed, he could reveal the meaning of the Christ-truth directly, apart from any connection with Jesus. Yet it is the basic Christian belief that he has bound the two together. But *how?* In what manner? *How* does the historical Jesus *become* the Christ of faith? Is there a power residing in bare historical facts to *generate* subjective meaning? If so, why does faith arise in some and not in others? Or are historical facts a kind of *occasional* or *tangential* cause of faith, the *originating* cause being the immediate working of the Spirit of God? Or shall we adopt the view of Karl Löwith of the University of Heidelberg and say that historical facts, *in themselves,* are utterly without meaning, and that objective history *derives* meaning solely from the interpretative act in the mind of the observer, who, so to speak, reads meaning into the facts of history.[19]

This is a difficult problem, and one which involves the whole question of epistemology and the interpretation of history. I am inclined toward a kind of critical realism, by which I mean that the Christ picture or Christ reality *was present* in the inner spiritual life of the carpenter of Nazareth, but that only faith can lead one to a redemptive discernment of this reality, this meaning. Jesus himself seems to say as much when he commented upon Peter's confession of his messiahship as being the result of God's revelatory influence upon him. "Flesh and blood (i.e. history) has not revealed this to you," said Jesus, "but my Father who is in heaven" (Matthew 16:17).

If we accept this statement of Jesus as true, then must we not say that some kind of existential leap is here involved? Must we not say that there is no continuous development from an objective study of the Jesus of history to the decision of faith to accept him as Christ and Lord? Is not Karl Löwith correct when he says that "no historian as such can possibly discover that Jesus is the Son of God?"[20]

In any case, if it is Jesus, the carpenter of Nazareth, who is the Christ, if *he* is the one whom *God* has made *our* Lord and Christ, then tradition assumes an indispensable role, for we today have no other means of knowing about Jesus except through objective historical witnesses. This is the principal reason why a place of primary importance must be attached to the *handing down* of the original accounts of Jesus' deeds and words, however knotty this problem has become in modern biblical scholarship. This essential connection of faith with the figure of Jesus imparts to tradition a kind of authority; but this is the authority of a regularizing function and is not to be confused with the kind of authority which one experiences when led, through the medium of tradition, to a personal confrontation by Christ the Lord, our only absolute authority.

There seems always to be a tendency to relax the field of tension between these two dimensions of faith by emphasizing one at the expense of the other. The Montanists, Anabaptists, pietists, mystics, and, we might add, the rationalists and some contemporary European existentialists, have magnified the dimension of subjectivity (construed in one way or another) to the neglect of the historical. So that Hans Hermann Walz, a follower of the Bultmann school, can say that theological existentialism has possibly not yet adequately dealt with the problem of the *historic* continuity of the faith. Yet must we not say that the existentialists are correct in their insistence that to know Christ, in the responsible commitment of faith, is really the *basic meaning* of entering into the historical stream of the church's life?

On the other hand, stand those who have so emphasized the objective, outer history of the church's tradition as to neglect this dimension of the church's inner history, the history of *faith*. The broad movement of Catholicism has been guilty of this, as have also some of the liberals, and the exponents of Protestant orthodoxy.

We can perhaps bring the problem of holding together these two dimensions of the traditioning of Christian experience to a sharper focus if we restrict our attention for a moment to the preaching aspect of the *paradosis* of the gospel. Let us ask the question: what does it mean to communicate the gospel?

The word "communicate" here takes on a unique meaning. In common parlance the word "communicate" signifies merely an interchange of thought between two persons. A reporter learns about the successful projection of Sputnik, for example, and he hastens to *communicate* this to the public through his newspaper. The thing that makes the communication of the gospel unique is the addition of the eschatological dimension. The gospel is no bare fact of past history, and gospel preaching can therefore never be the work of a mere reporter. Christian preachers are not reporting bare facts of the past; they are *proclaiming the gospel;* and through this testimony *God himself acts* to speak to those who respond in faith.

This is the paradox of the Word made flesh. The New Testament presents this living personal Word made flesh not as a mere person of the *past* of whom we have reliable historical testimony; but also *as he is constantly present,* in the word of the church which proclaims him, in power. And the Christian *tradition* therefore can never be *mere historical transmission;* it is rather the continuity of the Christian proclamation of the Word, in which and through which God continuously acts and speaks. For Paul, this is one of the main aspects of the life of the risen Christ. That Christ is risen means that he is the ever-living Spirit of the church, and that he speaks through the preached word. Therefore, says Paul, "We are ambassadors for Christ, God making his appeal through us" (2 Corinthians 5:20).

There are now four major perversions of the communication or *paradosis* of the gospel. These perversions are: biblicism, historicism, dogmatism, and rationalism.

The first perversion is *biblicism.* One may know the Bible from cover to cover; he may hold it to be absolute and infallible truth; he may stand in the pulpit and quote scripture with amazing feats of memory, and fail utterly to proclaim the gospel. For the Bible, *as a historical book,* is not the living word of God. The Bible is rather a human witness to God's Word made flesh, and should be used for what it is, not for what God never intended it to be.

The second perversion is *historicism.* This is the error which regards the object of faith to be something wholly historical. This view forgets that the word of God is never a mere historical fact. Hearing the word of God is an eschatological event. To be sure, one may study the historical events on which the revelatory activity of God rests, from an objective, scientific point of view. And such study is vitally important. But the historical Jesus, so *viewed,* apart from faith in him *as Christ and Lord,* could have no more saving significance than any other historical event. The *object* of saving faith is not merely a historical Jesus; it is "Jesus Christ our Lord"; it is the redemptive word of God which we hear, *in and through* the historical Jesus. The task of Christian preaching is therefore not merely one of *reconstructing past history* and getting people to believe that these historical things did happen once upon a time in the long, long ago. It is rather to learn how to bear our witness faithfully so that others may hear and heed the saving Word of the gospel.

The third perversion of *paradosis* is *dogmatism*. This is the erroneous view which holds doctrines or creeds to be the object of the Christian faith. According to this view, which has unfortunately been quite popular throughout Christian history, Christian faith is simply belief in the truth of a set of teachings. This is, of course, the business of philosophy; and if this view of dogmatism were correct, there would be no essential difference between religion and philosophy, for it is the primary business of philosophy to deal with the truth-value of propositions. No, the gospel is something more than philosophy, and faith is vastly more than belief in dogmas and creeds. The object of faith is not dogmas, even biblical dogmas. The object of faith is Jesus Christ.

To be sure, we recognize the positive value of the great traditional doctrines of the church. They function to preserve the integrity of the teachings of the church. They are useful in view of the ever-present danger of misrepresentation by the whims and fancies of cantankerous individuals. They serve to keep the faith within the bounds of true catholicity. Yet we must never forget that whenever faith is defined, not as trust in and obedient response to Christ as Lord and to the leading of his Spirit, but as punctilious adherence to doctrinal formulas, the church has then and there betrayed her Lord, and distorted God's revelation through him.

The fourth perversion is *rationalism*. This is the view which reduces the gospel to *nothing but* a republication of timeless, general truths; or as John Locke put it, Christianity recovered from obscurity the truths of natural religion which all men can recognize. Rationalism thus breaks the back of revelation in a radical way, and the gospel becomes *just another historical* expression of universal, natural religion, and a problematical expression at that, due to its involvement with miracle stories, its naïve view of history, its union with myths drawn from the Graeco-Roman world, etc.

However, the era of rational autonomy has spent itself in the Western world. We are recovering from the spell of the Enlightenment, and are now aware that the gospel, God's saving Word in Jesus Christ, is a personal event which, although it includes the sphere of reason, also transcends it. The object of saving faith is not timeless, general truths; the object of faith is a *special word* which God has spoken and continues to speak through Jesus Christ.

We say then that our task of *handing on* the gospel is not biblicism: quoting and expounding the Bible; it is not historicism: giving a factual report about an objective Jesus of history; it is not dogmatism: propagating the Disciples creed (heaven forbid that such a thing should exist!); it is not rationalism: elaborating timeless, general truths. We need the Bible, but not biblic*ism;* history, but not historic*ism;* Jesus, yes, but not Jesus-*ology;* constructive theological analysis, but not dogmat*ism;* reason, but not rational*ism.* We must avoid these *isms,* these perversions of the gospel which serve as a hindrance to an effective communication of the gospel. We must avoid the error of absolutizing the relative.

What then is the church's task? Her task is *the effective communication of the gospel of God!* The thing to remember is that God himself is present and acting in this traditioning process of the confessing church. The proclamation of the church is not a mere human word; it *is* a human word, but one *in which* and *through which* God himself speaks. We obviously do not have the power to make the word of our feeble human witness the word of *God.* Only God can do this; and the message of the gospel is that he does precisely this. By the immanent working of his Spirit he speaks to man, through the witness to his grace borne by us.

Take a simple example: the church's proclamation of God's word of forgiveness. No mere human word could possibly communicate the act of divine forgiveness. Only when one hears *God's* word is forgiving grace actually communicated. As Luther was fond of putting it, the Pope could tell one a thousand times that his sins are forgiven but he would still not know, in the assurance of *faith,* that God has forgiven him. Only *God's* word can bestow forgiving grace.

The traditioning of the gospel, thus, through the church's proclamation, serves as a medium of the continuous aspect of God's revelation in Christ. There is a kerygmatic quality about preaching. It does arouse in others the desire to have the same experience. But the main point is, as Schleiermacher put it, that "the impression which all later believers received in this way from the influence of Christ . . . *was just the same impression which his contemporaries received from him directly.*"[21]

One thing further needs to be said about the problem of *faithfully* passing on what we have learned of Jesus Christ. The Catholic view of tradition fallaciously construes the *kerygma* (that which is to be handed down) as an infallible deposit of truth, and the *paradosis* (the manner of transmission) as infallibly handing down, interpreting and preserving for all generations this body of absolute truth. The fallacy of this Catholic objectivism becomes evident when we bear in mind that the function of both *kerygma* and *paradosis* is to mediate the *experience* of Jesus as Christ, not to impart infallible information. The subjectification of the truth of Christianity, as personal encounter, is essential to the actual *paradosis* of Christianity. Without this subjectification of the Christ-truth, the *paradosis* would be but an empty shell.

Although the Catholic understanding of faithfulness, in handing on the gospel message, is unacceptable, there *is* a faithfulness here that is more important. Yet there can be no automatic guarantee that the tradition will be faithfully passed on. It can only be *faithfully* passed on by those who strive sincerely to bear their witness so as to point to, and describe, the historical evidence on which their faith rests, and the reasons which led them to their decision in response to the evidence, *in such a way* that this same evidence is made available to their hearers, so that *Christ* may confront them and call them to decision. This is the meaning of *faithfulness,* in the transmission of the gospel. And God acts, using such witness as a means by which to lift the hearer into the personal communion with himself, which is the relation of faith.

Such *faithfulness* one finds in the Apostle Paul. To the Thessalonian church Paul wrote: "We are bound to give thanks to God always for you . . . because God chose you from the beginning to be saved, through sanctification by the Spirit and belief in the truth. To this he called you through our gospel, so that you may obtain the glory of our Lord Jesus Christ. So then, brethren, stand firm and hold to the traditions which you were taught by us, either by word of mouth or by letter" (2 Thessalonians 2:13-15).

Scripture as a Norm Over All Subsequent Tradition

The truth of the Protestant belief that scripture possesses a normativeness over all subsequent tradition rests upon the fact that in the order of salvation God has established a fixed historical center from which the redemptive influence of Christ forever radiates, namely, the life, death, and resurrection of Jesus.

To be sure, scripture itself is a form of tradition. Scripture is *essentially* a part of the ongoing proclamation of the church. Oral and written teaching concerning Christ originally performed the same function, and differed only by accident. Basically, the historical foundation of Christian experience rested in tradition, in the *paradosis* of church proclamation of Christ. Scripture, *because it represents preaching,* is a traditioning medium through which faith is generated in those addressed. Protestants have not always been sufficiently aware of this intimate relation between the Bible and church tradition. In the patristic times, the biblical writings were identified with the church's tradition.

An adequate Christology, however, demands that we affirm also more than this about the function of scripture. But we cannot say that the superior normativeness of scripture lies merely in the fact that the biblical writings derive from the *apostolic period* of the church's life. Schleiermacher was correct in contending[22] that if we regard the church during the apostolic age as a unity, its thinking cannot supply a norm for later ages. Indeed, said Schleiermacher, the thought of *the entire church* of a given period is purer and more perfect in subsequent periods of the church's life, for in the primitive church many foreign elements still characterized the mind of the church, due to Jewish and Hellenistic influences. We cannot therefore regard the whole wide stream of oral tradition in the apostolic period as normative.

In the midst of this impure stream, however, flowed a purer current, namely, the presentations of Jesus Christ given by his immediate followers. If the object of Christian experience is *Jesus Christ*, no subsequent proclamation can share fully in the unique position which the witness of the immediate followers of Christ hold. More reliably than any other testimony, these writings preserve, for all times, the historical facts upon which the revelation of God in Christ forever rests. *In this sense* these writings must be regarded as canonical. *In this sense* the church can never again produce the canonical, relatively open though the total canon of scripture, as we know it, should remain.

Christology thus demands an *evangelical definiteness,* and such definiteness can only be preserved by recognizing this unique position and value of the biblical witness. Only such evangelical definiteness can secure the church against a sheer theological caprice and uncontrolled relativism which would make it possible for one to affirm anything and everything as Christian.

127

It should be obvious now that it is not the modern science of history alone, but the very evangelical genius of Protestantism which inspired, and continues to inspire, the work of biblical criticism. The structures of religious experience in Catholicism and in the mystical spiritualists lack this profound historical incentive which grows out of the Christological concern of Protestantism.

Jesus Christ as the Tradition

One of the thrilling and hopeful things which has grown out of the revival of Protestant interest in tradition is the new ecumenical awareness that although we are divided by our separate traditions, there is *one common tradition,* one thing in common, which is "handed down" by all of our traditions, namely, the redemptive power of God in the gift of Jesus Christ. Indeed, the formation of the World Council of Churches was possible because, as we got out of our theological isolationism and became acquainted with one another's traditions, we were all driven to the conclusion that, *divided* though we are by separate traditions, we are actually *united* by the *one true tradition;* Jesus Christ, crucified and risen, is *the* tradition at the heart of all of our separate traditions.

This discovery, which has grown out of our *initial* attempts at historical understanding and appreciation, has already wrought wonders in the cause of unity. And *continued* growth in such understanding and appreciation holds tremendous promise for the future in the cause of Christian union. As Albert Outler writes,

Our common history—the history of the witness of faithful men to God's redemptive love in Jesus Christ—stands over against our partisan histories and separate traditions. It rebukes those who are content with their separate histories and those who claim that in their *separate* histories the *whole* of the common history may be found.[23]

We are now beginning to recapture an understanding of the fullness and many-sidedness of Christian tradition, "along with a humble recognition both of the partial and limited character of each denominational tradition and of the imperfection of vision from which each denomination must suffer even in its attempts to grasp the fullness of tradition."[24]

We have thus become aware of our need for one another, aware of the fact that each of our separate traditions has its own unique contribution to make to the fullness of our common life in the body of Christ. We must no longer continue to bear our witness separately and in isolation from one another but *in the greater togetherness* of the church universal so that the lives of all may be mutually enriched by each, so that the strength of the church's witness to her Lord may no longer be weakened by division among her members.

Tradition and Freedom

Valid and valuable as the Protestant recovery of the total sweep of tradition is, we must also maintain a keen awareness of the perennial evils of tradition*alism*. These evils are essentially four: formalism, legalism, archaism, and absolutism.

Formalism seems forever to haunt the traditionalistic mind. The ongoing life of the Spirit forever quests for new and ever more adequate forms of expression and fulfillment. Christians who cling to the particular forms of yesterday as fixed and forever permanent soon find the term "Ichabod" written above the door of their church, for the life has departed.

Legalism is the ethical expression of formalism. The legalist fails to appreciate the moral need for authentic personal decision, under the leading of God's Spirit. Hence he overestimates and distorts the relevance of the formulations of moral principles which were framed to meet the ethical demands of yesterday's situation, but which will not suffice for today, because a changed situation calls for alteration in ethical formulations if they are to be adequate for effective ethical response to the novel situation.

Archaism represents that aspect of traditionalism by virtue of which the spirit of prophecy has died out. Instead of recognizing and accepting the fact of change in the divine ordering of history, the spokesman of archaism bemoans the fact that things are not what they used to be. Ostrichlike, he attempts to close his eyes to the present and live in the past. He pretends that today's world does not exist. As Daniel Jenkins says[25] instead of living "between the times," he lives "behind the times." The traditionalist is thus chained to the past and thereby lacks the facility of freedom to adjust *to* the present, to live creatively *in* the present, and to move toward the future with transfiguring vision.

By absolutism we mean that the traditionalist commits the unpardonable sin of attributing to the *outer forms* of the Spirit of life characteristics which belong exclusively to the inner nature of truth. Whenever the Spirit expresses itself in outward forms something is always lost. Hence the quest of the Spirit continues, for more adequate fulfillment. It is a fallacy to view the historical life of the church as a smooth, uninterrupted flow of perfect truth. To be sure, the life of the people of God will be found clustering about the visible Christian communities; yet these communities incarnate the Spirit in only relatively good ways, never perfectly. The spirit of reform must remain in the church if it is to be indeed Christ's church.

The salvation from these evils of traditional*ism,* however, does not lie in a method which calls for a relation to the past by way of abcission. James Moffatt correctly says, "Once men and women are content to become isolated from the deep influences of yesterday . . ., they are in danger of being reduced to the level of the artificial and the superficial."[26] Furthermore, it is from *history* that we discover "the direction in which the Spirit, who ever goes before the church, has been moving, and on what lines we are to expect to be led forward."[27]

Alexander Campbell was perhaps thinking of this danger of superficialism when he wrote that "our greatest error . . . is that we are *too Protestant* in our aversion to the doctrines and commandments of men."[28]

True it is that many modern advocates of freedom fail to realize that it was the Christian faith which first liberated man from the clutches of a fatalistic philosophy of nature and the wheel of the phenomenal world. Yet some have exaggerated man's independence and lost sight of the valid way of connecting past, present, and future.

The past which has conditioned us, the present in which we busy ourselves and act in responsible decision, and the future whose form we are to determine responsibly—all are bound organically together in the historical character of human existence. To ignore this *historical* character of human existence and fail to appropriate the heritage of the past is to deny the most basic truth about God the Creator. It is to fail also to grasp the character of man's true freedom. Man's true freedom is realized only in community. The independence of individual freedom can find fulfillment only in the responsible dependence of community; for in the Christian perspective man's freedom is inseparable from his destiny: the community of Christlike men. These two—liberty and love—must be held together. Christian freedom grows out of, and remains organically rooted in, the framework of Christian community, in its total historic sweep.

NOTES

1. I Clement 7:2; see Kirsopp Lake trans. *Apostolic Fathers* (New York: G. P. Putnam, 1925).
2. Daniel Jenkins, *Tradition, Freedom and the Spirit* (Philadelphia: Westminster Press, 1951), p. 15.
3. Martin Luther, *Ausgewählte Werke* (München: Chr. Kaiser Verlag, 1957), III, 411. Trans. R.G.W.
4. *Ibid.* IV, III, Trans. R.G.W.
5. P. T. Forsyth, *Faith, Freedom and Future* (New York: Hodder & Stoughton, n.d.), p. 17.
6. Paul Tillich, *Systematic Theology* (Chicago: University of Chicago Press), II, 88. Copyright 1957 by The University of Chicago and used by permission.
7. Council of Trent, 4th Session, April 8, 1546.
8. Heinrich J. Holtzmann, *Kanon and Tradition* (Ludwigsburg, 1859), p. 430, Trans. R.G.W.
9. Jenkins, *op. cit.,* pp. 128-9.

10. N. P. Williams, "Tradition," in *Encyclopedia of Religion and Ethics,* edited by James Hastings (New York: Charles Scribner's Sons, 1922), XII, 412.

11. F. W. Dillistone, ed., *Scripture and Tradition* (Greenwich: Seabury Press, 1955), pp. 148-9.

12. Karl Adams, *The Spirit of Catholicism,* trans. Dom Justin McCann (New York: The Macmillan Company, 1955), p. 229.

13. Probabilism is that ethical theory which says that where there is no specific moral command which gives a clear answer as to what to do in the moment of ethical decision, and where, in such cases, two lines of action may probably be the morally good thing to do, that one is acting ethically if he chooses the path of action which is *less* probably right than that path which seems to him to be *more* probably right.

14. It is not implied that *all* Protestants in the Puritan tradition have been guilty of the neglect of tradition here described. The familiar symbol of the Puritan with Bible in hand, however, is perhaps the best to use to indicate the partisan, sectarian outlook which many Protestants of this tradition developed.

15. Disciples of Christ must rethink and re-evaluate the restorationist aspect of their theology in the light of this criticism.

16. To borrow the popular Lutheran phrase in reference to the idea of the real presence of Christ in the sacrament of the Lord's Supper.

17. Daniel D. Williams, "Theology and Truth," in *The Journal of Religion,* Vol. XXII, No. 4, p. 388.

18. *Essays and Addresses* (iii. 34).

19. Karl Löwith, *Meaning in History* (Chicago: University of Chicago Press, 1949), p. 5.

20. *Ibid.,* p. 186.

21. Friedrich Schleiermacher, *The Christian Faith,* trans. H. R. Mackintosh and J. S. Stewart (Edinburgh: T. and T. Clark, 1928), p. 69.

22. *Ibid.,* p. 595.

23. Albert C. Outler, *The Christian Tradition and the Unity We Seek* (New York: Oxford University Press, 1957), p. 57. Used by permission.

24. Jenkins, *op. cit.,* p. 167.

25. *Ibid.,* p. 119.

26. James Moffatt, *The Thrill of Tradition* (New York: The Macmillan Company, 1944), p. 178.

27. Newman Smythe, *Christian Ethics* (New York: Charles Scribner's Sons, 1905), p. 79.

28. Alexander Campbell, *The Millennial Harbinger* (1847), p. 201.

PART TWO
GOD, MAN, AND CHRIST THE LORD

6

The God who Revealed Himself
in Jesus Christ

FRANK N. GARDNER

HOW difficult it is to write about God! The difficulty for the Christian does not rise from the scarcity of data, evidence, or experience. Rather, the difficulty rises from trying to write words about a reality overwhelmingly good and merciful with whom a Christian is intimately involved when one knows that words are puny in conveying the richness and the majesty of this reality. A man truly in love with a woman finds that it is actually impossible to use words with which to express the depth of his love and devotion. When a youth who has been surrounded all of his life by the warmth and compassion of understanding parents finds himself far from home and undergoes the experience of being homesick, he cannot find words to express his feelings. Even more truly is this the case in trying to write about the deepest and most vital part of our life—our life with God.

Quite well I know that we theologians have written millions of words about God. Yet I would profess that, for my own part, I feel much like Shakespeare who, in one of his sonnets, contrasts his own inability to praise his beloved, because he is moved so deeply, with the wordier courtship of his more superficial rivals.

135

> My tongue-tied Muse in manners holds her still,
> While comments of your praise, richly compil'd,
> Reserve their character with golden quill
> And precious phrase by all the Muses fil'd.
> I think good thoughts whilst other write good words,
> And, like unlettered clerk, still cry "Amen"
> To every hymn that able spirit affords
> In polish'd form of well-refined pen.
> Hearing you prais'd, I say, " 'Tis so, 'tis true,"
> And to the most of praise add something more;

So it is when we speak about God. There is the haunting sense of something "vastly more" beneath and beyond the ability of symbols and signs to express which always accompanies our task.

In consequence we find ourselves as Christians always trying to say something about which we feel nothing can adequately be said. Yet we are just as positive that something *must* be said. For, as Christians, we are impelled to communicate in conversation and proclamation how our lives have been changed by the God who revealed himself in Jesus Christ. We feel ourselves to be his witnesses. We feel that if we did not speak, even the rocks must cry out.

When we write of "conversation" and "communication," we are immediately confronted with the necessity of using words with precision and clarity so that meanings do not remain ambiguous. Otherwise conversation is not a two-way street and communication is never achieved. At the same time we run the risk of losing the richness of quality involved in speaking of God in our very attempts at precision. Perhaps all that we can hope to do is to use signs and symbols with sufficient precision to "point" towards the reality deserving our deepest commitment of life so that there shall be as little confusion as possible.

Religiously and metaphysically I hold that the doctrine that God is love is the most adequate doctrine. All that follows is simply argument and testimony in behalf of this doctrine.

Just when I reached this conclusion I do not know. In a sense, having been reared in a Christian home, I have, perhaps, always "felt this in my bones." The intellectual clarification of the doctrine has been a slow development over many years. Shortly before his death in the early spring of 1936 my beloved former professor, Elmer Ellsworth Snoddy, stated that, rightly understood, this ancient Christian assertion was the most intellectually defensible of all the doctrines of God. Unfortunately, illness soon afterwards prevented his developing the argument to any real extent. Within a few years I read Charles Hartshorne saying the same thing in his *Man's Vision of God,* but his explication of the doctrine never quite satisfied me, although it was my privilege to be a student of his later on.

My intellectual pilgrimage along this theological road was hastened by the stimulus given me by Alfred North Whitehead's total philosophy but particularly at this point by that marvelous chapter in *The Adventure of Ideas* where he writes with insight of the marvelous intuition which Plato had late in life that the ultimate category applicable to divinity is not power or authority but love and persuasion, of the later embodiment of this doctrine in the life of a historical person, Jesus of Nazareth, and of the early metaphysical attempts at framing a consistent systematic explication of this doctrine by the Christian philosopher-theologians at Ephesus and Alexandria. As Whitehead described how this younger and less powerful idea sought to make its way in the midst of the older and more powerful traditional doctrine of God as a coercive agency and how it finally fell, a victim of the idea of God fashioned after Oriental despots and ruling Caesars, I was challenged again to investigate the validity and relative adequacy of the notion that God is love.

At about the same time I made the acquaintance of Barton W. Stone's writings. I was impressed with Stone's conversion experience following young Hodge's sermon from the text "God is love." This was as much an earthquake experience for Stone, as was Paul's vision on the road to Damascus, or Luther's insight upon rereading the Roman Letter, or Kierkegaard's hearing his guilt-ridden father confess his early sex sins. Further reading of Stone convinced me that this first of pioneers of the Christian Churches looked upon this doctrine as the North Star which gave direction to all that he wrote and did. I must confess that this insight caused me to feel a rush of hope that the Christian Churches had something to say, not only to a divided church, but to a divided world.

In pursuit of this idea I once again reread the Gospels. Now it became clear to me that the core of Jesus' life and teaching was to be found in his saying that everything that is of any importance or consequence flows from two basic and complementary life commitments. Said he, "You shall love the Lord your God with all your heart, and with all your soul, and with all your mind. This is the great and first commandment. And a second is like it, you shall love your neighbor as yourself. On these two commandments depend all the law and the prophets" (Matthew 22:37-40). I became convinced that the heart of the Christian gospel is that God loves, *is* love in fact, that God's love is magnificent and extravagant to men who really do not deserve such love, that this love of God is so warm and richly persuasive that, as it reaches men and as they are sensitive and aware, they will respond with love in their hearts to God—so much so, that, like God, they will love not only their friends and neighbors, but also their enemies. Children of God become extravagant in their love like their Father who is in heaven.

It now seemed to me that the beauty and lure of the very life of Jesus was to be found in the tender and compassionate elements of that life which radiated sensitive understanding, appreciative response, and creative love.

The story of the early Christians, as related in the canon, seemed to me to be primarily a witness as to how this spirit of God, the spirit of love, which they called the "Holy Spirit," which was in their leader and Lord, had entered their lives and made them changed men. The Book of the Acts of the Apostles might be better entitled "The Acts of the Holy Spirit in the Life of the Apostles." Here the account of Peter's visit to the Gentile

Cornelius is especially illuminating as are Paul's many expressions in his writings of the change wrought in his own life by the "Spirit of the Lord Jesus." Under the spell of the great Reformers most of us Protestants emphasize the pre-eminence of faith. Luther's diligent study of Paul, however, overlooked the greatest of the early missionary's testimony—that love was supreme even over faith. Perhaps if the great Reformer had recognized this, he would have been glad to have shaken hands with an equally courageous reformer, Zwingli, when they could not come to agreement about the nature of the Lord's Supper. Since he failed to recognize this, he scorned to do so. As a consequence, most Protestant bodies also have been great on faith, but small on love. Truly, Paul was a complex man. Yet when the chips were down and he summed up what was most important, he did it in these words, "So faith, hope, love abide, these three; but the greatest of these is love."

Yet it remained for the unknown elder of an early Christian community to state the thesis most emphatically and clearly.

Everyone who loves is a child of God and knows God, but the unloving know nothing of God. For God is love; and his love was disclosed to us in this, that he sent his only Son into the world to bring us life . . . God dwells in us if we love one another; his love is brought to perfection within us. Here is the proof that we dwell in him and he dwells in us; he has imparted his Spirit to us.

Here is a doctrine of direct immanence. This is no derivative image—only a shadow of the real thing, as in Plato. This is the doctrine of divine incarnation. It is a doctrine of God actually in man and in the world. This is no "ersatz" deity which the writer proclaims is in intimate involvement with men and the world. It is the true God himself. He boldly proclaims that *God is love in man and the world.*

The further I explored this realm of understanding, the deeper grew my conviction that the doctrine of God as love ought to be taken seriously, really seriously, and not as simply a nice poetical or sentimental expression, after which one could return to emphasis upon God as coercive power and authority. In fact, the notion of God formulated upon the basis of the latter categories has become repugnant to me. It seemed to me that most of us Christians have made a grievous error. We begin by assuring others and ourselves that God has revealed himself in Jesus Christ. Now, quite ordinarily, this would seem to mean that we can learn something about the character of God from Jesus. This would seem to mean that Jesus can tell us much about God. This would seem to mean that if we would seek what God is like, we ought to listen to Jesus and look into his life. But this we have not usually done, for, you see, we already know what God is like from other sources. We already know that he is judge, ruler, and all-powerful after the image of earthly monarchs. We have even defined him in *omni* terms—omnipotent, omniscient, omnipresent, and omnieverything. He is conceived after the static perfection models in philosophy, or in abstract structures coldly remote from the daily struggles of men. Having so conceived of God to begin with, there remains nothing that Jesus can teach us about God. So we reverse the procedure and fashion Jesus Christ in the image of our already held doctrines of God. The so-called infancy gospels show how this process was developed even in the early days of the church. Its later development is familiar to all of us. While sophisticated treatments of this process are given by many theologians, the horrible result among so many of the laity is that Jesus Christ has become a composite portrait of a zombie, Superman, the archangel Gabriel with his trumpet of judgment and doom, with a little flecking here and there of a sentimental "dear Jesus" coloring.

Yet I realized that if this doctrine that God is love is to be taken seriously we must explore the meaning of love at deeper levels than we customarily do. The word itself carries so many meanings to so many people that to say, "God is love," is to really say nothing. The word is ambiguous; it lacks precision. To many it indicates that the user of the word "love" is expressing nothing more than a warm and sentimental feeling in front

140

of which he wishes to bask in animal security. True, one may mean nothing more by "love" than a sentimental feeling. He may equate love with sex or lust. Or he may mean all the other counterfeits of love.

This business of talking about love is something everyone talks about. And usually we use the word as if everyone understood it—that understanding what is meant by the word "love" is really a very simple thing. Quite ordinarily one finds that people believe that to love is simple but that to be loved is most difficult. In our marketing orientation many of us believe that we are not loved because we are not attractive enough. We look upon attractiveness as being based upon such things as looks, dress, intelligence, money, social position, or prestige. Actually we fail to realize that the basic problem is not the difficulty of being loved but the difficulty of loving; that one is loved only if one can love, if one's capacity to love produces love in another person, that the capacity for love, not for its counterfeits, is a hard, arduous, and exacting achievement.

True human love is often confused with the counterfeits of love. The counterfeits of love are what people mistake for love. Among these counterfeits are such emotions as dependence, submission, domination, possessiveness, the craving for control, sexual greed and lust, and the inability to be alone. True human love is the capacity for and the strenuous attempt at the experience of concern, responsibility, respect, compassion, empathy, and understanding of another person, plus an intense desire for that other person's growth in meaning and value.

The difficulties which we face as persons and the difficulties societies face as societies, whatever may be the symptoms of our difficulty, are rooted in our real inability to love. As Erich Fromm, among others, has reminded us, analytic therapy is essentially an attempt to assist the patient to gain, or regain, his capacity to truly love.

Love, if it be true love, cannot be restricted to any one person. If we love only one person, or if we love only a few intimates, and do not love our neighbor or a stranger, we demonstrate that our love for one person is an attachment of submission or domination—but not of love. Furthermore, if we love our neighbor but do not love ourselves, we reveal that our love of our neighbor is not genuine. True love is based on an attitude of affirmation and respect, and if this attitude does not also exist towards ourselves (we are also human beings and neighbors), it does not exist at all.

Our tradition has it that Jesus never lost an opportunity to emphasize true love, its necessity, and its roots in the love of God.

"You have heard that it was said, 'You shall love your neighbor and hate your enemy.' But I say to you, Love your enemies and pray for those who persecute you, so that you may be sons of your Father who is in heaven; for he makes his sun rise on the evil and on the good, and sends rain on the just and on the unjust" (Matthew 5:43-45).

"If you love those who love you, what credit is that to you? For even sinners love those who love them. And if you do good to those who do good to you, what credit is that to you? For even sinners do the same. And if you lend only to those from whom you hope to receive, what credit is that to you? Even sinners lend to sinners, to receive as much again. But love your enemies, and do good, and lend expecting nothing in return; and your reward will be great, you will be sons of the Most High; for he is kind to the ungrateful and the selfish. Be merciful, even as your Father is merciful (Luke 6:32-36).

The plea of Jesus is for us to truly love, for this is what God is constantly doing. His disciples who lived the life of true love and compassionate concern were filled with the Holy Spirit and found their lives changed and made radiant—so much so that throughout the rest of the New Testament this life of the Christian is spoken of as filled with "glory." In spite of sin, death, suffering, war, anxiety in the world, the Christian knows and experiences glory. The word "glory" is a much neglected word in theological vocabularies these days. We seem to relegate it to Negro spirituals while our mouths savor the bitter taste of the gall of sin and the sour taste of the vinegar of "man's helplessness." I rarely read the work of a theologian these days who emphasizes the glory of the Christian life or "the glory which shall be in us." Perhaps this is another bit of evidence that modern man and modern Christians have not learned to truly love.

When we manifest a genuine concern for another's growth and good, when we seek with sensitivity to put ourselves in his place—to view the world through his eyes, to feel his hopes, disappointments, and joys when we share in his life itself, an astonishing thing happens. We find that we ourselves undergo a process of change and become different persons. We find that the world no longer seems the same, nor do we seem the same to ourselves. We discover that we now view ourselves and our world-in-process from different perspectives than we are able to see customarily. We find our world of appreciation expanding and growing so that persons and events we formerly were unable to appreciate or grasp with interest are no longer matters of indifference to us. We find we have new ideas, new insights, and new understandings. Felt qualities seem to be multiplied and meanings with diverse nuances are now grasped where before they were not. In brief, we find that we are undergoing a process of dynamic change such that there is a new unification of our personalities out of interaction with a diversity of meanings and values. This creative process of unification of diverse values operative in us results in a new synthesis of meaning and value. We find ourselves to be newly emergent "wholes" rising out of the previous synthesis of personality into a new structure. The "old" has become "new." The old diversity of structure has not disappeared in the sense that there is nothing left. Rather it is a case of growth whereby the old structure is transformed into a new creative synthesis. The values of diversity have been preserved, but they have not been preserved intact as they once were. Rather they have been preserved through a kind of creative transformation such that we are aware of our immediate derivation from the past and feel continuity with the past, yet we are just as aware of the fact that we have been changed and are different.

When persons love truly, they will be changed. Life will take on new depths of quality and meaning. The texture of life will become increasingly complex and rich. We may be so changed that what we once hated we now treasure.

We find that we do not cause these changes to occur. We cannot even predict *how* we will be changed. We *can* predict only that when we love truly, we *will* be changed.

The witness of the New Testament is that the early Christians underwent the same kind of transforming experience. Peter, a hesitant Jew still refusing to have real and sensitive relationships with non-Jews, underwent a transforming experience following which he said, "God has shown me that I should not call any man common or unclean." He spoke kindly to a non-Jew, entered his house, spoke with him about Jesus Christ, and later when he was taken to task by Jewish Christians still unconverted and accused of "visiting with men who are uncircumcised," defended himself by telling of his transforming experience and of the fact that these non-Jews had received the Holy Spirit just as had the Jewish Christians. He concluded, "God gave the same gift to them as he gave to us when we believed in the Lord Jesus Christ; who was I that I could withstand God?" With this, his opponents were silenced.

A similar transformation of life and attitude with a corresponding expansion of meaning and appreciation was experienced by the Apostle Paul. As Saul of Tarsus he was a person who had integrated his life around the law. This term symbolized the entire system of value for a devout Jew. The law summed up all that was most important for a Jew. But Saul, the Jewish religious and cultural devotee, was confined to the level and circumference of value and meaning enclosed within the tradition of Judaism. Because it had made him what he was, he loved it and became a zealous defender of it against what seemed to him to threaten it. Since the early Christians seemed to threaten all that he appreciated and held dear, Saul harried and hounded them. But the Holy Spirit of love which came to him through

Jesus Christ wrought a creative change in Saul. He ceased being a hater of non-Jews and became the first great missionary to non-Jews.

Paul's transformation he describes in his own words,

[I am] a Hebrew born of Hebrews; as to the law a Pharisee, as to zeal a persecutor of the church, as to righteousness under the law blameless. But whatever gain I had, I counted as loss for the sake of Christ. (Philippians 3:5-7)

I have been crucified with Christ; it is no longer I who live, but Christ that lives in me. (Galatians 2:20)

For in Christ Jesus you are all sons of God, through faith. For as many of you as were baptized into Christ put on Christ. There is neither Jew nor Greek, there is neither slave nor free, there is neither male nor female; for you are all one in Jesus Christ.

(Galatians 3:26-28)

And because you are sons, God has sent the Spirit of his Son into our hearts crying, "Abba! Father!" So through God you are no longer a slave but a son. (Galatians 4:6-7)

But far be it from me to glory except in the cross of our Lord Jesus Christ, by which the world has been crucified to me, and I to the world. For neither circumcision counts for anything, nor uncircumcision, but a new creation. (Galatians 6:14-15)

To get the full impact of these last words of Paul think of an Episcopalian saying, "For neither apostolic succession nor the want of it is of any importance, but only a new creation," Or think of a Lutheran saying, "For neither the Augsburg Confession nor the want of it is of any importance, but only a new creation." Or think of a Roman Catholic saying, "For neither the Mass nor the want of it is of any importance, but only a new creation." Or, finally, think of Baptists and Disciples saying, "For neither baptism nor the want of it is of any importance, but only a new creation."

To venture to commit one's life to the creative and transforming work of God when one cannot foresee the results of God's working, seems senseless to most people, and to most Christians by name. One can already see and appreciate the structure of values he has inherited and achieved in his culture and nation. The goods of life which one knows and values are difficult to relinquish in order for one to go with God. It must have been difficult for Abraham. It must have been difficult for Paul. It takes an act of faith and commitment to God. Because it is so difficult, Paul writes much about faith to his early Christian friends. Yet out of faith and commitment comes the "new creation" as Paul describes it. We are born again. Our old self is dead. We now live in newness of light. We are new, the world is new, and we have become a greater new synthesis of value and meaning.

As a Christian I can only testify that when I have done my best to have this attitude of understanding, empathy, compassion, and love towards other persons—whether these persons be those in my family with whom I live intimately every day or whether they be strangers of all colors of skin, of all kinds of economic levels, of all grades of education, of all types of morals—and when this attitude is expressed in activities of concern for the growth and good of these other persons, I have been transformed into a new person day after day and year after year. It is an extraordinarily difficult task, especially with some people. But I find that when I so live, my world expands, my mind is alive with new insights, and I am brought into closer community with the other person who is my neighbor.

On the other hand, I can also testify that when I have been primarily preoccupied with my own welfare, when I have refused to enter into sympathetic interaction with others, when I have become absorbed in defending my own system of ideas or values, when I have been self-concerned, then I have not grown, I have tended to become fixed and static. Jesus' words have been true in my case, "He who finds his life will lose it, and he who loses his life for my sake will find it."

In recent years I have been increasingly interested in some findings in the sciences which seem to indicate that this process of creative transformation which we all experience is also operative at other levels. Elementary particles brought close together interact with each other so furiously that they can be separated only with great difficulty. Further, in the process of their interaction with each other they take on the characteristics of each other, and seem to be a composite of the characteristics of all the others. In biological growth such as that of a plant, there is a creative process by which various chemicals, gases, etc., are restructured in constantly new syntheses through a highly interactive process. It is an amazing thing to witness a rosebush produce a rose from carbon, water, potassium, phosphates, oxygen, hydrogen, nitrogen, sunlight, and hundreds of other diverse events. In the growth of the human mind and in the growth of personality the same fundamental creative process seems to be operative. In human life what we have called "love" seems to permit this creative process to work freely and without serious hindrance.

Since this creative reality is what produces good in our lives and seems to be operative throughout the structure of the world in the same transforming fashion, we seem to have some clue as to the character of God. The majesty and goodness of God towers far above our pygmy ideas of God, usually fashioned in some way from our own image of ourselves. He cannot be confined to the structures of meaning involved in terms of impersonality or of personality. A descriptive definition of God would be the following: God is that creative reality (or operative process) unifying diverse events, qualities, and values through time and history in such a way that the values of diversity are preserved and enhanced in constantly emerging new syntheses of structured value. Or, putting it religiously, "God is love." This is the result of love in human life.

Here a significant distinction needs to be made. We must not confuse God as love, with man's love. We may be made in the image of God, but *we are not God*. Human love is the attitude and manifestation of concern for the good and growth of others. It is characterized by mutuality, empathy, helpfulness, openness of interaction, and compassion. When we so love others, we know God, for it is then that we begin to realize the working of God in our lives as he creatively transforms us. But it is God who does the transforming, not ourselves. It is God who unites these diverse values into new structures of good. In a sense we can prepare the ground and the soil, but it is God who does the growing. Yet it is by the very work of God that we exist at all. He called us into being and he worked in us long before we knew him. We can love only because he first loved us.

As our Lord saw, these two loves cannot be separated, though they are distinct. We must love the Lord our God with all our hearts and our neighbors as ourselves. God's love is one intersecting plane. Man's love for man is the other intersecting plane. At the juncture of the intersection is where God is found. At the juncture of the intersection is found man's understanding of his true nature and destiny as a son of God.

At last I have arrived at the place where I can say that for me there is far greater depth of meaning in the words "God revealed himself in Jesus Christ" than I can ever put into words. It is this God of love who revealed himself in Jesus Christ. Truly he was the Son of God. But we are also sons of God. Our Lord called us his "brethren." And there is profound truth in the words of Paul that "All who are led by the Spirit of God are sons of God" (Romans 8:14). In a truly real and magnificent sense our Lord was "the first-born among many brethren" (Romans 8:29).

It is the proclamation of this God, his revelation in Jesus Christ, his continuing life in his body, the church, and the implementation of this kind of living and loving (which is the fruit of the Spirit) in the daily life of all mankind which is our task as Christians. Only so can all men everywhere have peace, hope, opportunity, justice, and the good life. It is this God revealed in Jesus Christ who is both the source of the good news and the center of its message.

7

The Nature of Christ's Authority

GLENN C. ROUTT

THERE is solid theological ground for emphasis on the centrality of Christ in the life and thought of the church, conceived in terms of the supremacy of personal faith over all creedal expressions and theological formulations as the criterion of membership in the body of Christ. J. H. Garrison declared, "The exaltation of the Lordship of Jesus Christ above human opinion [is] the very Magna Charta of our religious liberty."[1] It is also the basis of Christian unity, as the ecumenical movement in our time is becoming increasingly aware.

Perhaps it needs to be made explicit from time to time that the question of the lordship of Jesus Christ is also the question of his authority. This paper is an attempt to make somewhat more explicit the implications of the lordship of Jesus Christ with special reference to his place in the life and thought of the church.

The Problem and Need of Authority

P. T. Forsyth once said, "Our idea of authority lies so near the heart of life that it colours our whole circulation."[2] How the idea of authority has colored our thinking can be seen in our attitude toward such seats of religious authority as the Bible,

149

the church, tradition, creeds, ecclesiastical bodies, reason, experience, and Christ himself. But perhaps we have not paid enough attention to a prior question: not what is the *seat* of authority (to use James Martineau's phrase) but what is the nature of religious authority for the Christian?

The *problem of authority* in religion can be stated as follows: Is there any *accessible source* of *religious truth* which is *wholly authoritative?* and, if so, what? This statement of the problem allows for the possibility that the *source* may be either inside or outside the human mind. The word "accessible" means "capable of being arrived at and understood by the human mind, assisted or unassisted, corporate or individual." The use of the phrase "religious truth" implies a distinction between religious and other sorts of truth. The use of the term "wholly authoritative" means it possesses the character of universality and validity so that choice and action are not grounded in individual caprice.

Some religious leaders have been guilty of thinking of authority in purely negative terms, as something entirely external and coercive. In a sense this is true and good. But in a more fundamental sense it is misleading. Is liberty man's chief end? Is authority a curse? A moment's reflection tells us that liberty without authority is impossible. Life itself is impossible without authority. Authority is ultimately a religious question: What is valid authority? Who shall be Lord of the human spirit? Alexander Campbell with his negative attitude toward the creeds turned to the Bible saying, "I have endeavored to read the Scriptures as if no one had read them before me, and I am as much on my guard against reading them today through the medium of my views yesterday, as I am against being influenced by any foreign name, authority, or system, whatever."[3] Thus Campbell, while not opposing the authority of the Bible or reason, did reflect a negativism in his idea of the nature of authority. He recognized the need of authority, but was largely concerned to locate it properly and to affirm freedom.[4]

Ultimately the religious authority is decisive for questions of theology and morality, for society, for the church, for man as man. Questions of truth and of right are questions of authority. Indeed the inner character of all periods of history, and especially our own, is the struggle for valid authority, inasmuch as the question of authority is the question of truth, of reality.

The problem of authority in religion was one of the central issues of the age of the Protestant Reformation. Prior to the reformers the church of the Middle Ages thought the problem was solved. The task of theology was to elucidate the truth which had been authoritatively revealed. Thus the Thomistic synthesis of reason and revelation was made possible. The same pertains to fundamentalism today. The question whether there *is* an authoritative source of religious truth was not seriously raised. The issue was rather simply, what is the *locus* of authority?

Part of Luther's significance as a reformer lies in his challenge of the authority of the church by the authority of the Bible and conscience. But he did not doubt the need of authority. The same is true of Wycliff, Hus, Zwingli, Calvin. They all arrived at theories of authority which opposed that of the Catholic church. They could succeed only by providing a substitute theory. The Reformation hinged on this.

In the matter of valid authority the church today has a vast service to render to religious freedom, as in the past in the period of the Reformation. While we are not unmindful of the time the church has rendered a disservice, nevertheless, at its best the church has served the cause of religious freedom "by providing an authority whose very nature creates freedom—the authority, that is, not of the Church itself but of its Gospel and Saviour."[5]

Whenever the church has subordinated freedom to authority, she has become coercive and has begun to degenerate. But when the church subordinates authority to freedom, her decline is no less sure. It is only when the church proclaims and lives by the divine authority that she is able to become the agent of liberat-

151

ing power. Only then does the church maintain her holy character and arrest the tendency to decline into a secular institution. It has been well said, "There is only one thing greater than Liberty, and that is Authority."[6] I would add "valid authority."

Thus the church cannot avoid the problem of authority, for to do so would be to lose sight of her Lord and her gospel and to become bogged down in all manner of proximate issues and side-show activities. It is important to put aside some of the negativism with respect to authority and to face seriously the question of true authority. To face the question as a positive demand rather than a negative evasion is perhaps the first qualification for discussing the subject.

What is the positive demand? It is the demand of the soul for its rightful lord. It is the demand of the will for moral sanction. It is the demand of the mind for truth. In a word, it is the demand of man for God.

Thus authority is bound to revelation. That means it is a religious and theological matter before it ever becomes psychological, social, and political. It all turns on what makes authority authoritative without being authoritarian, that is, without destroying freedom but rather fulfilling it. It is not enough to say that reason, or experience, or the Bible, or the church is the seat of authority. That does not answer the demand of why they are authoritative and in what sense.

The Nature of Religious Authority

It is commonly regarded that religious authority is by nature coercive, exercising some degree of compulsion over thought and action with or without our consent. Actually religious authority must always be joined with consent before it can function, otherwise it *is* sheer coercion. This means that religious authority cannot be separated from personality. Authority is part and parcel of man himself, we are under its sway either from within or without.

Sabatier has introduced the distinction between "religions of authority" and "the religion of the spirit." But this is a misleading distinction in that it is not an issue between authority and no-authority, but only between the forms of authority. Bertram Lee Woolf in a careful study of the conception of authority has described two forms of authority as being either that which is "uncriticised, and therefore in a sense external," or that which is

assimulated and more or less completely grafted into, and which now forms part of an organic whole with, the individual activity. Thus the authority of the Church may be replaced by that of "reason," or the Bible or some other more or less complex conception, but in no case is there left a mere vacuum.[7]

The description of an internal and external form of authority raises the question as to how they are to be related. If authority is purely internal, then the question of subjectivism is raised in its acutest form. If it is purely external, the question of personal freedom is raised. If it be remembered that the question is more than one of logic but is one of experience involving the total personality, we may facilitate the discussion.

The experience of authority, like that of revelation, is characterized by its quality of personal encounter and response. Religious authority is something we recognize and respond to. It has a practical as well as a theoretic character. Like faith it is not merely intellectual but also volitional and emotional.

Perhaps the nature of religious authority is best understood in its relation to faith. Faith is the internal response to God who is other than man. There is a certain immediacy of recognition and obedience. In this experience the personality is enlarged, the object of faith becomes the new center of personal life. The external authority becomes the internal authority, as when Paul says, "The love of Christ constrains us." Authority thus augments and completes freedom, the bondage in which there is perfect liberty. Here we have the Christian experience of the authority of Christ, at once the greatest conceivable authority because it

153

dominates the whole inner life so that one can no longer call his life his own, and yet experienced as compatible with the greatest conceivable liberty. Indeed, the completeness and absoluteness of the authority of Christ is the very condition of perfect liberty.

For Christians the question of religious authority is the question of the lordship of Christ. The redeeming Christ becomes his own authority with us, not because we have proved him true or worthy but because he has proved us and made us worthy. The nature of Christ's authority is that of a person for a person, and this is established only in faith. *"Our only authority must be faith's object itself in some direct self-revelation of it."*[8] This and this alone is what makes authority really religious. Here the internal and external aspects of authority are established in the sole object of faith and not simply in some outside though indispensable witness to it. God in Chirst is our ultimate authority, but without the witness of the Bible and church, reason and experience, how would we know this God? Thus we cannot casually pass over the process by which the Christian comes to the recognition that the ultimate authority is to be found in the Christian revelation. Because the Christian in his arrival at a valid authority and object of faith is guided by a number of witnesses and moved by a variety of influences including the *Bible, church,* and *tradition,* and his own *rational insight and experience,* we need to inquire in what way are these authoritative for him.

The Authority of the Bible

In the course of our quest for valid authority we move not in a vacuum but in a living tradition and continuum of experience which bear witness, even though at times they may be made false claimants to ultimate authority. The Bible has been misused in that manner.

Since the question of authority is the question of revelation, and since the chief Protestant authority is the revelation of God in Christ to which the Bible bears witness, we must ask (1) what is the relation between the revelation of God and the biblical record, including the Old and New Testaments? (2) What is the relation between the biblical record of revelation and the church, including her tradition? and (3) what is the relation between both Bible and church to the experience of the individual, including reason, conscience, and faithful response?

Hubert Cunliffe-Jones distinguishes three senses in which the word "authority" is used. Using the factors of "right" and "power" as the essential constituents of authority, Cunliffe-Jones differentiates between (1) final authority, (2) educative authority, and (3) the authority of power.

There is the final authority in which right and power are united, there is the educative authority which has right, so far as its truth has not been assimilated but no power, and there is the authority of power, hardly to be found in complete isolation from right, but not primarily dependent upon it.[9]

It is in the first sense of the word, final authority in which right and power are united, that we are interested.

In what sense is the Bible finally authoritative? Can the Bible have final authority for the Christian so that he cannot dissent from it? Surely, we must say, only in so far as it points to the authority of God. As we previously urged, authority is bound up with revelation. While the Bible may have educative authority, it is as the witness to the revelation of God that it becomes authoritative for us. It is the God of the biblical revelation who is our authority, *this* God and not some other claimant.

But who is this God? Where specifically do we find him revealed in the Bible? Every person and every group appeals to the Bible selectively, even those who most vigorously advocate plenary inspiration. But what is the principle of selection? Often it is a principle derived from some source outside the Bible in the prevailing culture or a dominant system of philosophy.

In recent years we have seen a quite different approach to the Bible by those who fully accept the methods and results of

155

biblical criticism. This has led to a sounder understanding of the nature of biblical authority. It begins by recognizing that the biblical writers were men of faith who were telling the "Story within the stories," the story or drama of revelation and redemption through the mighty acts of God culminating in Jesus Christ. One implication of this way of looking at the Bible is that it has brought forth a new emphasis on the unity of the Bible as the drama of salvation, as gospel. At times the emphasis becomes overemphasis, so that there is the temptation to force upon the Bible a unified view of God and man and history which overlooks the element of diversity. Nevertheless, it is a positive gain to recognize the unity of the Bible and the fact that its uniting center is the gospel of God. We need not insist that all parts of the Bible are equally helpful to our understanding of the center. And we would avoid forcing the whole Bible into a unified christological pattern. But the Bible as a whole is about the gospel of God which finds its fulfillment in Christ.

It is important to reiterate that the Bible itself is not the gospel or the revelation of God. It is the witness, the record. We do not say "merely" the witness and record. It might even be better to speak of the Bible as the sacrament of the word, the reading and preaching of which is a means of grace. Herein lies the authority of the Bible—that it is a *means* of presenting him who is the final authority for life. The Lord of life must be found in life, in personal communion with the personal God. The final authority must be a communing Person, it cannot be a book, or a creed, or even a church. If it were otherwise, we should indeed need an infallible book or an infallible see or an infallible man because faith would then be primarily assent. We should then need documents, not sacraments.

It is in this connection that we can see the significance of the apostolic witness and interpretation in the New Testament. The revelation of God in Christ, we must say with P. T. Forsyth, includes both the gift of himself and the interpretation of it.

This gift and interpretation was itself an essential part of the whole historic act, of the unitary revealing act of God in Christ. The revelation was to go on in the special and apostolic Word of revelation. The apostolic interpretation is an integral part of the revelationary fact, process, and purpose, a real though posthumous part of Christ's own continued teaching.[10]

Seen in this light, the New Testament is more than a record of revelation; it may become a sacramental function of the revelation itself. By the Spirit the apostles' interpretation of revelation becomes the self-interpretation of the revelation. "It is Christ explaining Himself," says Forsyth, "it is the Saviour still preaching His salvation not only unsilenced by death but in the fulness achieved by its conquest."

The implications of this view for the doctrine of inspiration seem obvious enough. "The Apostles were not mere channels but agents, not vehicles of Christ but members of Him." The apostles participated in the revelatory event; they were within Christ's finality and therefore authoritative and normative *in that sense and in that way*—agents of Christ and the Spirit necessary for the historic revelation. "If they are final for the historic fact, they are no less final for its central interpretation."[11] Their interpretation was a part of Christ's finished work, and every aberration of the apostolic interpretation does something to dissolve the meaning of the historic revelation. The church seems to have sensed this in all ages and therefore has rightly resisted every dilution of the apostolic interpretation.

The Authority of the Church and Tradition

Let us now turn to the question of the relation of the church to the Bible as it bears on the matter of authority. While it is true that the church produced the Bible, it is more fundamentally true that both the church and the Bible were the result of the gospel. The revelation of God that comes to us through the Bible is authoritative for both the Bible and the church. As Canon Wedel has put it,

The Bible as book appeared within the Fellowship. It is, therefore, true to say that the Fellowship came first. The Fellowship was responsible *for* the Book. But the Fellowship is also responsible *to* the Book, for the Book contains the living Word of God to man.[12]

Thus the authority of the church, like that of the Bible, lies in its participation in the authority of Christ and his gospel, not in its institutional prestige. Protestantism has always known this, although it has not always remembered it. In its insistence that the church must always remain under the revelation that is known through the Bible, Protestantism has recognized better than Rome the nature of the church's authority. Barth has said it well,

If then, apart from the undeniable and singular aliveness of the Church, there exists over against it a concrete authority whose utterance means not a talking by the Church with herself, but a talking to the Church, which compared with the Church may hold the position of a free power and so of a criterion, obviously it must be distinguished precisely by its written scriptural nature from the mere spiritual and oral life of a Church tradition and given a place before it.[13]

Some of Barth's tendency toward "biblicism" may be detected in this statement, but the idea of the church standing under an authority which it does not control is an essential element in the Protestant concept of religious authority.

On the other hand, sectarian Protestantism has been guilty of seeking to justify its sectarianism through irresponsible use of the Bible. Where the Roman church has rightly seen that the Bible needs interpretation, that is, that the revelation cannot be seen as revelation except through the eyes of faith, and this means by the whole church, Protestant sectarianism has cut itself off from that whole tradition. Protestants have been inclined to oppose tradition and Scripture, and Disciples of Christ are no exception to this.

Sectarianism's revolt against tradition can be understood. Perhaps the basic objection has not been to tradition as such but to traditional*ism* as an *external* authority. To that extent the objection is valid, but it has resulted in isolation from our corporate and historical experience by its failure to recognize adequately the positive value of tradition. In a recent course in the history of Christian thought, reference was made to Reinhold Seeburg's *Textbook of the History of Doctrines* as required reading for the course. The students thought it amusing when it was announced, "Brethren, you're going to plow this, stumps and all." But after several hours of reading they did not find it so amusing. And surprisingly it was not the stumps that bothered them. Their main difficulty was that they could see little relation between this tradition and their own special tradition. Too many have been inclined to believe they could jump back into the Bible, leaping over all of the intervening centuries. Or, if they have recognized the need of tradition, it has been largely limited to their own tradition. Actually, of course, no one has completely avoided it. We are bound to use tradition of some sort, and this not merely of necessity but of privilege when tradition is drawn from the Bible and rests upon the authority of the God there witnessed to.

In his recent book, *The Christian Tradition and the Unity We Seek,* Albert Outler has urged Protestants to use the *total* Christian tradition as the criterion of its lesser denominational parts. There is a new attitude toward tradition emerging among Protestants which seems healthy. H. Richard Niebuhr gives a description of this new attitude when he writes:

Tradition has assumed a new significance for Protestants in a period dominated by the historical understanding of human life. So long as the Church was understood as primarily institutional, in terms of its parallelism to a state rather than to a cultural society, and so long as tradition meant resistance to reform, conflict between the principles of traditional and Scriptural authority was inevitable. But in our time tradition is conceived otherwise than it was in the sixteenth and eighteenth centuries. It appears in a different form partly because the problem of social continuity has become as great for us as the problem of change and reform, but even more because the historical cultural character of human existence has come into fuller view. We know tradition now not only in the form of social rigidities resistant to change but as the dynamic structure of modifiable habits without which men do not exist as men. Tradition means a society's language, its conceptual frames of reference, its moral orientation in the world of good and evil, the direction of its science, the selection of the best in its literature and art. We know tradition as a living social process constantly changing, constantly in need of criticism, but constant also as the continuing memory, value system and habit structure of a society.[14]

This discussion of tradition has already assumed the proportion of a digression for this paper, but it is made to emphasize that tradition may be a spiritual bond uniting the present with the past so that there is no such a thing as an isolated Christian. Tradition is, as James Moffatt put it, "the vitality of a continuing way of life." Without tradition the Christian easily loses his Christian identity and suffers from a kind of amnesia. According to Albert Outler a man receives a blow on the head; he forgets who he is. He knows *that* he is, but he does not know *who* he is. He has lost the "vitality of a continuing way of life" and can only wander in comparative meaninglessness and aimlessness. His only hope is to recover his past in order to establish his identity and hence his purpose for living, otherwise he is not truly a man. Similarly, the Christian attains spiritual existence only because he stands in historical relations. The historical character of human life is that it is lived in three tenses at the same time, past, present and future. The spiritual character of the Christian life is that it is the life of faith (past), love (present), and hope (future) at the same time.[15]

We have begun our inquiry into the nature of the church's authority by pointing to the importance of tradition in order to show that the source of the church and her tradition is the covenant-act of God in Christ. Neither the church nor her tradition is finally authoritative of itself. Again, as with the Bible, we must look to God in Christ for our final authority. We may ask with Outler,

Is there an actual and real authority for all Christians which stands above our competing authorities, beyond the reach of our manipulation and control, but genuinely present, actively operative? Is there a center and source of authority which is rooted in concrete fact and Christian history—and yet *not located or* circumscribed by human institutions and traditions?[16]

If we put Outler's question, we might well take his answer:

There *is* just such an authority for *all* Christians. It is the origin and center of our faith and our community. It is God's self-manifestation in Jesus Christ who possesses all men who receive him (John 1:12). It is God's prime act of *tradition*—or 'handing over' Jesus Christ to share our existence and to effect our salvation.[17]

Let it be said that just as there is no church without the Christ, neither can there be Christ without the church. Christ and church go together, with the primacy belonging to Christ who "loved her and gave himself for her." The church is perhaps better designated as the "body of Christ" than as "the extension of the principle of the incarnation." Not that the latter is untrue, but that it may too easily be construed to mean that the church possesses a holiness the equal of Christ and hence an authority the equal of his. Rome has misconstrued the designation in this way. We may, indeed, speak of the church as a sacrament of Christ, as is the Bible, as is the apostolic witness through the centuries. Jesus Christ, who is the basic sacramental reality, the "Word become flesh," is himself sacramentally present in the church and her living tradition. Tradition may well be more than history; it is *Heilsgeschichte*. It may be a means of grace to us men and for our salvation. This sacred tradition shapes us and makes us; as a sacrament it makes God present. Here, then, is to be found the nature of authority in the church and her tradition—that she witnesses to the covenant-act of God in Christ. The creation of the church is part of the gospel, of God's self-revelation, which is our final authority.

A question remains. How shall we relate ourselves to that

body of tradition which lies outside the Bible? Here we must recognize the distinction between God's tradition of Christ ('handing over,' *paradosis,* Jesus Christ) and the traditions of men. Within the ecumenical context a special opportunity presents itself. Having declared ourselves bound only to God's prime tradition in Christ, and free from bondage to any specific segment of the postbiblical tradition of men, we are free to let all traditions open their meanings to us. We can rejoice that God's tradition (gospel) is carried on through the denominational traditions, and at the same time recognize the partiality of their respective witnesses, including our own. The way to the unity we seek may well be here. Are we open to moving among the various streams of Christian tradition without losing sight of the total tradition while keeping all traditions under the judgment of the prime tradition, the act of God in Christ? We have the assurance that once we are in Christ all things are ours (1 Corinthians 3:21).

The Authority of Reason and Experience

Having spoken of the objective sources of authority in the Bible and church, what of the individual who must make response and indeed decide whether to accept the authority of Christ or the Bible or church or whatever? The individual must finally make his own decision in matters of faith, but it is important to know that he does not make them alone. His response to the Christian revelation is made, at least in part, within some Christian community. He stands at a point of convergence of many influences, some distinctly Christian, others distinctly non-Christian, and still others a curious mixture of both. If his concern is to know the nature of Christ's authority and to make a genuine decision for or against it, he must do so under the conviction of the validity or invalidity of the Christian claim. This is the critical task. Are there standards for critical analysis so that the decision is not arbitrary? Which of the influences converging on the individual will be decisive? Can the note of authenticity and truth, and hence authority, be heard from a position external to the Christian revelation? Is reason able to discren? Is reason foreign to faith?

The relation of reason to faith and revelation is one of the unresolved issues in Christian thought. But surely it would be acceptable to say that Christian faith is the individual's response to God's revelation in Jesus Christ. And while it is not a "blind" response, the point to be made is that faith does not wait for reason's verdict before responding. The verdict, the decision, is in the response. It is not the verdict of reason alone, although reason is involved in the act of faith. As an "act" of faith the response is of a volitional as well as a cognitive character. It is useless to argue as to which comes first, since they are correlative, but there is a certain primacy in faith in that faith does not simply wait for reason to review Christ's claims and then allow them if it is satisfied. Indeed we do not know how valid his claims are until we have met them and surrendered to them. There is the element of "risk" in faith. To be sure, faith has the character of rational assent because the total personality, including reason, is involved. But for this same reason faith is not merely assent but also trust and obedience, *fiducia*. It is man's recognition of his rightful Lord and final authority and commitment of his total person in loyalty to him, thereby gaining the full use of all his powers.

The true sacrifice of the intellect consists, not in cutting reason's throat with the knife of revelation, but rather in the loyal acceptance of unpleasant and even disturbing facts in the ultimate assurance of faith that all truth, however unedifying at first sight, must in the end reveal the same God who was manifest once for all in Jesus. It is exactly by submitting itself to learn and take account of facts as they are, without imposing upon them its preconceived idea of what they ought to be, that Christian intellect is trained in the self-denial by which it also enters God's Kingdom. If the intellect has not the utterly sincere love of truth, it can never learn the full truth of love.[18]

Thus it is not "reason" that faith would oppose, but the imperialism of the rationalist or dogmatist who would impose his limitations on what truth must be.

The authority of reason and experience, we may say, does not lie in themselves as such. It is not on the subjectivity of experience, even the experience of faith, that authority is based. That would be to ground authority in something human, in a mode of consciousness. It is not "*I* know in whom I believe," but "I know *in whom* I believe." Certainty and authority have this objective reference. "For the autonomy and finality of mere experience is an end to all authority. A real authority, we have seen, is indeed *within* experience, but it is not the authority *of* experience, it is an authority *for* experience, it is an authority experienced."[19] That is, the experienced authority is my experience, but the authority thus experienced is not me nor the experience itself. This is the point often missed by the "pneumatists," "enthusiasts," and "spiritualists" who point to *their* experience to establish certainty. It is not faith as much as faith's object, God, who is the Christian's authority. Thus faith, like reason and experience, the Bible and the church, points beyond itself to its proper object.

The Nature of Christ's Authority

We have now looked briefly at the various *loci* of authority which have at times been presented as final authorities for the life and thought of the church. We have urged that in none of them is the claim to final authority justified, but that in all of them there is a certain indispensableness. They all point beyond themselves to God, man's ultimate authority; they all may serve as the occasion of revelation, hence are authoriatative in that sense and in that way. We have now to inquire into the nature of Christ's authority.

It would be well to begin by reminding ourselves that because man is a sinner in need of redemption, the primary purpose of revelation is not information but salvation, the reconciliation

164

of man with his rightful Lord, his final authority. Furthermore, salvation is not merely from sin in the negative sense but also for the fulfillment of man's possibilities. It is the Christian claim that God in his redemptive work through Jesus Christ is moving toward the accomplishment of his purpose. The Christian rejoices in this and freely acknowledges Christ as Lord, for under his authority he finds his greatest freedom and the fulfillment of all his powers of being. To say that Christ is Lord is to say that he exercises a legitimate control over personal life; the control is legitimate because it does not destroy life but re-creates it. Man knows he can trust and obey this authority because Christ has shown himself to be trustworthy by his love for the one he claims for himself. Because Christ's "perfect love casts out fear," the believer confidently "commits his way unto the Lord." With this hope and confidence, born of faith, the external authority is transformed into an internal authority. Christ's authority is the authority of grace, of a love which "while we were sinners" died for us. This is the authority of holy love, the only valid authority for the soul, because it does not dominate but sets free; it does not restrain but constrains; it is not a new law but a new life. Thus if we would understand the nature of Christ's authority, it must be in terms of God's redeeming activity in and through him. It is God's love, meaning his holiness, his justice, and his mercy which we see in Christ and which now constrains us. It is not enough to say he is Savior; he is also Sovereign. His sovereignty is his saving work, and by that work claims, or reclaims, us for God.

His is no external authority. External authority renders men impotent, both intellectually and morally. Christ's authority, even more in his death than in his life, is invincibly compelling; never more than when disobedience makes our consciences ashamed. His is also a redemptive authority, which delivers from inward conflict, breaks down rebellion, and renders us free to obey.[20]

The authority of Christ is not ultimately his own, but of "him that sent me." He who "spoke with authority" acknowledged it as "given to me." Paul Tillich has given forceful expression to this in a sermon[21] based on Luke 20:1-8, the colloquy with the chief priests, scribes, and elders who asked Jesus, "By what authority do you do these things, or who is it that gave you this authority?" In this conversation on Christ's authority, Tillich points out, the surprising thing is that no answer was given by Jesus; or rather, the refusal to give an answer was the only answer Christ could give because to have engaged in a comparison of credentials with these religious leaders would have been to discuss the matter in the wrong terms. He did not ask them what the source of their authority was; had he done so they could have replied by pointing to their wide knowledge of the scriptures, or to their great wisdom and experience, or to their priestly consecration, and they could have challenged Jesus to produce as good or better claims to authority. Instead, Jesus asked "Was the baptism of John from heaven or from men?" They could not answer without outraging the popular recognition of John as a prophet called by God, or admitting to a source of authority beyond their own special claims. In either case the recognition of God as the ultimate authority was demanded. As Tillich puts it,

That which makes an answer impossible is the nature of an authority which is derived from God and not man. The place where God gives authority to a man cannot be circumscribed. It cannot be legally defined. It cannot be put into the fences of doctrines and rituals. It is here, and you do not know where it comes from. You cannot derive it. You must be grasped by it. You must participate in its power. . . . We can only point to a reality, as Jesus does.[22]

The two questions, "By what authority?" and "Who gave you this authority?" raise the matter of the nature and source of Christ's authority. "By what authority?" means "What *kind* of authority?" Is it like that of the rabbi or is it something special? Hence follows the second question, "Who gave you this authority?" which means "What is the *source* of your authority?" Since the nature and source of Christ's authority was something Jesus could not claim as a possession, he did all that was necessary—pointed beyond himself to God.

This does not mean there are no preliminary authorities giving direction and protection and which can serve as media of the God who is Spirit. It is only that these preliminary authorities do not have unconditioned authority in themselves. Indeed,

> Even the authority of Jesus the Christ is not the consecrated image of the man who rules as a dictator, but it is the authority of him who emptied himself of all authority, it is the authority of the man on the Cross. It is one and the same thing, if you say that God is Spirit and that *he* is manifested on the Cross.[23]

It is not enough to say that the authority of Christ is the impression of his personality, his teachings, his God-consciousness upon men. That is all true and must be affirmed. The New Testament writers go to great lengths to record the words and deeds of Jesus throughout his public career. The cross could not be understood without a knowledge of the person who died on it. But there is more.

> The crucifixion of Jesus set men thinking more than anything else that had ever happened in the life of the human race. . . . it made them think of the redeeming love of God.
> Not simply of the love of Jesus, but of the love of God. . . .
> . . . There was no distinction: the two were one and the same thing. In discoursing of the love that was shown in the Cross of Christ the New Testament is never able to stop short of tracing it upstream to the eternal love of God dealing sacrificially with the sins of the world.[24]

Here, then, is the nature and source of authority to which all preliminary authorities for Christian faith point and from which they derive their validity. Here is no negative, external authority but one which is positive and internal—Christ for us and in us. It is not a limitation but a liberation; not a fetter but a freedom. It is an authority in which right and power are joined; right because he seeks only man's good, power because he is able to accomplish our good. "It is in this nature and action of the Cross that the solution lies of the question of authority for Christianity, for history, for ever. It lies in the absolute holy right of the new Creator of Humanity. . . . Our great authority is what gives us most power to go forward; it is not what ties us up most to a formal past. It is of Grace and not of Law. It cannot be a doctrine, nor a book, nor an institution; it must, for a person, be a person."[25]

This is not merely the authority of one who lived long ago and far away. It is the living Christ made contemporary through the witness of the Bible, the church, reason, and experience, as the Holy Spirit re-creates the original revelation so that we are led to say, "My Lord and my God!" "No man calls Christ, Lord, except by the Spirit." Here we are touching upon the mystery of revelation, of the activity of the Holy Spirit in guiding us. Some may still want to protest that we are, after all, "cutting reason's throat with the knife of revelation." But it must be reiterated that the guidance of the Holy Spirit by which Christ is acknowledged as Lord, does not come to a passive mind but to one actively engaging all its powers as it hears the testimony of Scripture, of the apostolic and witnessing church. Mystery there is; but it is mystery with meaning, grounded in historical fact. Says Outler,

. . . To talk about history, mystery, and the Holy Spirit all in one breath may seem to 'modern men' to compound fuzziness. . . . And yet, for historical Christianity, the plainest meaning of the Holy Spirit's 'office' is: God at work in the living present revealing to us the meaning of the Christian past, centered as it is in Self-revelation in Jesus Christ. In this representation, the Spirit gives meaning to *that* revelation in the life of the church *today*. The work of the Holy Spirit is to bring men up-to-date: to make them contemporary witnesses; to transform Christian history into personal faith.[26]

It is this personal faith in Jesus as the Christ which is the criterion of all preliminary authorities. It is the constraint of

Christ's love which is the bondage in which we are free and the bond of unity in which we are brothers in the body of Christ.

NOTES

1. *Reformation of the Nineteenth Century,* p. 508.
2. P. T. Forsyth, *The Principle of Authority* (London: Hodder & Stoughton, 1912), p. 1.
3. *Christian Baptist,* 1825.
4. *See* D. Ray Lindley, *Apostle of Freedom* (St. Louis: The Bethany Press, 1957) for a well-illustrated and documented presentation of Campbell's position on the nature of authority.
5. Forsyth, *op. cit.,* p. 9.
6. *Ibid.,* p. 19.
7. B. L. Woolf, *The Authority of Jesus* (London: Allen and Unwin, 1925), p. 16.
8. Forsyth, *op. cit.,* p. 22.
9. Hubert Cunliffe-Jones, *The Authority of the Biblical Revelation* (Boston: Pilgrim Press, 1948), pp. 3-4.
10. Forsyth, *op. cit.,* p. 149.
11. *Ibid.,* p. 150.
12. T. O. Wedel, *The Coming Great Church* (New York: The Macmillan Company, 1945), p. 99.
13. John Bennett, "A Protestant Conception of Religious Authority," *Union Seminary Quarterly Review,* 1951.
14. H. Richard Niebuhr, *The Purpose of the Church and Its Ministry* (New York: Harper & Row, Publishers, Inc., 1956), pp. 87-88. Used by permission.
15. *See* Emil Brunner, *Faith, Hope and Love* (Philadelphia: The Westminster Press, 1956), p. 13.
16. Albert Outler, *The Christian Tradition and the Unity We Seek* (Oxford University Press, 1957), p. 110.
17. *Ibid.,* cf. Rom. 8:31-32; 4:24-25.
18. O. C. Quick, *Doctrines of the Creed* (London: Nisbet & Co., Ltd., 1938), p. 321.
19. Forsyth, *op. cit.,* p. 83.
20. R. H. Stracham, *The Authority of Christian Experience* (London: Student Christian Movement Press, Ltd.), p. 198.
21. Paul Tillich, *The New Being* (New York: Charles Scribner's Sons, 1955 and London: Student Christian Union Press, Ltd.), pp. 79-81.
22. *Ibid.,* p. 88.
23. *Ibid.,* p. 91.
24. D. M. Baillie, *God Was in Christ* (New York: Charles Scribner's Sons, 1948), pp. 184, 189.
25. Forsyth, *op. cit.,* pp. 13, 15.
26. Albert Outler, *The Christian Tradition and the Unity We Seek* (New York: Oxford University Press, Inc., 1957), p. 54.

8

The Lordship of
Jesus Christ over the Church

RALPH G. WILBURN

IN this chapter we are concerned to explicate the lordship of Jesus Christ. We are not concerned, however, with the entirety of Christ's lordship, such as his relation to the cosmos, to all history, or to the whole of human society and culture. We are concerned mainly with his lordship over the church.

The Church Created by the Power of God
in and through Jesus

The redemptive power of God's lordship, at work in and through Jesus, brought the church into being. The theological center of this new community was expressed in its first proclamation by the Apostle Peter: "Let all the house of Israel therefore know assuredly that God has made him both Lord and Christ, this Jesus whom you crucified" (Acts 2:36). To appreciate the structuring of the faith of this new religious fellowship we must grasp the meaning of the terms of this Petrine confession. The term "Jesus" is the proper name of that historical figure to which the New Testament witness points. Christianity did not yet emerge, however, with the birth of the historical Jesus, nor yet with his vocational development in Nazareth. Christianity came

170

to birth when those who were drawn to this figure were led to make the affirmation of faith: that Jesus is *Messias,* that *Messias has come,* and that therefore the new age of righteousness has already begun, in the life, death, and resurrection of Jesus, though the consummation awaits his immanent return.

The term *"Messias,"* or *"Christos"* (the Greek translation), is a theological term drawn from Judaism. It was the concept by which the original Christians expressed their understanding of the transhistorical significance of Jesus. The meaning of the term *"Messias"* had been construed in a variety of ways by different Jewish groups. Yet basically it meant "the anointed one," who by virtue of receiving a special unction from God would be enabled to establish "the reign of God" in Israel, and through Israel in all the world.

This twofold character of the Christian faith should always be borne in mind. The basic revelatory "event" on which Christianity forever rests is twofold: (1) the historical person Jesus, born under the reign of Herod and crucified under Pontius Pilate, together with the antecedents of this fact in the history of Israel; and (2) the reception of the redemptive meaning of this person *as the Christ of God.* Thus fact and faith or history and interpretation are held indissolubly together.

In reference to the knotty problem of the Jesus of history and the Christ of faith, which lies at the heart of this event, three fairly definite things can be said. (1) It was the revelatory impact of Jesus' personality which created the gospel picture of him. (2) However much faith may have embellished or altered the facts, a substantial analogy remains between the picture and the reality which generated it. And (3) since it is the Jesus picture of the gospels which remains the perennial fountainhead of Christian proclamation, the analogy between it and the historical Jesus must be sufficiently accurate to perform the redemptive work which God has thereby performed, and continues to perform. The gospel portrait of Jesus must therefore be an *ade-*

171

quate expression of the transforming power of the New Humanity *established in Jesus.*

To the title *Christos* in the Petrine confession is added also the term Lord *(Kurios)*. The use of this term as a qualification of the designation "Jesus Christ" points perhaps to the most profound thing about the Christian confession. This places Jesus the Christ in very close relation to the Eternal, for the term *Kurios* was used as a translation of *Jahweh* in the Septuagint.

Some form of the phrase "Jesus Christ our Lord" stands at the heart of the gospel according to Paul. In the numerous passages where the term is used, the basic thought which runs through them all is that of the power and authority of the living God himself, who acts to reveal himself to us, through the life, death, and resurrection of Jesus, and to lift us into that abiding communion with him which is life eternal, a relation in which the lordship of God becomes redemptively effective over our hearts and lives.

It is this relation with God, established and mediated by the power of God in Jesus, which brought the church into being. Pentecost means, basically, that those who had come to the empowering faith that Jesus is Christ and Lord, through the experience of the resurrection, were formed into a closely knit and compact religious group. The one whom death had taken from them really triumphed over death; indeed he was restored to them, in Spirit. And they now knew him, immediately, as the living presence, whom death could not conquer. By the power of this Living Presence they were bound together in their faith, hope, and love.

Thus the church came into being, centered in faith in Jesus as the crucified but risen Lord, the abiding presence and empowering might of his indwelling Spirit, the hope of the Lord's immanent return, and meanwhile their sense of mission, grounded in an awareness of being the eschatological community, the new Israel, the "people of God."

The Unity of Christ and Church

That the church came into being bound together by the living presence of its Lord implies a vital unity between Christ and church. It is not possible to speak about Christ *as Lord* apart from the religious relation which he sustains to the church, for the understanding of Christ *as Lord* is possible only from the standpoint of faith. In the religious sense in which we here use the term "Lord," Christ *is* Lord only when he *becomes* Lord *for somebody*.

To be sure, God is mysterious and in his transcendent majesty is beyond man's comprehension; yet it is an error to separate this "hidden" God from God revealed, the God who acts to place himself in relation to us. Thereby he *becomes* God *for us*.

Here we touch upon the deepest quality in the life of the Eternal, namely, not merely God's will, as Creator, to be Lord over all things, but to be Lord over man in a more spiritual way. Man, he made in his own image. It is therefore not enough for God to be Lord over man in the sense in which he is Lord of all creatures. He wills to be *our* Lord in being known and freely and joyfully acknowledged as such,[1] for only thus can he really be *our* Lord in the religious sense of the term. God wills to be not merely Lord *over* man, but Lord *of* man.

Similarly, apart from Christ (by "Christ" we mean primarily God himself in his self-revealing mode of being), apart from Christ's lordship there would be no church; for, as William Temple aptly puts it, the church "is the representative, in the historic order, of that infusion of Divine power into human nature which begins with the Divine act of the Incarnation."[2] Wherever Jesus Christ *lives* among men and exercises his lordship, eliciting faith and obedient response, *there* is the church.[3]

Christ and church, then, are correlatives, Christ is not Lord apart from the church; and the church is not church apart from Christ. But the unity between Christ and church is more intimate still. It is amazing, really, how intimate this unity is, according to the New Testament. For example, the Johannine Christ said

173

to his disciples, "I am the vine, you are the branches" (John 15:5). This is, to be sure, an analogy. But the analogy does say something. It obviously says that just as the branch has no life in itself, but *only as part of the vine,* so the church has no life or spiritual power *in itself,* but *only as it derives its life from, and is sustained by, the Christ-reality.*

Part of our difficulty in understanding the relation between Christ and church arises out of our individualistic presuppositions, which cause us to think of Christ mainly as just an individual alongside his followers, who are other individuals. If, however, we bear in mind that by the term "Christ" we mean a structure in the life of God, we can see that in some sense, as Anders Nygren argues, "Christ is the whole, and the disciples participate in Him,"[4] or in the power of the New Being in him, as Paul Tillich puts it. The Eternal God is infinitely more than just another individual. He is the Eternal Spirit "in whom we live and move and have our being." Just so, we may say that Christ *is* the Spirit in the saving power of whose life the church participates. Something of this participation in the power of the new Being in Christ is evidently what Paul had in mind by using the phrase ἐν χριστῷ some 164 times in his writings.

This same organic unity between Christ and his church is indicated by the New Testament use of the phrase "the body *(soma)* of Christ." There are three uses of this phrase in the New Testament. Its first and most natural usage concerns the physiological structure of Jesus' historical existence. Thus in the Gospel of John we read that "The Word became flesh and dwelt among us" (John 1:14). Similarly, in 1 Peter 2:24 we read, "He himself bore our sins in his body on the tree."

The second use of the phrase is found in the eucharistic passages in which Jesus said, "This is my body."

Third, Paul wrote that Christians are "the body of Christ and individually members of it" (1 Corinthians 12:27). Rudolf Bultmann argues convincingly that *soma,* for Paul, "can denote both the body and the whole man, the person,"[5] and that

174

man is called *soma* in reference to "his being able to control himself and be the object of his own action." After an analysis of numerous passages in Paul, Bultmann concludes that "The *soma* can be described as the actual tool of action; thus 2 Cor. 5:10 says, 'that each may receive according to what he has done through the *soma.*'"

This basic meaning of *soma* evidently determined Paul's concept of the church as the *soma tou Christou*. As Bultmann puts it, this phrase "expresses both the unity of the church and the foundation of this unity in an origin transcendent to the will and deed of individuals and hence expresses its transcendental nature."[6] The phrase serves to express "the comprehensive historic complex, instituted by the salvation-occurrence, into which the individual is placed."[7] The phrase also contains an eschatological meaning, for said Paul, "if any one is *in Christ,* he is a new creation" (2 Corinthians 5:17).

While there are various nuances of meaning in these three New Testament uses of the phrase "the body of Christ," the primary meaning in all three uses would seem to be the same. Just as the *soma* of a man is constitutive of the being of man, or just as the *soma* of a man is a way of being, so also the church, the *soma tou Christou* is constitutive of the being of Christ in history, or it is the way or means of Christ's presence and action in history. And just as my *soma* is the means of accomplishing the purposes of my will, so also the *soma* of Christ is the instrument of his spiritual wisdom and power. Basically, the term "Christ's body" carries this existential or instrumental meaning, whether it be the physiological structure of Jesus, the sacramental form of the eucharist, or the empirical community of the church itself.

It is saying too much about the unity of Christ and church, however, to affirm in an unqualified way that the church is "a continuation of the incarnation," due to the imperfections which characterize the church, inasmuch as its life is continually being fashioned out of the life of the world and is always partially determined by its involvement in the cultural situation. The empirical church is consequently never *de facto,* but only *de jure* wholly free from sin. Hence the life unity of Christ and church, though real, is an ambiguous unity. "God *is* at work in you, both to will and to work for his good pleasure" (Philippians 2:13), but this immanental working of God is never wholly lucid and pure.

Yet the church *is* that realm in the context of human relationships in which the Spirit of Christ is *in process of being incarnated.* In this sense the church does represent the immanental aspect of the presence and action of Christ. Nygren hardly expresses it too strongly when he writes that "*in its essence* the church is nothing other than the presence of Christ."[8] In its wholeness, of course, the church is many things (including its own sinfulness) other than Christ. But the "essence" of the church's life is the presence of Christ and the power of his lordship. Take the presence and power of Christ out of the church and what would remain but a spiritual corpse?

The Transcendent Fullness of Christ's Lordship

The organic unity of Christ and church is a unity which contains within itself both immanental and transcendental aspects. When we look more closely at the historic prolongation of Christ's own activity in the church, we are confronted by a wealth of diversity in the understanding of its meaning and the forms of its expression. This fact points beyond itself to the transcendent fullness of the Christ-reality. The church is part of the wholeness of Christ; yet the fullness of the Christ-reality is infinitely more than the church. The significance of this transcendence can perhaps be made clear in four ways.

First, what we mean ultimately when we speak of "Christ" is the eternal *Logos* of God, the Christ who is himself the Living God, or more precisely, a structure in the life of the Eternal. This distinction between God and the *Logos* of God, who nevertheless *is* God, is already found in the opening verses of John's

176

Gospel. This Living God, to quote A. N. Whitehead, contains within himself "the unlimited conceptual realization of the absolute wealth of potentiality."[9] And because he does so, because God is infinite, he is of necessity transcendent in the sense that he can never be *wholly* identified with the world of actuality. Though creation and redemption mean that this Lord is creatively at work in the process of time and history, he is always something more than the cluster of meanings and values realized at any level of the process of the world of actual becoming.

There is here both identity and distinction, both immanence and transcendence. But the point is that no form of finitude can ever fully contain or exhaustively actualize the infinite Lord of all life and history. In this respect God is absolutely infinite: in the infinite creative depth of His being.

Second, the Christian experience is bound to a particular concretion of the infinite One in history; it is anchored to God's self-disclosure in Jesus. As Christians, we must say, "Jesus Christ our Lord," for the Eternal Christ, *as we know him,* has become real *for us* through the life, death, and resurrection of Jesus. And therefore the Christ-reality, as we have been led to grasp it, has gathered into itself, and has been determined by, the remembered events of the life of Jesus.

We are therefore forced to draw yet a second distinction in our Christology, namely, the distinction between two Christs as it were. We must distinguish, though we cannot separate, between the Christ who is himself the Living God, and the Christ whom we know as a historical quantity, the Christ-Jesus, through whom the Eternal God enters into our history. The personality of Jesus, while there is nothing docetic about it, nevertheless bears witness to the cosmic Christ-reality, of which in the very nature of the case the historical Jesus could only be a partial expression, due to the limitations of historical existence, as such.

In fact, Jesus as a finite historical self, pointed beyond himself to this transcendent reality, by refusing to be called good,[10] and (if we may trust the Fourth Gospel) by insisting that even his presence among the disciples constituted a kind of limitation, a barrier which had to be removed before they could experience the Comforter, the fuller measure of the Spirit.[11] This Spirit was to lead the disciples to higher levels of community than Jesus, as a historical figure, had been able to achieve.[12]

We must say then that while Jesus constitutes a decisive and authentic disclosure of the ultimate meaning of human existence, in terms of the dynamic of *agape,* the place of Jesus in the Christ-reality is not such that one can bluntly equate the historic Jesus with God. The personality of Jesus does not exhaust the creative depth of divine life. Yet it does authentically open up this divine depth to human view.

Yet a *third* aspect of the fullness of Christ's lordship lies in what John Baillie has called the Subjecthood of God. This means that the religious relation is, at its heart, something infinitely deeper than a relation in the I-it dimension of reality. In the I-it dimension, as Martin Buber says, "I perceive something, I am sensible of something, I imagine something."[13] But one steps into another dimension of being when he no longer knows a something, but instead utters the word "thou." When subject addresses subject, man "takes his stand in relation." Here we approach existence at its deepest level, in the meeting of an I with a thou.

Here, then, we come upon a profound aspect of God's transcendence, his transcendence of the subject-object structure of the phenomenal world. Is not Buber correct when he writes: "God is the Being that . . . may properly only be addressed, not expressed"?[14] To a degree this is true of our fellow men. They confront us, not as objects, but as subjects; here subject faces subject. And when they are present, the second person mode of speaking is alone appropriate. Of course, in their absence we do speak to another about them in the third person. But the Eternal One is always present; he is omnipresent. As John Baillie says, "God is the eternal Thou by whom we are at every moment being addressed."[15] This is a profound kind of transcendence,

178

for by his very nature the "Thou" cannot become an "it."

This I-Thou character of the relation to the living Lord involves a fullness of meaning which defies our theological attempt to state it adequately. A feeble analogy would be the richness of quality and meaning involved in the love relation between husband and wife. No verbal symbols can adequately describe or fully delineate the concrete fullness of this relation, for the personal "I" always transcends the "me" of objective description.

This leads to the *fourth* thing to be said about the fullness of Christ's lordship, namely, that it infinitely transcends any and all of our Christologies, vital and important as they are. Some Christologies stress the moral value of Jesus as the Master Teacher. Some emphasize the disclosure of God himself in Jesus' life, death, and resurrection, a confrontation which challenges us to decision. Others see in Jesus the founder of the institutional church which mediates grace through its sacraments.

In our efforts to *describe* the abiding essence of Christ's lordship, we seem to be involved in interminable debate. The embarrassment under which theology must speak, at this point, is due to two things. *First,* it is due to the fact that all theological effort inevitably shares the limitations of the existential situation within which such effort takes place. *Second,* it is due to the impossibility of capturing the ineffable fullness of a living, subject-to-subject relation in concepts and propositions, the logic of which is really appropriate only to the subject-object structure of being. By its very nature a subject cannot become an object. Yet it is *as object* that affirmations must deal with religious truth. This probably means that all valid theological affirmations must be capable of being recast in doxological form. All "he" expressions about God must be convertible into "thou" expressions. This means that the Christian doctrine of God is something quite different from a mere composition of expressions about God as an object of theoretical knowledge. And they are thus different because Christian affirmations about God are grounded in the mighty act of God with us and upon us, which is grasped in faith.

However, we must be on guard lest we permit this Pauline admission "now we see in a mirror dimly . . . [and] know in part" to glide imperceptibly into a skeptical kind of relativism which would destroy the faith. The miracle of revelation *does take place,* by the grace of God. God does speak his saving word, enabling us to hear. This does not mean that God gives a lecture course in systematic theology, or that the Holy Spirit hands down to us a polished creedal statement. Yet *he does speak;* he does illumine our minds, authentically, about himself and his purposes for our lives. As H. Richard Niebuhr says, "if we cannot say anything adequately, we *can say some things inadequately.*"[16] And this is perhaps the important thing after all: that we do bear our witness to this eternal truth, stammering and inadequate though it must be.

Furthermore, if we cannot capsule the abiding essence of the Christ-reality, we can certainly describe the historical structure within which this Christ manifests himself. The Christian experience of God contains an ineffable element; yet it is inseparably connected with, and mediated by, *historical* processes which can be put into words and sentences; and this gives the Christian experience a *dependable definiteness.* The Jesus whose saving influence is interpreted in so many ways is, after all, a definite historical figure, whose life, teachings, and death are of a piece; he is the Jesus Christ of the New Testament.

The Church in Permanent Dialogue with the Lord

The vision of the transcendent fullness of Christ's lordship leads us to recognize yet another fundamental distinction within the unity of Christ and church. Basic to the structure of this unity is the fact that the church's being is always being-in-radical-dependence. The church can maintain itself *as church* only if it remains in permanent dialogue with its Lord. The source of the church's origin, the ground of its present existence, and the basis of its ultimate consummation lie *beyond* itself. Its being is being-in-radical-dependence upon the supremely great Other-than-itself. Its being is *being-in-response,* in response to the call and power of this divine Other.

Christ, then, *remains* Lord of the church. Speaking the truth in love, the church is "to *grow up in every way into . . . Christ, from whom* the whole body . . . makes bodily growth (Ephesians 4:15-16). Christ is "the head of the body," that "in everything he might be preëminent" (Colossians 1:18). Growth in this body is development *from the head,* and *toward* the head. The "fullness of Christ" is not the church's condition, but her goal. That Christ is the head of the church expresses "the eschatological reserve" which characterizes the church's situation in the world.

It is imperative, therefore, that the church maintain the dialogue with its Lord, through his continuous self-revelation in the gospel. The proclamation of Christ's lordship is always a matter of life and death for the church. As W. A. Visser t'Hooft says,

Where the King is not proclaimed or is proclaimed only in a pious but irrelevant manner, the Church loses its birthright. It becomes the lonely Church, the Church in monologue, the sick Church, which does not realize its own sickness. But where the Kingship is actually recognized, where in sober realism and radical self-criticism the Church dares to face the judgment of the Lord, there the Church discovers the true measure of his grace and is born again through his creative action.[17]

Two important implications are to be drawn from this fact that the creative source of the church's life lies always beyond itself.

First, whenever the church fails, for any reason, to listen to the word of its Lord, to respond to *him,* to be judged by *him,* to be continually renewed in its spiritual life by *him,* it forfeits its birthright and lapses into a self-sufficient kind of existence. In this way it falls prey to the principle of the demonic. The principle of the demonic asserts itself whenever any form of finitude

181

ceases to point beyond itself to the Eternal, becomes self-enclosed, and presumes itself to perform the functions of the Eternal.

This demonic distortion of the church's existence has assumed different forms. The church may permit itself to be reduced to an *all too human* community for the mere promotion of her own moral ideals. This was the danger in the old liberalism. Or it may allow itself to get caught in the trap of doctrinal absolutism. This is the form which the demonic distortion assumed in orthodoxy, both Catholic and Protestant. Or again it may identify its own institutional structure and sacramental appurtenances with the Christ-reality. It may *equate* the body of Christ with the visible, hierarchical church—as in Roman Catholicism, in which the church fancies itself to be so at one with its Lord that it comes to think that when it speaks *ex cathedra,* its own voice is the very voice of God.

Whatever form this demonic lapse from its exalted destiny may assume, the result is the same: the church becomes imprisoned in its own system, directs its gaze away from its transcendent Lord and fixes it on itself thereby losing its highest privilege, namely, to be "re-called, re-formed, and re-created,"[18] by the exhaustless creativity of the Christ-reality. It may still be a powerful sociological, or even political, force in history, but it is no longer able to serve the cause of God's kingdom.

The church must therefore constantly be on guard against the tendency to domesticate the Eternal, to capsule or enclose life's ultimate in the idol of book, creed, church, or sacrament, and thereby bring it under the control and manipulation of man, for this is tantamount to a demonic denial of the lordship of God over man.

There is perhaps no greater danger that has dogged the church throughout its career in history than this. Like Laodicea of old,[19] it is always tempted to overestimate its own accomplishments, to take pride in the victories it has won, and to succumb to the tempter's suggestion that it can move forward under its own steam and by its own wisdom and power.

Second, when the church ceases to carry on the dialogue with its Lord, it blurs and distorts the frontier between the church and the kingdom of God. At this point we must grasp the important distinction between the "already" and the "not yet" of the redemptive working of God. The church does indeed have much to say about the "already" of its inheritance. The church *is* an eschatological fact, in history. Christians *have* "tasted the powers of the world to come."[20] The gift of the Holy Spirit *does* represent an "earnest" of the future.[21] This "already" of our inheritance is the time of the reign of Christ; and the church is an instrument of this reign, poor and unworthy though she be. The church is the community which knows of this reign and which proclaims it with power. So that to the extent to which the Spirit of Christlike love and righteousness are present and operative in the empirical life of the church, to this extent the kingdom has become an empirical reality.

Yet all these glorious realities of the "already" of the church's being become sadly distorted if they are not held in tension with the "not yet" of its destiny. The church *is* constituted by the *power* of the kingdom, present and at work in it, but other powers in the life of culture and society also manifest themselves in the character of the church. Due to the powers of finitude and sin, the church is always a mixture of good and evil, of Christ and anti-Christs. So that to the extent that the church is still *en route,* so to speak, to the extent that its fellowship is yet an imperfect manifestation of love and righteousness, the kingdom cannot be identified with the church.

When, therefore, Karl Adam writes that "the church is the realization of the Kingdom of God on earth,"[22] that the church "*is* the Kingdom of God,"[23] and that "in the papacy" the church "grasps and realizes itself as the one Kingdom of God, as the one Body of Christ on the earth,"[24] we can only reply that a church which so thinks of itself is to be pitied, for it has lost touch with the blessed hope of the gospel, the hope for something more and better than its present self. And when Congar

183

writes of the church as "the extension of the life of God . . . God's life itself . . . the divine society itself,"[25] and when Vonier calls the church "so perfect, so definitive as the glorified Christ is in his perfection,"[26] Protestants can only reply that such beliefs weaken rather than strengthen the church. Such a church is so much at ease with its own present estate that it has lost touch with the kingdom. The church which thus blurs or eradicates the distinction between the "already" and the "not yet" of its life blocks the creative working of God and proves itself to be sterile in relation to the final purposes of God.

The church which refuses to exist in this tension between the "already" and the "not yet" proceeds to resolve it in one of two ways. Either it follows the precedent of Roman Catholicism and eliminates the tension by absolutizing the relative *status quo;* or with the Christian Gnostics it becomes radically otherwordly, developing an escapist kind of religion. The former allows the "already" to swallow up the "not yet," thereby forfeiting the blessedness of hope. The latter permits the "not yet" to eliminate any positive significance to the "already," thereby losing the relevance of the kingdom to historical existence. Both ways terminate with a static view of history. Both fail to develop a dynamic view of historical existence. This failure results in the loss of the ability to use the kingdom as a fulcrum by which to move history.

At this point of relation between church and kingdom we touch a profoundly significant aspect of the church's need for continuous dialogue with its Lord, as it "strains forward to what lies ahead" (Philippians 3:13). The goal of the kingdom it to embrace all creation in an ultimate unity.[27] This ultimate lordship of God gives to the church its most profound task. Because its Lord is the only God and Lord, who is King over all, the kingdom is the ultimate basis of the validity of Christian ethical action. This is what makes Christian ethics religious, in the deepest sense of the term; and it is what bestows upon the church its brightest hope and its deepest spiritual strength.

The Task of the Church under the Lordship of Christ

What now, we ask finally, does the lordship of Christ over the church mean in regard to the church's mission? What kind of church will it be which takes Christ's lordship seriously?

First, it will be a church in which the doxological quality colors its entire life and thought. The church is first of all a worshiping community, a community which, in its liturgy, confession, and entire existence, manifests the lordship of God in Christ. It seeks to praise him, to offer its sacrifice of adoration and thanksgiving. For it is he who has gathered us together from the four corners of the earth to be sons and daughters of the Most High. It is he who has drawn us to the foot of the cross and constituted us a fellowship of forgiven sinners.

In worship the church also expresses the secret of its inmost being, and is renewed and inwardly reinforced as the "people of God." In worship the church is confronted by the Presence of its Lord, who thus *becomes real* to us, as the vital center of our lives, individually and corporately. Thus we are redeemed from the persistent tendency to center our beings in ourselves and come to experience the New Being which is "in Christ." In worship the church experiences the eschatological hiddenness of being "with Christ in God."

Second, the church which takes Christ's lordship seriously will be keenly aware of its *kerygmatic* function, aware that one of its basic tasks is the effective proclamation of Jesus Christ as Lord. That is, it will be a confessing church, by which we mean that it is blessed with the assurance of the victory of the cross and the resurrection, and is therefore able, without hesitancy or confusion, to proclaim the victory of the Lord and the relevance of this victory to the concrete problems of historical existence. As Reginald Fuller says, "What God does through the church's proclamation is precisely to make his eschatological action in the past history of Jesus present and available."[28]

185

The pulpit and classrooms of such a church will not be used for soothing messages calculated to make either church members or nonchurch members feel good. The pulpit will be used to preach *in such a way that the King's message can be heard,* calling people to repentance and challenging them to decide for Christ, amidst the conflicts of the social order.

When the lordship of Christ's Spirit is denied by "practical" compromises with the world, the pulpit of the confessing church will call such denials by their true name, even if it thereby loses its cultural respectability and prestige, or perhaps *especially* when this is the price it must pay for proclaiming the message of its King, who was himself crucified for speaking under the same divine constraint. It thus becomes the church's exalted privilege not only to believe in Christ, "but also to suffer for his sake," (Philippians 1:29).

The *kerygmatic* function, however, is expressed not only in the church's pulpit and classroom, but also in its sacramental celebrations. For whatever else baptism and the Lord's Supper mean, they are powerful symbolic ways of *proclaiming and fulfilling* Christ's lordship. The meaning of baptism is inseparable from the cross and resurrection of Christ and the resultant crucifixion of the old self and emergence of the new "in Christ." When Paul wrote: "We were buried therefore with him by baptism into death, so that as Christ was raised from the dead by the glory of the Father, we too might walk in newness of life" (Romans 6:4), he as much as said that the same eschatological power which was at work in the resurrection of Christ is operative in the emergence and growth of the new life of faith.

Similarly, at the table of the Lord, Christ is *re-presented* afresh, through the symbols of his body and blood. Hence, in the eucharistic act we *"proclaim* the Lord's death until he comes" (1 Corinthians 11:26).

In pleading thus for a *confessing* church, we do not mean a *confessionalist* church. A *confessionalist* church is one which permits itself to get caught in the fallacy of orthodoxy, for it

186

comes to consider *its own confession* as an ultimate. Such confessionlism turns out to be a hindrance to the Lord, who wills always that new light shall break forth from his Holy Word, as an effective answer to the new needs of new situations, in the shifting structures of man's historical existence. On the other hand, a *confessing* church is one which confesses Jesus Christ as Lord, listens continuously to hear his word, and to learn its relevance to concrete situations in existence. The confessing church is aware of the inadequacy of past confessions as answers for the present. It will be continuously formulating fresh expressions of the meaning of Christ's lordship for the present, and will never permit itself to get bogged down in traditionalism, nor to become anachronistic.

Third, the church that takes Christ's lordship seriously will itself become a dynamic thrust of creative community in the larger social order. To take the lordship of Christ seriously means to accept, and seek to fulfill, the ethical imperative which Christ imposes, namely, to seek our neighbor's good. Such a church will reflect the universality and unity of the people of God. It will be a church which seeks to establish and maintain all social relationships by the high ideal of Christlikeness.

The source of this ethical character of the church's being lies in its heritage of Judaism, which held religion and morality to be inseparable, and in the understanding of God as a moral Being, a Being, that is, who has a fundamental stake in the moral human venture, the God of righteousness and holiness, who gave the law and the prophets. It lies also in the luminous moral example of Jesus' own life among men, and in the consequent moral implications of fellowship with Christ.

The ethic of this community is therefore eschatologically grounded, yet also dynamically related to the present, actual world. As Paul expressed it, "Our commonwealth is in heaven" (Philippians 3:20). It is there, in the Christ who has been made Lord over all, that our ultimate commitment lies. It is Christ whom we serve as King, above and beyond all other values and

187

authorities which impinge upon us in history. Nevertheless, this is the *kind* of transcendence which has a positive bearing upon historical existence. The Christian Lord is no gnostic Savior who inspires in his devotees an escapist attitude toward historical existence.

The concrete socio-historical situation in which the church finds itself, at any given time and place, must first be understood in terms of our best and highest scientific understanding of human existence. Christianity itself does not supply us with this wisdom; yet such wisdom is indispensable for Christian ethics. Of course, at the level of such scientific understanding one has not yet reached the question of *Christian* ethics. *Christian* ethics comes into being when, beyond scientific description, we face the crucial question: what does the love of God disclosed in Jesus Christ demand of me *in* the given situation? In this way all moral values are exposed to the light of God's perfect love, with its redemptive power of judgment and mercy. And when in humility and repentance we accept the impact of this love, Christ's kingly power transmutes all of our fragmentary values and brings them into a new order of being, whose definitive principle is Christlike love, in all its radical inclusiveness and depth.

Through the church, which takes this ethical demand seriously, Christ exercises his lordship to lift our sinful world (of which the church is also a part) to higher levels of mutual love and appreciation, to the abolition of artificial human barriers of race, class, and nation, and thus to foster and promote that participation in the Spirit which is the seed and promise of the coming kingdom. Thus, to borrow Fuller's words, "as Jesus by his human obedience provided the occasion in and through which God wrought his mighty act of redemption, so the church, by her obedience, provides the occasion through which God continues and renews his act of redemption. Thus mission and Christ's lordship go together."[29]

It is important also to remember that the Christian ethic is an expression of the lordship of Christ. The Christian ethic is

188

not a legalistic ethic. For the church, the decisive "salvation occurrence" has already been given, in the event of Jesus Christ. The ethical life of the church must be seen as a *product* of this occurrence. Hence justification is by faith, and not by works of law. Yet the salvation is paradoxically both a gift and a demand. It is a *gift*, for its source lies in the free grace of God's forgiveness, which moves us to repentance and endows us with inner power to break the walls of pride and self-centeredness, making us a "new creation" in Christ. But it is also a *demand*, for the gift involves its personal appropriation through obedient response. The task of the church, without the gift, would drive us to despair, as the Apostle Paul learned the hard way. But the gift without the task would lead to a sentimental antinomianism, which would be less than Christian, for it would leave human personality untouched and untransformed. With Augustine, then, we can say, "Give what Thou commandest, O God, and command what Thou wilt."[30] The paradox here is a profound one. But the fact that God himself works in us "both to will and to work for his good pleasure" in no way lessens the urgency and imperativeness of the demand: "Work out your own salvation with fear and trembling" (Philippians 2:12). Indeed, it underscores this urgency, by viewing it in the light of grace.

Fourth, a denomination which takes the lordship of Christ seriously will become conscience-stricken about its isolationist attitudes and its sectarian ways. It will share vigorously in the current quest to find new structures and forms which will manifest and realize more adequately the unity which is an essential part of the church, as given by God.

The problem of unity is dealt with in a chapter in Volume III of the Panel Series. We shall therefore not deal further with this problem just here. We do well to remember, however, that if Christians know and serve only one King, if by the intention of God they are fellow members of the one body, they dare not rest content with the present scatteredness and brokenness of

189

this body. The lordship of Jesus Christ means the *fellowship* of those who worship and serve him, in the *Una Sancta*.

NOTES

1. Cf. Matthew 11:25-26.
2. William Temple, *Christ in His Church* (New York: The Macmillan Company, 1924), p. 8.
3. Cf. Colossians 2:6.
4. Anders Nygren, *Christ and His Church,* trans. Alen Carlsten (Philadelphia: The Westminster Press), p. 92.
5. Rudolf Bultmann, *Theology of the New Testament,* trans. Kendrick Grobel (New York: Charles Scribner's Sons, 1954), I, 196.
6. *Ibid.,* p. 310.
7. *Ibid.,* pp. 310-311.
8. Nygren, *op. cit.,* p. 96.
9. A. N. Whitehead, *Process and Reality* (New York: The Macmillan Company, 1929), p. 521.
10. See Matthew 19:17.
11. See John 16:7.
12. See John 14:12; 16:8-11.
13. Martin Buber, *I and Thou,* trans. Ronald Gregor Smith (Edinburgh: T. & T. Clark, 1944), p. 4.
14. *Ibid.,* p. 81.
15. John Baillie, *Our Knowledge of God* (London: Oxford University Press, 1946), p. 221.
16. H. Richard Niebuhr, *Christ and Culture* (New York: Harper & Row, Publishers, Inc., 1956), p. 14.
17. W. A. Visser t'Hooft, *The Kingship of Christ* (New York: Harper and Row, Publishers, Inc., 1948), p. 103. Used by permission.
18. *Ibid.,* p. 100.
19. See Revelation 3:17.
20. See Hebrews 6:5.
21. See 2 Corinthians 1:22.
22. Karl Adam, *The Spirit of Catholicism,* trans. Dom Justin McCann (New York: The Macmillan Company, 1955), p. 15.
23. *Ibid.,* p. 34.
24. *Ibid.,* p. 42.
25. In *Chrétiens Désunis* (Paris, 1937), p. 59.
26. Quoted by Grosche, *Pilgernde Kirche* (Freiburg, 1937), p. 70.
27. See 1 Corinthians 15:28; Romans 11:32.
28. In *Encounter,* Fall, 1959, p. 448.
29. *Op. cit.,* p. 452.
30. Aurelius Augustine, *Confessions,* Book X, sec. XXIX.

The Lordship of
Christ over Society

GLENN C. ROUTT

A subtitle for this chapter might be: "The Life of the Church and its Apostolic Task in the Life of the World: A Discussion of the Ethical Dimensions of the Christian Gospel." As such, this chapter may be presumed to be a continuation of Dr. Wilburn's treatment of "The Lordship of Christ Over the Church" in the preceding chapter. We will presuppose Dr. Wilburn's excellent discussion, especially his exegetical section on the lordship of Christ, and invite your attention to certain emphases in his paper that have a direct bearing upon our topic and which may be taken as controlling factors in any consideration of the lordship of Christ in the life of the church and the world.

One important emphasis in Dr. Wilburn's exposition is "the thesis of an organic unity between Christ and Church." It is a matter of primary importance that this correlation of Christ and church be maintained in our theological constructions, for there is no church without the Christ, and no Christ without the church. To speak of the church as "the body of Christ" is to use a figure expressive of organic unity. As the human body is the instrument of the human will, so the *soma tou Christou* is the instrument of Christ's spiritual power. But the figure of speech has its limitation, and care must be taken that the organic unity between Christ and his church not be construed to mean an

191

identity without qualification. Thus when it is said that the church is the continuation of the incarnation and this is taken to mean that the church has a spiritual and moral stature equal to that of Christ, then we have extended the figure of speech beyond its theological limits. Reinhold Niebuhr has warned of the danger of idolizing the church by an uncritical identification of the church with her incarnate Lord:

The deification of the church is spiritually dangerous, however conceived. The Catholic doctrine that the church is an "extension of the Incarnation" represents a significant shift of emphasis from the Pauline-biblical doctrine that the church is the "Body of Christ." For when conceived as the body, it is clear that it remains subject to the laws of historical reality. Its ideal and norm is, that all its members should be perfectly coordinated to one another by being subordinated to the "head" which is Christ. But the actual realities always betray some of the contradictions which characterize historical existence. In history there is always "another law in my members, warring against the law of my mind." This war is certainly as apparent in the collective, as in the individual, life of the redeemed.[1]

Dr. Wilburn also has given warning of this danger when he says,

It is saying too much about the unity of Christ and church to affirm in an unqualified way that the church is "a continuation of the incarnation," due to the imperfections which characterize the church, inasmuch as its life is continually being fashioned out of the life of the world and is always partially determined by its involvement in the cultural situation.[2]

The dialectical relationship of Christ and his church is further indicated by Dr. Wilburn when he speaks of "the transcendent fullness of Christ's Lordship," and says, "The church is part of the wholeness of Christ; yet the fullness of the Christ-reality is infinitely more than the church.[3]

This affirmation of organic unity and its attendant warning are well taken. At the same time they can serve to indicate the dimension of the problem we have set before us in this paper,

192

namely, the life of the church and its apostolic task in the life of the world. On the one hand, the life of the church is the life of her Lord; on the other hand, the life of the church is "continually being fashioned out of the life of the world." This double relation determines the life of the church at all times. It is an abiding tension that sets both its possibilities and its problems, as we will hope to show.

The second emphasis we would ask the reader to bear in mind is that the church is in a continuous dialogue with Christ. The church is the listening and confessing community of faith; she is the receiving and the apostolic community of grace. The church on her human side consists of those who are forgiven sinners but nevertheless still sinners, *simul peccator et iustus,* and therefore is continuously in need of receiving anew the word of God in forgiveness and power. Thus there is not only an organic but also a dialogic relationship between Christ and the church.

The third emphasis is that the lordship of Christ over the church is the basis of the mission of the church in the world. Included in the mission, Wilburn points out, is the church's "dynamic thrust of creative community in the larger social order."[4] That is, "through the church, which takes this ethical demand seriously, Christ excercises his Lordship to lift our sinful world (of which the church is also a part) to higher levels"[5] of community. The words of Reginald Fuller are cited with approval to underscore this emphasis:

As Jesus by His human obedience provided the occasion in and through which God wrought His mighty act of redemption, so the church, by her obedience, provided the occasion through which God continues and renews His act of redemption. Thus mission and Christ's Lordship go together.[6]

The church is, therefore, not only in a continuous dialogue with her Lord, but also with the world. Indeed, if the church is to converse with her Lord, she must listen to what he has to say about the world. And if she is to converse with the world, it must be to speak of Christ who is Lord of the world.

We have lifted up these three emphases made by Dr. Wilburn in order to recall that the matter of the lordship of Christ over society has as its effective context the life of the church and its apostolic task in the world. The Christ who is Lord of the church is also the Christ who is Lord of the World. It is one Lord and one lordship, and though the two realms are distinguishable, they are not separable. We seek now to indicate the nature of the lordship of Christ over the world and the function or mission of the church in the manifestation of that lordship in the life of the world.

Christ, the Church and the World

In contrast to the lordship of Christ over his church, where that lordship is clear enough in that the church confesses and acclaims his lordship even in her betrayals of it, his lordship over the world is not clear at all. If, as Roger Shinn has said, lordship implies recognition and obedience on the part of its subject, then Christ's lordship over the world of man's societal relation is dubious. "If Christ is Lord of the world . . . He is a Lord unacclaimed, often disobeyed, sometimes despised."[7] Christians have always known this, but we continue to affirm his "hidden lordship" maintaining that in Christ God's sovereign act of grace has *made* him Lord. Christ *is* Lord and seeks recognition and obedience from the world. The church proclaims and manifests in her own life the lordship of Christ over the world. That is its message and its mission in the world. This proclamation of the lordship of Christ includes what is called Christian social action. Although the world may reject both the proclamation *(kerygma)* of Christ's lordship and the loving service *(diakonia)* of his church on behalf of the world, the church has no alternative but to remain faithful in its mission to "provide the occasion through which God continues and renews his act of redemption."

How shall the church think of Christ as Lord of the world? From the beginning Christians have claimed that God has ordained that "every tongue confess that Jesus the Christ is Lord" of all life.[8] The first thing that needs to be made clear is that the affirmation of Christ's lordship over the world is the affirmation that he is the Lord of all life. The Christian doctrine of creation is not a bit of prescientific cosmogony. In fact, it is no cosmogony at all. It is a purely religious affirmation of the absolute dependence of the world, all parts of it, upon God for its existence and meaning. The "orders of creation" are under the sovereignty of God. This bold affirmation is made as the confession of faith and not as a metaphysical statement to be debated. In acknowledging Jesus Christ as Lord, the Christian acknowledges a new relationship with life into which he enters wherein he is enabled to receive life as it is offered and which he receives as significant and good. Thus the Christian doctrine of creation is given a christological orientation, as all Christian affirmations must have. The proper starting point of the Christian doctrine of creation is not the opening chapters of Genesis but such New Testament passages as John 1:1-3; 1 Corinthians 8:6; Colossians 1:15-16; Hebrews 1:2.

To say the Christian doctrine of the world and man is a purely religious concept means that the true nature of the world and man can be seen only from the viewpoint of their relation to God. That relation is one of covenant, in which God in his grace calls his creatures into being and sustains them in his faithfulness. The created world is a covenanted world; it is in his hand and nothing can shake it from his eternal grip. "The earth is the Lord's and the fullness thereof."[9] Whatever meaning the world has, from the perspective of faith, it is to be found in relation to God who is its creator, judge, and redeemer. The world has no independent meaning of existence. Indeed, as Brunner has shown, creation itself should be understood in the light of redemption and fulfillment.[10]

More specifically, creation, that is the world and man, is seen by the eyes of faith from the standpoint of the revelation of God in Jesus Christ. In creating the world, God has covenated himself with his world. In Christ God has renewed and fulfilled the covenant broken by man's disobedience. Christ is at once the revelation of God's faithfulness and of man's unfaithfulness; and the good news of the gospel is that God has not abandoned the world but has redeemed it.

On the one hand, we must say the world *is* redeemed; it *is* reconciled. In Christ the world has become involved with the gospel; it is not an optional matter whether it wants to be involved. The Christ-event has occurred; there is no neutral ground on which the world can stand. It can only accept or reject what has taken place once it knows of it; but it cannot alter the fact that the Christ-event has taken place. The world is under the lordship of Christ; there is no realm of life outside his lordship. Dietrich Bonhoeffer has said:

There are not two realities, but only one reality, and that is the reality of God, which has become manifest in Christ in the reality of the world. . . . The whole reality of the world is already drawn into Christ and bound together in Him. . . . The world is not divided between Christ and the devil, but, whether it recognizes it or not, it is solely and entirely the world of Christ.[11]

This, then, is the truth about the world that the gospel proclaims. On the other hand, the world has not yet recognized its rightful Lord, nor does it obey him. In the New Testament the "world" is generally seen to be in opposition to God; it is the world that is at enmity with God and rejects his Christ (John 1:10; 7:7; 14:17; James 4:4; 1 John 5:19; Romans 1:16); it is the world that has been judged, overcome, and reconciled by Christ. But "the world knew him not" (John 1:10). Therefore, we can only say that the world stands under both the "already" and the "not yet,"[12] and that God is seeking to bring to complete fulfillment the covenant relation he has with his world.

The biblical revelation of God is that he is a seeking God, one whose love is prevenient, who takes the initiative and does not merely wait to receive those who turn to him. The redemptive initiative of God is seen in his special relation to Israel, the "people of God," chosen as the servant of God with a unique mission in the world. God's righteousness is linked with his mercy and grace in the election of a people and the creation of a covenant. The righteousness of God has redemption as its goal. Thus the people of the covenant, the "church," is that community which out of obedient love and loyalty to God acts to "provide the occasion through which God continues and renews his act of redemption."

The redemptive activity of God in and for the world took a decisive form in his act in Jesus Christ. Christian faith affirms, "God was in Christ reconciling the world to himself, not counting their trespasses against them, and entrusting to us the message of reconciliation" (2 Corinthians 5:19). "For God so loved the world that he gave his only Son, that whoever believes in him should not perish but have eternal life."[13] Thus Christ is the saving act of God in the life of the world.

The people of the "new covenant," the church of Jesus Christ, is the community of believers called into being by faith in the resurrected Christ whom they affirm as Lord. The church is the continuing witness to and instrument of the gospel of God's redemptive activity in the world. "In and with the world, but not of the world" describes the dialectical character of the church's relation to the world. Christians have been called out of the world of disobedience and decay into the realm of God's redemption where obedience and life are the abiding features. They are already citizens of God's kingdom and wait for the full manifestation of his lordship. "Our commonwealth is in heaven, and from it we await a Savior, the Lord Jesus Christ" (Philippians 3:20).

This distinction between being "in and with the world" and being "not of the world" has significant implication for the ethical dimension of the gospel. It is important because the fact of being "in and with the world" determines that the church must concern itself with the ethical problems of how to live in the world as redeemed men. Though "not of the world" the

197

church is a mission in and to the world, the world of people. As D. T. Niles has put it, the world is the object of God's concern; he created it, he loves it, he judges it, he redeems it.[14] The church, as her Lord, exists in, with, and for the world, to proclaim the gospel in its fullness, witnessing in word and deed that Christ is both judge and redeemer of the world. It is not the building of a "Christian society," as such, nor even "Christianizing" the world that is the church's primary mission. Rather it is to "evangelize" the world; and that means, as Bonhoeffer says,

Man is challenged to participate in the sufferings of God at the hands of a godless world. He must therefore plunge himself into the life of a godless world, without attempting to gloss over its ungodliness with a veneer of religion.[15]

Thus the church should not think of herself as being the only sphere of Christ's reign, nor even that Christ exercises his lordship exclusively through his church. The world of man's cultural achievements is also the dominion of Christ and is within the realm of God's grace. The most important emphasis of the church's evangelistic task is not to draw hard and fast the distinction between the church and the world, but to declare the newness of humanity in Christ. In so far as the world is "godless," its life is in defiance of its rightful lord and is under the judgment of God. But the world is also God's creation and he is its Lord, not its destroyer. In both senses of the term "world" as it is used in the Bible—whether the realm of sin and evil, or the realm of God's creation and redemption—the world is under the lordship of God and his Christ. The redemption accomplished in him is on behalf of the whole world and not merely the church.[16]

Man's Sin and Redemption and its Implication for Christian Ethics

The specific Christian understanding of man holds together three central affirmations: man is created in the image of God; man is a sinner; man is reconciled to God. As the "Image of

God" man sustains a unique relation to God, a relation of personal and moral responsibility. To say that "man is created in the image of God" is to say that man's being is one of responsible freedom. It is relationship to God in which he stands as one to whom he must respond. As Brunner says,

> The fact that man must respond, that he is responsible, is fixed; no amount of human freedom, nor of the sinful misuse of freedom, can alter this fact. Man is, and remains, responsible, whatever his personal attitude to his Creator may be. He may deny his responsibility, and he may misuse his freedom, but he cannot get rid of his responsibility. . . . Responsibility is part of the unchangeable structure of man's being. That is: the actual existence of man—of every man, not only the man who believes in Christ—consists in the positive fact that he has been *made* to respond—to God.[17]

This is the deeper meaning of "Image of God." Man's true nature is that of existence-in-love. Hence the commandment, "You shall love the Lord your God with all your heart, and with all your soul, and with all your mind. This is the great and first commandment. And a second is like it, You shall love your neighbor as yourself" (Matthew 22:37-39).

Man is a sinner. He lives in contradiction to the image of God. He denies his responsibility, but does not escape it. Instead of his life being an existence-in-love, it is an existence-in-opposition. Estranged from God, sinful man does not do God's will because he cannot do it; and he cannot do it because he has fettered his freedom. This is man's guilt and his bondage. Again Brunner has said it well,

> God calls man into existence in order that he may respond to Him aright—not in order that he may respond wrongly or rightly. Man is not destined to choose between faith and unbelief, obedience and disobedience; God has made man in such a way that he can respond as God wills him to do. A certain freedom of choice, which makes this response possible, only becomes visible when the wrong response has been made. . . . Man ought to know nothing of this freedom save in the form of the generous love of God. The fact that he is aware of this freedom of choice is already the effect of sin, and of separation from his connexion with God.[18]

This is the deeper theological meaning of "original sin." We might say man discovers his freedom after he has stumbled over it.

Since man is in this tragic state of estrangement from God through guilt and bondage, the resolution of the tragic impasse is and must be an act of liberation and restoration. This act is a gift of God, not a self-development by man of his potentiality. That God has so acted is the meaning of the incarnation and atonement. By this act of God two things are accomplished which man could not do for himself: (a) The guilt of sin is forgiven. The righteousness of God, in judgment and mercy, brings to man the recognition of his rebellion and of the divine acceptance. (b) The bondage to sin is removed and with it comes the gift of power to affirm God's lordship, in whose service is perfect freedom. Man's freedom is in God and for life. Thus forgiveness has the positive meaning of power—power to accept and affirm life, and power for moral action. By this "double cure" man's true relation to God is renewed, the lost image of God is restored and the gift of common life in the community of faith is received. This act of God's grace is received in faith, and by it man's whole existence is changed. This is the deeper meaning of salvation by grace and justification by faith.

The Lordship of Christ and the Christian Ethic

The ethical dimension of the doctrine of redemption by the grace of God received in faith is that Christian living is by "faith working through love" (Galatians 5:6). The Christian ethic is the ethic of gratitude to God expressed in love of God and love of neighbor. "We love, because he first loved us (John 4:19). It is the ethic of free and grateful response. Thus the Christian ethic, in the words of Paul Lehmann, has as its primary question, not "What does God demand?" but "What does God do?" This puts the emphasis upon "gospel" rather than "law," or rather it sees "law" within the context of "gospel."

Seen in this light the Christian ethic is described as "the disciplined reflection upon the question and its answer: what am I as a believer in Jesus Christ, and as a member of his church, to do?"[19]

It is essential to note that it is as a believer in the lordship of Jesus Christ within the community of his church that the Christian acts. That is, as man's true nature as image of God is existence-in-love, redemption, or restoration of the image of God can never be interpreted merely in individualistic terms. It is true that man can experience this restoration as an individual only as he personally receives the act which is done on his behalf by recognizing and obeying the lordship of Christ. But since the nature of God is love, and since man's true being is understood in terms of the covenant relation in which he lives, man's redemption must be understood primarily in terms of community. Love means community, and the harmony of life with life. Thus the meaning of "redemption" is "re-created community," or reconciliation. Community and true humanity thus understood are synonymous.

The act of God in Christ is an act of judgment and reconciliation; it is also an act of creation by which true community under the lordship of Christ is made possible. This is the meaning of the kingdom of God. In so far as the kingdom is an accomplished fact by Christ's appearance in the world, the New Testament speaks of the kingdom as a present reality. In so far as the world has not given recognition and obedience to the lordship of Christ, the kingdom is a future hope. Both the present and the future aspects of the kingdom, the "already" and the "not yet," are maintained. One might say that the Christians are those who are ahead of the times, or that the Christian lives in the time between the times. The church is in culture to "run ahead" of the present disorder and to resist the world's attack upon the lordship of Christ. Commitment to the lordship of Christ means, as it were, taking up a position on the battle line against the world's idolatrous rebellions against its rightful Lord.

But the church also knows that the Christ has already overcome the "powers" of the world. The kingdom is a present actuality brought into historical existence by the victorious word or act of God. At the same time the church knows that the kingdom in its historical manifestation is not yet universal, and so the church remains the church militant and missionary. It lives in the eschatological hope of the consummation when "at the name of Jesus every knee shall bow, in heaven and on earth and under the earth, and every tongue confess that Jesus Christ is Lord, to the glory of God the Father" (Philippians 2:10-11).

At the World Council Assembly in Evanston a reporter asked some theologians, "If Christians believe that the most important event in history has already happened in the life of Jesus, what is the motivation for living now?" That is a penetrating question. Christians will answer that this most important event which has its climax in Jesus the Christ is yet unfinished. It is still going on, and we are a part of it. It has become our life now; his lordship has changed everything. The power of evil is broken and we are free.

Anders Nygren has used an analogy in another connection[20] that seems to be serviceable in this connection as well. It has to do with the announcement of the liberation of Norway from the Nazis. When the report was received that the decisive battle had been fought and that Hitler's forces had been put to flight, though this battle had taken place in a land not their own but on their behalf, they were free. Nazi troops were still in Norway, but their power had been broken. For a while the people of Norway would have to suffer the Nazi occupation, but having the foretaste of freedom they began to live as free men, rejoicing and taking heart while adding their efforts to the final consummation of the world's costly gained freedom. So, too, the church of Jesus Christ lives in the midst of the alien powers of sin and darkness, but it lives under the assurance of a victory already won and the hope of a glory yet to come, working and praying "thy kingdom come, thy will be done, on earth as it is in heaven."

Here, then, is the keenest incentive to action the church has. It is not that the kingdom depends upon the efforts of men alone. Indeed, we will never in this life reach such sanctity and power. But the eschatological hope deepens the sense of obligation to the point that we can say with Paul, "Woe is me if I preach not the gospel," and "I am under obligation both to Greeks and to barbarians" (Romans 1:14). "For what we preach is not ourselves, but Jesus Christ as Lord, with ourselves as your servants for Jesus' sake" (2 Corinthians 4:5). The universality of the gospel demands that the church sees her task in universal dimensions. "We do not take the gospel to someone to whom Jesus does not already belong, and if to be within the Church is to be a person for whom Jesus died, then the Church is coextensive with mankind."[21] In Christ there is a "new creation," a new humanity (2 Corinthians 5:17).

Thus while the world's opposition to God is not wholly overcome in the present, the world is nevertheless under the lordship of Christ, *Christus Victor Kyrios Christus*. But it must not be overlooked that Christ's lordship over the world takes on the "form of a servant" (Philippians 2:7). Christ's lordship has its power and authority in the humble and obedient service he gives to God and the world. It is by this that he asks to be known and recognized as having come from the Father, appointed by God to show the world the measure of the Father's love for them. The Servant-Son has his presence in the world as Servant to those whom he seeks recognition as Lord, to the glory of the Father.[22]

The church's missionary and evangelistic task is to declare this to the world to the end that the world may believe, recognize, and obey the true Lord of life. Paul Tillich has said that the work of the church in the world is to transform its own latency into its own manifestation all over the world. P. T. Forsyth has caught all of the essential motifs in a lyrical passage which we may use to summarize and prepare us for the transition to our next consideration—the implication for Christian ethics of the lordship of Christ:

The power that claims and saves us is beyond history, from before the foundation of the world. The first missionary was God the Father, who sent forth His Son in the likeness of sinful flesh. That is the seal and final ground of mission—the grace, the ultimate, unbought, overwhelming grace of God, the eternal heart and purpose of the Father who gave us not only a prophet but a propitiation. The second missionary was the Son, the apostle of one profession . . . the true primate of the apostles, of those that He sent forth from the bosom of the Father to declare Him; who exiled and emptied Himself in this foreign land of earth, and humbled Himself to death, even the death of the Cross. And the third missionary is the Holy Ghost, whom the Saviour sends forth into all the earth, who comes mightily and sweetly ordering all things, and subduing all lands to the obedience and kingdom of Christ. And the fourth missionary is the Church. And these four missionaries are all involved in the one divine redemption to which we owe ourselves utterly, which is the ground of the divinest claims on us, and makes us debtors, and nothing but debtors, forever and ever. These go forth together into each other, into all the world, into the depths of the soul. And the soul is saved in going forth from itself into this one living fellowship and through it in love, sacrifice, and blessing to all the world.[23]

Up to this point we have been concerned to say with Dr. Wilburn that the lordship of Christ over the church is the basis of the apostolic task of the church in the world, and that included in that mission is the church's "dynamic thrust of creative community in the larger social order." Further, we also hold that "through the church, which takes this ethical demand seriously, Christ exercises his lordship to lift our sinful world (of which the church is also a part) to higher levels of community." And in the words of Reginald Fuller "the church, by her obedience, provides the occasion through which God continues and renews his act of redemption." In a word, then, the lordship of Christ over his church and the world is the fundamental category of the Christian ethic and mission.

With this basic agreement in mind, we must now ask with Brunner whether Christ's lordship is exercised in the same way in both the church and the world. When Dr. Wilburn says that "through the church, which takes this ethical demand seriously, Christ exercises his lordship to lift our sinful world (of which the church is also a part) to higher levels of community," and when it is said that the mission of the church is her "dynamic thrust of creative community in the larger social order"—we ask, Is there any difference between the lordship of Christ over his church and his lordship over the larger social order? Brunner rejects as "very questionable" on New Testament grounds the contention that we ought to have "an optimistic hope in the gradual penetration of the world by the forces of the church and the kingdom." Brunner's counter proposal is:

The Kingship of Christ—yes, in all things first of all! But this slogan . . . will produce something very different from Utopia or "ecclesiocracy," if we add: the direct Kingship of Christ through the Gospel, in the Church, the indirect Kingship of Christ through the Law in the world.[24]

We have already pointed to a tension that exists in that on the one hand God's victorious act in Christ has "overcome the world." But on the other hand there is a continuing struggle between Christ and the hostile "powers" of the world. Brunner holds that, indeed, Christ is Lord of both church and world, but in so far as the world does not recognize and obey its Lord it is not ruled by his grace but by the law. Christ is received as Lord in the church; but in the social orders of the world there are many, indeed most, who do not receive him as Lord. Obviously, then, Christ can not exercise his lordship in both realms in exactly the same way.

Oscar Cullmann, however, contends that Brunner has affirmed only the obvious when he points to the difference between Christ's lordship over the church and his lordship over the world. Arguing for "the christological foundation of the state" on New Testament grounds, Cullmann says the relation of the two realms of church and state is more complex than mere separation or intermixture. As Cullmann sees it:

Christ rules over the Church, and he rules over the entire world. The Church stands nearer to him, for it is His Body. The State also belongs to the same "order," to His Lordship, but it stands at a greater distance from Him, since its members do not know of the Lordship of Christ. This duality reminds us of the fact that the Kingdom of Christ, when we speak in respect of *time,* is not yet the Kingdom of God, which only at the end, when Christ shall have subjected all things to God, will succeed the Kingdom of Christ. Only in the Kingdom of God will there no longer be two realms, for there God will be "all in all" (1 Corinthians 15:28).[25]

Although a distinction between the kingdom of God and the kingdom of Christ may be made with respect to *time,* with respect to God's *realm* of redemptive activity no such distinction is made in the New Testament, says Cullmann.

There is in the New Testament no dualism between a realm where God is Lord and a realm in which Christ is Lord. The pagan State does not know that it belongs to the Kingdom of Christ. Nevertheless, according to the New Testament, it can discern its task . . . the State also stands within the redemptive history.[26]

In a similar vein, Claude Welch argues against "the supposition that the relation of Christ to the church can be determined apart from His relation to the whole of mankind, or that the line runs simply from Christ to the church and thence to the world," so that Christ's lordship is restricted to the church. Welch holds with Brunner that "the church is not the only form in which God's rule is exercised; He is Lord over all societies and all forms (e.g. the state)." But, contrary to Brunner, Welch adds, "moreover this Lordship of the whole world is not something apart from Christ, but in Him."[27]

In terms of the meaning of the lordship of Christ for Christian ethics the problem may be stated thus: What is the relation between "gospel" and "law" in the lordship of Christ? How can a Christian social ethic based on the gospel be developed?

206

How, if at all, can the norms derived from Christology be the norms governing the social orders of the world?

It should be obvious that the ethical aspects of the church's life and mission are not secondary but integral. We have suggested as a possible subtitle of this chapter, "The Life of the Church and Its Apostolic Task in the Life of the World: A Discussion of the Ethical Dimensions of the Christian Gospel." If P. T. Forsyth is right when he says "the soul is saved in going forth from itself into this one living fellowship and through it in love, sacrifice, and blessing to all the world," then perhaps we would not be wrong in saying that Christian ethics are *koinonia* ethics, the ethics of the Christian fellowship when it takes "the form of the servant." We have four general points to make about this.

I. Christian Ethics as Koinonia Ethics

We have said, following Paul Lehmann, that the Christian ethic has as its primary question not "What does the gospel demand?" but "What does God do?" This puts the emphasis upon "gospel" more than on "law." In Christ, God has re-created the covenant relation with his people. The Christian ethic, as a covenant-ethic, is thus a manifestation of the lordship of Christ. The context of the ethic is the fellowship of the covenant in Christ, the *koinonia,* which is the concrete result of God's revelatory and redemptive activity in the world and for the sake of the world. "God is faithful, by whom you were called into the fellowship *(koinonia)* of his Son, Jesus Christ our Lord" (1 Corinthians 1:9).

This means, as we have said, that Christian ethics is "the disciplined reflection upon the question, and its answer: What am I as a believer in Jesus Christ, and as a member of his church to do?" The answer to this question is given within the context of the *koinonia,* and is summed up in the words "do the will of God in your specific relationships and situation." But a second question is raised immediately: What is the will of God which I am to do? A *koinonia* ethic approaches this question by pointing rather than defining. It points to specific events in which the meaning of love is made evident, to the activity of God in the world.[28] This means that the norm of Christian behavior is not abstract but concrete, not speculative but existential, not individualistic but social. The divine imperative is derived from the divine indicative; what the Christian is to do is determined in the light of what God has done and is doing.

The connection of the Christian *koinonia* with the Christian ethic is made explicit in Ephesians 4—6 where the manner of Christ's relation to the church is the pattern for the Christian's behavior. Thus "the *koinonia* is a fellowship of working together for the gospel,"[29] a "partnership in the gospel" as the Apostle Paul put it. We may draw a formula: the *kerygma* (the gospel message of the lordship of Christ) is received and proclaimed in the *koinonia* (the Christian fellowship) through its *diakonia* (Christian service) in word and act in both the church and the world.

II. The Source of Christian Love in the Koinonia

The gospel and the ethic of the *koinonia* have their common source in the righteous and gracious reconciling work of God in Christ. "All this is from God, who through Christ reconciled us to himself and gave us the ministry of reconciliation (2 Corinthians 5:18). "We love, because he first loved us" (1 John 4:19). The gospel is the covenant-call of God, calling men into a new life of fellowship in the community of Christ, a community of grace and of faith. Thus the *koinonia* is not itself the initiating source of Christian love but is the *result* of God's call ("election").

The dominant theme of the Old Testament is that God's righteousness is manifest in his entering into a special relationship with the people of Israel. This covenant relationship was one of divine promise and human decision, of grace and free will. The dominant theme of the New Testament is that of a new and renewed covenant made in Christ which marks the coming of the kingdom. This new covenant is also one of divine promise and human decision, and as such indicates the continuity of the disciples of Christ as a covenant community with the people of God, Israel. Thus all biblical ethics are the ethics of the covenant, the ethics of grace. In the Bible the source of law and love is not found abstractly by defining God as justice and love but by receiving and participating in God's just and loving activity in creating and sustaining the covenant community.

As the source of human love is the divine love, so the motive of human righteousness is "grateful obedience": "We love, because he first loved us." Man's love of God and man's love of his neighbor is born of God's love of man. "The People of the covenant acted primarily from a total response to God which may be described as grateful obedience or obedient gratitude."[30]

III. The Measure of Christian Love

In the most developed biblical view, justice is redemptive and not merely punitive. God's justice is related directly to his love. Thus in the Bible the view of justice is invaded by the vocabulary of salvation, and human justice is related to the divine justice so that the latter is normative for the former.

The connecting link between divine righteousness and human justice is the covenant. . . . God's righteousness becomes the plumb line for measuring the righteousness of human relationships. Since the covenanted community has no charter for existence apart from God's act, the foundation and constitution of her justice must be laid in his righteousness.[31]

In the teaching of Jesus the righteousness required of men was derived from and measured by *God's* love.[32] In the thought of the early Christians, the measure of man's righteousness was given a *Christo*centric determination: Jesus has *become* the righteousness of God. The theological expression of this was the lordship of Christ:[33] the ethical expression of it was that Christ

209

is the prototype of divine love.[34] Thus we concur with Paul Ramsey's observation:

Differences in New Testament theology, however, should not be emphasized, since in getting to know the origin, and more decisively, the meaning, of Christian love the important point to see is the unanimity with which men of the Bible applied a supernatural measure to all obedient love.[35]

IV. The Meaning of Christian Love

If Christian love cannot be defined but is best described in the manner of Paul in 1 Corinthians 13, we may speak of it in terms of the ways it embodies itself to create and sustain the community and harmony of life with life. Love would then be spoken of in terms of personal life in its actual unity. Thus, again, the meaning of Christian love is found in the context of *koinonia;* in terms, that is, of what God has done and is doing in the life of the world—overcoming the self-destructive, demonic forces in life. As such, the meaning of love is stated in terms of forgiveness, reconciliation, and justice.[36]

Love means forgiveness; the acceptance and being accepted in spite of sin, and the opportunity of a new moral beginning. It is a gift, unmerited and uncalculated—"not counting their trespasses against them" (2 Corinthians 5:19). Love means reconciliation: the harmony of life with life, the reunion of that which is estranged. It is the concrete result of the movement of love in forgiveness toward community. Love means justice: the concrete way from forgiveness to reconciliation. It is God's righteousness manifest in the various structures and relations in the *koinonia* and in the larger social order.

Christian love, *agape,* is concerned for the neighbor's good, and for the neighbor's own sake. The "good" is not determined primarily by an abstract calculation of superior values, but by a concrete meeting of neighbor need. Christian love for the neighbor does not ask "Who is my neighbor?" but recognizes the neighbor in every man and seeks to prove himself neighbor to the man.

Christian love does not aim at self-realization. It does not "lose its life" *in order to* "find it." This prudential motive is eliminated by the words "for my sake and the gospel's." Here the Christian ethical orientation is the same as Christ's and the gospel's orientation: the neighbor. Thus *kerygma* and *diakonia* merge in the neighbor. Christian love does not use the neighbor as a steppingstone to God, as a means to gaining salvation. Salvation comes as the consequence of loving God and neighbor, but it can not have self-realization as its primary motive.

Christian love is responsive love; it is "faith working through love" in gratitude to God, seeking the neighbor's good. As Luther put it, "Our faith in Christ does not free us from works, but from the false opinions concerning good works, that is, from the foolish presumption that [our own] justification is acquired by works."[37] Jesus said, "The good man out of the good treasure of his heart produces good" (Luke 6:45). Commenting on this, Albert Rasmussen has said, "but they will not be the treasures of God unless shared, expressed, and made decisive as we confront our obligations under God."[38] Here, again, the meaning of Christian love is found in the life of the *koinonia,* spelled out in terms of what God is doing and has done in the world, calling for concrete behavior in response to this divine action, this "new thing" that has taken place and is continually taking place.

The Life of the Church and its Apostolic Task in the Life of the World

It has become quite common to point out the failure of the Christian church in meeting effectively the challenge of the moral and social chaos of our time, its failure to help create a healthy social order, to stem the tide of secularism and barbarism so-called. Much of this criticism is vital and well taken. But much of it is misleading because it stems from misconceptions as to the nature and function of the church in society. On the one extreme is the opposition of the church and the world. At the other extreme there is the thought, in the form of Catholic Modernism and Liberal Protestantism, which emphasizes the adaptability and accommodation of the church to the world. The one finds the idea of a Christian world a contradiction in terms; the other sees a Christian society the goal of the historical process, the kingdom of God established on earth. It is not surprising, therefore, that we should find a polarity of thought concerning the function of the church in society when we remember the dialectical character of the church's relation to the world given in the New Testament. We seek now to draw some of the implications and problems for the life of the church in the world of culture that result from this complex relation.

The conception of the function of the church in society must center around an understanding of the underlying and permanent tension between these two points of view; that is, there is a basic tension that makes possible such a polarity of thought as we have indicated. Furthermore, it is contended that a too easy resolution of this tension in terms of one or the other pole will result in a one-sided conception of the function of the church in society. This is what has been done; it is also that which must be avoided. A survey of the attitudes toward the world historically held by the churches would indicate the vacillation that has marked the life and thought of the church.

I. Historical Attitudes of the Churches Toward the World

The early church with its eschatological expectations took no interest in trying to reform the existing social structures. Rather they attempted to actualize the ideal of love in their personal relations as they waited for the "end of the age." Paradoxically, perhaps, their attitude "constrained by the love of Christ" contained a revolutionary element without a desire for revolution.

The monastic movement was an attempt to overcome the world by abandoning it. With little or no concern for the reform of the existing social structure, the monastic concern was largely that of the individual's transcendence of worldly conditions by seeking inner peace in this life and eternal bliss in the next. Thus the heroic rigorism of the ethic of Jesus became monastic asceticism and world indifference.

The attitude of medieval Catholicism was determined by its ideal of the Christian unity of civilization in which the church asserted its rule over the whole domain of human existence. The focus of this ideal was that of a Christian religious community, a *corpus Christi,* in which the religious idea worked itself out directly in a sociological form: a *corpus Christianum.* But still there was no great interest in large-scale social reform. The existing order was accepted, with attempts made to curb only the worst of its excesses. Thomas Aquinas gave the theoretical basis for this synthesis of *corpus Christi* and *corpus Christianum,* a reconciliation of this-worldly and otherworldly morality, of natural law and divine law, of free will and grace.

The attitude of Lutheranism was determined by Luther's view that the church's function is entirely "spiritual." That term was taken to mean the individual's redemption, not society's reformation. Social institutions are willed by God in the interest of fallen man's temporal welfare. These institutions of society are all more or less corrupt, due to human sin, but God permits them as means of punishment and as means of correction. At any rate, only God can change or redeem them. Thus, while there is no unity or separation of church and society, there is to be a harmony. The interest of each is interwoven, and each needs the other. But the individual Christian has no obligation to work for the redemption of the social order. Rather he should respond to the divine grace and witness to its availability to all men through the church's sacraments, rejoicing in his assurance of justification.

The attitude of Calvinism was one of spiritual detachment from the things of the world, combined with victory over the world while remaining in it. In contrast to Lutheranism, Calvinism stressed the need of the church for providing not only the means of grace but of Christianizing the community by placing its whole range of life under the control of Christian purposes and regulations. Thus the Calvinists showed a keen interest in the affairs of the world. It was to glorify God, preserve and make effective one's election, and produce the "holy community."

Pietistic sectarianism, registering a sense of moral outrage at the way in which official Christianity (the church) had compromised with the world, sought to achieve, on a small scale and on a voluntary basis, a community life that would be in harmony with the Christian ideal. It was to be a "holy experiment" in Christian living, day by day, in harmony with the teachings of Christ. The ascetic ideal of the pietists was not the "destruction of the sense of life and of natural self-feeling, but a union in love which is not affected by the social inequalities and struggles of the world."[39] The attitude of pietistic sectarianism, then, was one of detachment from the world in order to practice "holiness" and to avoid the secularization of religious energies by being "of the world."

The ideal of Liberal Protestantism is that of the adaptability of the Christian faith and ethic to the world. The gospel is a "social gospel." The tension between the church and the world is not between a "redeemed society" (church) and a "fallen society" (world). Rather the church is the agent functioning in a growing society for a progressive Christianizing of the social order. Liberal Protestantism heartily affirms the social responsibility of the church, the improvability of man and the world, and the relevance of the absolute ethic of love to the social problems of the world.

II. The Dialectical Relation of the Church to the World, and the Resulting Ethical Tension

Christians have traditionally spoken of the gulf between the church and the world. Consequently there has always been a note of "contempt" for the world on the part of the church. The world is the domain of evil and the church is the domain of love and holiness, it is said. Because of her holiness the church must remain apart from the world in order not to be too conformed to the world, that is, secularized. But, on the other hand, the church is loving. She is the instrument of God in love to save the world and is the bearer of the kingdom. Therefore, the church has "contempt" for the world and at the same time suffers for the world in love. She remains apart from the world and at the same time seeks its redemption. She is at once the holy community and a loving community.

The holiness and love of the church give rise to the ethical tension. The church, as a holy community, is "not of this world." But at the same time the church lives and loves in a world where perfect love is not possible, sin being presupposed. This is the resulting tension in the ethical life of the church: she must preserve the eschatological, ultimate, and perfect character of the love for which she stands, but she also must live in a world where such love is not a simple possibility. Again, the history of the church shows a tendency to resolve prematurely this ethical tension either by a too complete withdrawal from the world, or by a too simple conformity to the world. In Catholicism there developed the idea of a dual morality as a way out of this tension. There is one morality for the ordinary man; there is another and higher morality for those called to live the true life of the kingdom. This is the perfectionist element expressed in monasticism. Protestantism rejected the idea of a dual morality and insisted on one morality for all men. But in modern Protestantism there has been a subtle return to the idea of a dual morality for clergy and laity. In order to give expression to the perfectionist element in Protestantism there arose the pietistic sects. Thus, the ethical tension in the life of the church has given rise on the one hand to monasticism and on the other hand to pietism. It seems that both have become distorted because they have attempted to destroy or to deny the tension.

This tension is essential to the Christian faith and the ethical life of the church. But in practical situations such tensions are intolerable; decisions must be made. We must maintain the tension and yet at the same time make Christian decisions and actions in particular situations possible. The ethical tension can be maintained and at the same time surmounted for practical purposes by a more realistic understanding of the dialectical relation of the absolute of Christian love to the relativities of specific historical situations calling for ethical action. This has the strength of avoiding ethical legalism and false perfectionism on the one hand and ethical irrelevance on the other. It sees the imperfection of all our ethical decisions, thereby helping to avoid the peril of pharisaism; at the same time, it encourages one to deal with the relativities of life without feeling that such activity is wholly sinful in itself.

III. Principles and Problems of Christian Social Strategy

A number of principles and problems complicating any determination of a Christian social strategy may be listed: "Faith working through love" is taken by most Christians to be the basic principle of Christian ethics. But there is no general agreement whether love implies a particular *pattern* of action or implies the *intention* to do that which is best for all in a particular situation.

The gospel of Jesus Christ is the criterion of Christian ethics. But there is no general agreement on the nature of that gospel and its implications for ethics. Thus there is the problem whether the strategy of Jesus is to be followed by those living in a very different situation, with functions and expectations different from those of Jesus.

The "righteous" activity of God is the wellspring of Christian action. But there is a difference among Christians whether the righteousness and judgment of God are made effectual directly or through human media, and whether God works through those whose resistance to evil represents divine judgment as well as through those who follow the strategy of nonresistance.

The "way of the cross" is considered by all to be the way of the Christian. But it is not agreed whether the "cross" is to be understood as a method or as a consequence for those who follow it.

Grace is the power that makes for righteousness. But the relation of grace to freedom is debated, and to what extent we can count on the grace of God to change the hardness of man's heart.

Sin is the negative context in which Christian action must occur. But there is disagreement about evil persisting even among the "redeemed."

The church is the creation of God to be the agent of redemption in the world. But there is a difference of opinion with respect to the relation of the church to the world.

The Christian is under the divine imperative. But how the responsibility of the Christian is discharged is disputed, whether he is responsible for the immediate measures which seem necessary for the public order, or looks to and witnesses to the long-run vocation of the way of love which stands beyond the immediate situations.

From this listing of principles and problems we may conclude that the over-all problem confronting us is that of the absolute and the relative in Christian ethics, and how we can go beyond this simple alternative.

IV. THE PROBLEM OF THE ABSOLUTE AND THE RELATIVE IN CHRISTIAN SOCIAL POLICY

Paul Tillich has described the Christian ethic as the ethic of *kairos*—the ethic of "the historical moment in which something new, eternally important, manifests itself in temporal forms, in the potentialities and tasks of a special period."[40] The term *"kairos"* is taken out of its rather general biblical sense of any period of time and is used by Tillich in a more special theological sense of a period of time *in which the presence and will of God is recognized*. Thus any moment of time (occasion) may

217

be a "right time," a *kairos,* "but only love is able to appear in every *kairos.* Law is not able because law is the attempt to impose something which belonged to a special time on all times." "Love, realizing itself from *kairos* to *kairos,* creates an ethic which is beyond the alternatives of absolute and relative ethics."[41]

Speaking to the same problem and along lines similar to those of Tillich, H. Richard Niebuhr holds that the Christian ethical decisions can not be based on purely rationalistic considerations, although they are not made without reason.

They are rather undertaken and attained in the movement from consideration to action, from insight to decision. Each believer reaches his own "final" conclusion, in resolutions that involve a leap from the chair in which he has read about ancient battles into the middle of a present conflict. No amount of speculative insight into the reasoning and believing of other men, and no continuation of consideration of the imperatives and values issuing from Christ and culture, can relieve the Christian individual or the responsible Christian community from the burden, the necessity, the guilt and glory, of arriving at such conclusions in present decisions and present obedience.[42]

This "social existentialism" does not imply that decisions are made in isolation from the thinking and deciding of other men and groups. On the contrary, the Christian is aware of his relatedness to other men in a historical situation, and knows he must decide within the context of faith and history the freedom of faith and the contingencies of culture.

They are made, it appears, on the basis of relative insight and faith, but they are not relativistic. They are individual decisions, but not individualistic. They are made in freedom, but not in independence; they are made in the moment, but are not unhistorical. . . . The recognition and acknowledgment of our relativity, however, does not mean that we are without an absolute . . . to whom all their relative views, values and duties are subject.[43]

The specific problems of social living calling for Christian ethical decision and social policy are determined, therefore, by the principle of love on the one hand and by the changing *kairoi* on the other. In this context, the absolute of Christian love must be related to the relative of the changing situation. The one must not be confused with the other, nor swallowed up by the other. Here the problem is that of allowing love to be in permanent criticism of every specific social policy without destroying the basis for concrete decision and action. How can the absolute maintain its transcendence of every concrete situation and at the same time be made relevant? Love itself demands laws and institutions in order to provide guidance and effective channels of action. These laws and institutions for the actualization of love in special situations are the concrete meaning of justice. "From this it follows that justice is the secondary and derived principle, while love, actualized from *kairos* to *kairos,* is the creative and basic principle."[44]

John Bennett finds the problem of bridging the distance between the absolute of love and the relative approximations of justice in society to be complicated by a combination of factors.[45] First is the interior one of self-centeredness expressing itself in hostility, prejudice, indifference, and so forth. Then there is the added factor of the wider immorality of social groups in conflict, as compared with the narrower immortality of individuals.[46] A third factor is the cumulative results of past evils so that the past dogs us as a handicap creating vicious circles of evil. Fourth, because we live in a mixed society of Christians and non-Christians, there is often no standard of ethical judgment beyond a general common denominator of average moral insight. This common denominator has been described as "enlightened selfishness" which is somewhere between the "unenlightened selfishness" of raw egoism and the "enlightened unselfishness" of intelligent good will. Moreover, Christians differ among themselves as to the meaning and measure of Christian love. A fifth factor is that in social situations we often have to deal indirectly with large masses of people, which tends to make for impersonal relations and for insensitivity. A sixth factor is that in broad social situations there is often an absence of a concentrated sense of responsibility, in which only a comparatively few feel the full force of the moral obligation. Moreover, Christians often differ among themselves regarding social objectives. A seventh factor is that there are always morally neutral considerations for which we have no specific Christian insight, such as those of technical problems of production, marketing, cost-price, etc. An eighth factor is that of the difficulty in predicting actual consequences. How groups will react to suggested policies is almost impossible to determine with accuracy. A ninth factor is the way of competing values and the problem of determining what points should be controlled by what values: how to weigh, for example, the values of freedom and security, of justice and order? A tenth factor is the limitation imposed by the historical circumstances in which a Christian church may find itself, as for example, the possibilities of action open to a church living in comparative social security as compared with one living under persecution or tyranny. Similarly with respect to the individual and his duty within his vocation and life-situation, we must live and act within the particularities and limitations of our conditioned existence.

V. Christian Strategies in regard to Social Problems

In the light of the foregoing moral and morally neutral factors Christians have had to devise their strategies as they have sought to bridge the distance between the absolute and the relative in ethics. To discuss these strategies would entail a history of the relations of church and culture as for example, H. Richard Niebuhr's modern classic, *Christ and Culture*. In regard to these strategies, we may follow John Bennett and describe them generally as (1) the Roman Catholic strategy, (2) the strategy of withdrawal, (3) the strategy of relevance without transcendence, (4) the strategy of the double standard, or the irrelevance of Christian ethics to public life, (5) the strategy of relevance with transcendence.[47]

The Roman Catholic strategy[48] is a mixed one, having at least three elements. First there is the idea of a dual morality. Here there is a different set of standards for the clergy and for the laity. These two orders are thought to be closely correlated, each supporting the other, but the vocational asceticism of the monk who has found an oasis of sanctity within the vast desert of the secular world serves that world through his prayers and merits. The laity and secular priests who are involved in the life of the world support the institutions of the church which make possible the withdrawal of the monk. A second element in the Roman Catholic mixed strategy is the adaptation of human reason or natural law into the ethical teaching of the church. It is felt that human reason is free enough of sin to permit the church to speak with confidence and accuracy on specific ethical issues, that the Christian position can be determined unambiguously. A third element in the Roman Catholic strategy is the authoritative role of the church in pronouncing on particular social choices. Here again it is felt that the church is free enough of sin to permit it to speak with confidence and accuracy on specific ethical issues.

The strategy of withdrawal is not confined to the Roman Catholic Church. Within sectarian Protestantism there are those who practice at least a partial withdrawal[49] into relatively self-sufficient communities. The idea of a double standard is not admitted, although there is a kind of double standard recognized —one for those of the sect and another for Christians not of the sect. Within this strategy there are variations. For example, there are the more radical advocates of withdrawal who would create a permanent opposition between the Christian and the world. Their interest is not to save the world but to save men from the world. Therefore they have little to say to the problems of social justice as embodied in the structures of society. On the other hand, there are the less radical groups practicing a selective withdrawal. They refrain from participating in some areas of the life of the larger community, but participate actively in other areas.

221

The strategy of relevance without transcendence[50] is one which identifies Christianity with certain social programs, movements, or institutions. Catholic and Protestant exponents of this strategy see no moral ambiguity in social policies involving large mixed groups, and consequently no need for any permanent opposition between Christianity and the social order.

The strategy of the double standard[51] is one which affirms the relevance of Christian ethics for personal living but denies the relevance for public life. This strategy is based on the assumption of a basic conflict between the church and the world, a permanent opposition, with few opportunities for direct influence by the church upon the structures of society.

The strategy of relevance with transcendence is one "which takes account of the universality and persistence of sin and the elements of technical autonomy in social policies" while preserving the tension between Christian ethics and social policy.[52] This strategy seeks to deal with the ethical problems in ways which avoid the weaknesses of the other four strategies. It recognizes the relativity of solutions without giving up the absolute demand.

John Bennett sees five ways in which the Christian absolute of love can be related to the decisions of social policy when this strategy of relevance with transcendence is followed: First, Christian love can control motives. Even in the more impersonal relations it is possible for private interests to be made subordinate to the welfare of all when "faith working through love" is made central.[53] A second element in this strategy is that Christian love may provide the necessary accompanying attitudes, e.g. humility, which greatly modify actions and their effects.[54] A third element in this strategy is the kind of guidance Christians can have through the rigorous criticism of existing institutions and practices, including those in which the Christian himself is deeply involved.[55] A fourth element in this strategy is the necessity of charting better possibilities for approximation of the Christian norm so that compromises will not have to be made. "These are not absolute and all-inclusive goals but the next steps that our own generation must take."[56] These "next steps" have been described as "middle axioms" and "proximate goals" in order to indicate their relation both to the absolute goal of love and the relative situation.

They are an attempt to define the directions in which, in a particular state of society, Christian faith must express itself. They are not binding for all time, but are provisional definitions of the type of behavior required of Christians at a given period and in given circumstances.[57]

A fifth element in this strategy is the kind of individual action and the action of smaller groups of Christians that can be taken "to counteract some of the consequences of what we must do as citizens or in some official capacity by action of another kind."

We have contended throughout that a one-sided view of the function of the church in society can be avoided only by maintaining both the opposition and the adaptability of the church to society; her holiness and her love. If our presentation of the basic biblical doctrines is substantially correct, we believe our insistence on the basic tensions in the faith and life of the church is legitimate. Also, we believe the variety of attitudes historically held by the churches witnesses to the presence of this tension: that the church in holiness must oppose the world and in love she must embrace it. Both emphases are needed, not as a patchwork compromise but because of the very nature of the relations of the church and the world.

As a broad conclusion to the problem of the function of the church in society in general, we see that the church as a corporate body can and must do a tremendously important work for establishing a better society, but this work is largely indirect.

On the other hand, the church working through individual Christians can and must take direct action towards this end. At the same time, the improved society will not be the full realization of the kingdom. It will be Christian only in a qualified way. But neither will it stand in direct antithesis to the kingdom.

The true relation between them will be rather of a dialectical kind. In so far as it approximates the kingdom ever so little, it will be a development for which we must thank God. Yet we must never confuse this imperfect fulfillment of an earthly hope with the hope that is eternal, for "here we have no continuing city."

Conclusion

We have carried our discussion to the limits of space permitted us, and find ourselves confronted with problems for which there are no ready solutions. We have sought to indicate the possibilities and limitations the church labors under in its attempt to be obedient to her Lord. Certain guiding principles have become evident. In summary, these controlling principles are: (1) There is an organic relationship between Christ and his church. (2) There is a dialogic relationship between Christ and his church. (3) The lordship of Christ over his church is the basis of the apostolic task of the church by which his lordship is manifest in the life of the world.

If the church is to serve in joyful obedience in the world in which she finds herself, she will continually remind herself that she is under the kingship of Christ. In this she will know in whose hand she rests and by whose power she works, and in her obedience to the Lord in whose service she is called she will be strengthened by the firm confidence that she "by her obedience, provides the occasion through which God continues and renews his act of redemption." She will continue in her dialogue with her Lord, beseeching him for the gift of his Spirit, that she may continue her other dialogue with the world.

Knowing that Christ is Lord of the church and Lord of the world, both being his creation, the church will enter into the grace of his new creation in faith and obedience. Knowing, too, that this new creation in the community of faith is God's gift to the world, she will joyfully accept her inescapable responsibility to declare this good news to the world. Christians who are called out of the world into a new community under the lordship of Christ will not conform themselves to the world in its present form. But by living in the world, encouraged by the promise of Jesus and by his declaration that through accepting his lordship over the world they, too, can overcome the world and its afflictions, "and no one will take your joy from you" (John 16:22), they will fulfill their calling to take "the form of a servant."

We do not, on that account, despise the world of man's cultural life. The Christ who is the Lord of the church is also the Redeemer of the world. The world is where the church meets "the brother for whom Christ died." That brother is man, all men, in culture, in their historical existence, living in the world which God in his grace has created and endowed with meaning and purpose within the covenant relation, and which by his grace will be fashioned into his kingdom.

NOTES

1. Reinhold Niebuhr, *The Nature and Destiny of Man* (New York: Charles Scribner's Sons, and Hertfordshire: James Nisbet and Co. Ltd., 1948), II, 144-145.
2. Chapter 8, p. 175.
3. *Ibid.,* p. 176.
4. *Ibid.,* p. 187.
5. *Ibid.,* p. 188.
6. Reginald Fuller, "The Church under the Lordship of Jesus Christ," *Encounter,* Vol. XX, No. 4 (Fall, 1959), p. 452.
7. Roger Shinn, "The Lordship of Christ and American Society," *Encounter,* Fall, 1959, p. 459, Cf. John Godsey, *Ibid.,* p. 438.
8. Cf. Philippians 2:8-11; John 1:3, 10; Hebrews 1:2, 3; 2:8; Colossians 1:15, 20; Ephesians 1:10; 1 Corinthians 8:6; 2 Corinthians 5:10, 19; Romans 5:18; Revelation 1:5; 17:14; 1 Peter 3:22.
9. Psalm 24:1. Cf. Thomas Wieser, *Encounter,* Fall, 1959, pp. 484ff.
10. From *The Christian Doctrine of Creation and Redemption* (Dogmatics, Volume II) by Emil Brunner, Jr., Olive Wyon. Published 1952, The Westminster Press. Used by permission.
11. From *Christ and Time* by Oscar Cullmann, Jr., Floyd Filson. Copyright 1950, by W. L. Jenkins. The Westminster Press. Used by permission.
12. Wieser, *op. cit.,* p. 492. Cf. Cullmann, *op. cit.,* p. 734, passim.
13. John 3:16. Cf. Romans 5:8.
14. D. T. Niles, *The Preacher's Calling to Be Servant* (London: Lutterworth Press, 1959), p. 131.
15. Dietrich Bonhoeffer, *Letters and Papers from Prison* (London: S.C.M. Press, 1953), p. 166.
16. Cf. Claude Welch, *The Reality of the Church* (New York: Charles Scribner's Sons, 1958), pp. 198-203.

17. Brunner, *op. cit.*, pp. 56-57.
18. *Ibid.*, pp. 60-61.
19. Paul L. Lehmann, "The Foundation and Pattern of Christian Behavior," in *Christian Faith and Social Action,* ed. by John Hutchison (New York: Charles Scribner's and Sons, 1953), p. 102.
20. Anders Nygren, *The Gospel of God* (Philadelphia: Westminster Press, 1961), pp. 29f.
21. D. T. Niles, *The Preacher's Task and the Stone of Stumbling* (New York: Harper & Row, Publishers, Inc., 1958), p. 111.
22. Niles, *The Preacher's Calling to be Servant,* Ch. 5. Cf. Karl Barth, *Church Dogmatics,* IV, 1, 2.
23. P. T. Forsyth, *The Essential Missionary Nature of Christianity.*
24. Brunner, *op. cit.*, pp. 316, 321. Cf. pp. 300-303.
25. Cullmann, *op. cit.*, p. 208.
26. *Ibid.*, p. 209.
27. Welch, *op. cit.*, pp. 199-200.
28. Cf. Romans 5:8-11; John 3:16; 1 John 4:9-11; 2 Corinthians 5:18-21.
29. Lehmann, *op. cit.*, p. 103.
30. Paul Ramsey, *Basic Christian Ethics* (New York: Charles Scribner's Sons, 1950), p. 13.
31. *Ibid.*, p. 5, Cf. pp. 8, 12.
32. Cf. Matthew 5:44, 45, 48.
33. Cf. Philippians 2:10; Colossians 1:15-17; John 1:3.
34. Cf. 1 Corinthians 13; Philippians 2:5-10; John 15:12-13; Romans 5:6-8, 10.
35. Ramsey, *op. cit.*, p. 21.
36. Cf. *Ibid.*, pp. 112-113.
37. *Works of Martin Luther,* The Philadelphia Edition (Philadelphia: Muhlenberg Press, 1943), II, 344.
38. Albert Rasmussen, *Christian Social Ethics* (Englewood Cliffs, N. J.: Prentice-Hall, 1956), p. 80.
39. Ernst Troeltsch, *The Social Teachings of the Christian Churches* (London: Allen and Unwin, 1931), I, 333.
40. Paul Tillich, *The Protestant Era* (Chicago: University of Chicago Press, 1948), p. 155.
41. *Ibid.*, p. 156.
42. H. Richard Niebuhr, *Christ and Culture* (New York: Harper & Row, Publishers, Inc., 1956), p. 233. Used by permission.
43. *Ibid.*, p. 234, 238.
44. Tillich, *op. cit.*, pp. 159-160.
45. John Bennett, *Christian Ethics and Social Policy* (New York: Charles Scribners Sons, 1946), pp. 15-31.
46. Cf. Reinhold Niebuhr, *Moral Man and Immoral Society* (New York: Charles Scribner's Sons, 1932).
47. Bennett, *op. cit.*, pp. 32-88.
48. *Ibid.*, pp. 32-41.
49. *Ibid.*, pp. 41-46.
50. *Ibid.*, pp. 46-51.
51. *Ibid.*, pp. 51-57.
52. *Ibid.*, p. 59.
53. *Ibid.*, pp. 61-65.
54. *Ibid.*, pp. 65-71.
55. *Ibid.*, pp. 71-76.
56. *Ibid.*, pp. 76-77.
57. W. A. Visser 't Hooft and J. H. Oldham, *The Church and Its Function in Society* (London: Allen and Unwin, 1937), p. 210.

☙10☙

Authority: Human and Divine

EUGENE H. PETERS

OUR topic is one which easily proliferates into a number of other important topics: e.g., law and gospel, reason and revelation, free will and grace, etc. Hence, we have every chance of "striking it rich" as we investigate "Authority: Human and Divine." At the same time, we have the problem of knowing where to begin and where to focus our attention. Our topic might be approached in several ways. Perhaps the way we have chosen will be as helpful to the reader as any of the others.

James Luther Adams contributes to *Religion and Culture: Essays in Honor of Paul Tillich* a most provocative chapter on "Rudolf Sohm's Theology of Law and the Spirit."[1] A review of this chapter will provide an introduction to our topic. Adams begins by calling attention to Luther's doctrine of the two kingdoms: there is the kingdom of God, which exists under the authority of the love and spirit of Christ and is guided by the Holy Spirit (in conjunction with Word and sacrament); there is the kingdom of the world, which exists under civil authority and is ruled by law. This doctrine was vigorously discussed before World War I and today is prominent once more. Discussion has centered about such questions as the role of the Holy Spirit or charismatic authority in the church; the place of sacrosanct legal authority in the church; the tendency of legal order in a Protestant church to deprive it of its evangelical character and freedom, and drive it toward Roman Catholic bondage to canon law; the danger that law in the church will lead to idolatry; the essential incompatibility of charismatic authority and divinely sanctioned legal authority, whether the latter officially establishes doctrine or polity.

Adams says that Rudolf Sohm (1841-1917) is a key figure for understanding this discussion. Sohm, an eminent German jurist and church historian, held that charismatic authority is wholly incompatible with "divine church law." Non-Lutheran Protestants may ask why the Holy Spirit need be defended against canon law. But, Adams explains, Sohm's understanding of charismatic authority is akin to conceptions of the Holy Spirit which are familiar in free-church tradition and especially in the "left wing" of the Reformation, to which many Protestant denominations and sects trace their lineage.

In his protest against the legalization of belief and practice in the church, Sohm appealed not only to Luther's doctrine of the two kingdoms but also to his doctrine of the invisible church. In fact, Sohm developed a theology of church history based on loyalty to or deviation from the norm of the invisible church. He traced the "fall" of the church from this norm, recovery of the norm in Luther, and its subsequent perversion in the Protestant churches. While the Anabaptists identified the "fall" with the alliance of church and state, and Harnack with the "acute Hellenization" of Christianity, Sohm held that the "fall" of the church is to be located in the advent of a legally constituted church under the episcopate.

Adams points out that Sohm's concern was to dissipate every confusion between the kingdom of Christ and the kingdom of the world. He maintained that whereas the primitive Christian *ecclesia* had excluded legal direction and restraint, the later church tended to become a second state, thus being secularized from within. Christ delivered men from the law. Hence, the Christian is under charismatic authority and is oriented primarily to an invisible church. Canon law, by contrast, is a form of authority which belongs to a visible church.

Any assembly of Christians is a manifestation of the universal *ecclesia*. Members of the Body of Christ are called by the Holy Spirit to various tasks. The organization of the church conforms to the distribution of gifts of grace. Thus, it is an organization given by God, not produced by merely human consensus. No bearer of charismatic gifts has a *right* to his office. Rather, he depends on permission from the assembly but not as if it were a sovereign or democratic body, for confirmation of leaders depends on witness coming from God. One obeys the Spirit in a response of love and not legalistically. The efficacy of the Spirit is inseparable from Word and sacrament. Since the *ecclesia* is obedient to a living rather than a dead Word, it is not bound to the past.

According to Sohm, the danger of idolatrous attachment to the visible church was present even in the primitive *ecclesia*. This danger can be met only by faith in the invisible church. Hence, Sohm saw in Luther's doctrine of the invisible church a corrective to the primitive *ecclesia* and to the legalization of Christianity. In appealing to this doctrine, Sohm emphasized that the Word and the Spirit work within the depths of the Christian's life, for the relation to God is personal, not legal. Accordingly, church polity is a secular concern and a matter of indifference to Christians.

Toward the end of the chapter, Adams calls attention to certain consequences of Sohm's divorce of Spirit from law. One consequence is that love and justice are disjoined. Nor is there connection between charisma and Logos. Hence, Sohm is not concerned with ways of relating charisma to the empirical reality in face of which it will offer love. Furthermore, he fails to indicate how response to the Spirit involves responsibility for the consequences of action or inaction. Nor does he consider how the Spirit brings about consensus among Christians. And finally, he is unable to discern whether one polity is more amenable to the workings of the Holy Spirit than another.

Adams' discussion of Sohm, which we have now reviewed, is valuable for our purposes because it puts before us a clear, if extreme, theological conception of "Authority: Human and Divine." For here, in Sohm, we have a doctrine which thoroughly separates the kingdom of God from the kingdom of the world. The one is personal, spiritual, inward, and invisible; the other is legal, secular, external, and visible. Not only is Sohm's theory clear-cut; in addition, it embodies a central motif of the Lutheran Reformation. To be sure, one may question whether Sohm's concept of the church is really in accord with Luther's.[2] I am not competent to judge this matter, but surely Sohm's fundamental concern is identical with Luther's: to avoid confusing the human and the divine, a concern which if neglected leads to idolatry. Furthermore, Sohm's theory of the two kingdoms embodies the basic principle of neo-Reformation theology. Adams states that Emil Brunner shows a marked sympathy with certain aspects of Sohm's outlook and that Rudolf Bultmann is at least somewhat favorable to Sohm.[3] Interestingly enough, Karl Barth attacks Brunner for supporting Sohm's antilegalism and demands *living* law in the church.[4] Barth's divergence from Brunner on this point cautions against a too simple classification of theologians.

Nonetheless, something of Sohm's dualism (though not in its acute form) undergirds the entire movement of neo-Reformation theology. For, as Langdon Gilkey says, the earliest emphasis of the movement "was a radical criticism of the 'liberal' union of culture and Christianity, and a corresponding assertion of the discontinuity of Christianity in all its aspects from the dominant thought-forms of Western life."[5] Hence, if liberalism represented to some extent a wedding of Christianity and culture, neo-Reformation theology represents a disjunction of the two. Neo-Reformation theology vests value, being, and authority in God rather than in man. God is seen as transcendent; man is seen as a sinner, powerless to save himself and thus dependent on

230

divine grace. Accordingly, the Word of God stands in contrast to and in judgment on the words of men.

Thus, in modern Christendom there are two widely divergent attitudes respecting human and divine authority, that of synthesis (represented by Protestant liberalism) and that of diastasis (represented by Sohm and neo-Reformation theology). Of course, theological opinion ranges in various ways between the extreme forms of synthesis and diastasis. One may say that ultimately the issue is the doctrine of the *imago dei,* that is, the status of man before God.

We see then that our topic furnishes an issue far wider than that of ecclesiastical polity. This can be illustrated by considering the underlying unity between Sohm in his polemic against "divine church law" and Brunner in his polemic against philosophy. As we saw, for Sohm the relation to God is personal, not legal. The same is true for Brunner, and since Brunner holds that the object of philosophy is the impersonal, timeless, abstract orderer of the world, he infers that philosophy can gain no access to God. A different way of apprehending is required, namely, Christian revelation. The abstractions of philosophy must be replaced by the unique and particular content provided by the disclosure of God in Jesus Christ. Through Christian revelation man comes to know for the first time what it means to live in responsible community with God and neighbor; at the same time, he recognizes what his actual estrangement from God and neighbor has been.[6]

Adams points out that, for Sohm, the legalization of the primitive *ecclesia* indicates "lack of trust in the power of the divine Spirit."[7] Sohm held that "Catholicism—any Christianity dependent on divine church law with respect to doctrine or polity—is precisely an expression of original sin."[8] For Brunner, the philosophic quest is an exhibition of human pride and self-deception: man's abstractions about God become identified with divine truth; they become his idol. Thus, as Daniel Williams remarks, "what Brunner has done is to show that the problem of the relation of the law and the gospel is basic to the under-standing of the problem of philosophical interpretation of our existence."[9] The break is not between philosophy and theology for Brunner, but between both of these and faith. Theology can point to Christian truth, but faith alone can possess it; the words of theology are not the Word itself.[10] Hence, while for Sohm there are two kingdoms, for Brunner there are two truths or words and a distinct way to apprehend each. However, Brunner says that Christian revelation enables one to recognize God in the creation. This concession suggests that in Brunner's thought there is a tendency toward some rapprochement between revela-tion and reason. But in general Sohm's attack on legalism in ecclesiastical doctrine and polity is of a piece with Brunner's attack on philosophy with its abstractions.

Brunner maintains that while the Christian man's thinking loses its independence, it gains a new freedom in dependence upon God.[11] This implies that for Brunner the question is not "either freedom *or* authority." Rather, the question is: either sinful, rebellious freedom, leading to idolatry of system (false authority) *or* true freedom found through faith in and surrender to God (true authority). The notion that in dependence on God we find true freedom would be regarded with both amusement and amazement by an existentialist like Jean-Paul Sartre. In any event, it places us on our guard against supposing that the neo-Reformers interpret freedom as a sort of limited autonomy. Actually, it is difficult to see exactly what these theologians mean by freedom.

We will examine the problem in a theologian who, though oriented toward Reformation thought, seeks to alleviate to some extent the divorce between Christ and culture. Paul Tillich is certainly not content with a diastasis between Christ and cul-ture: he contends that it is the function of theology to answer the questions of secular culture, particularly those of philosophy. Thus, Tillich's theological method is that of correlation. God is the ground or power of being. He is not severed from the world; he is the depth undergirding it. Man (and the world) leaves the ground of being in order to "stand upon" himself. This is the Fall; it is estrangement from God; it is to "exist," to stand out of essence. In this situation man loses that relation to authority which Tillich calls "theonomous." He becomes "autonomous," while the church (and perhaps other institutions) imposes itself "heteronomously" in the name of "theonomy." Thus, the warfare between church and culture is a result of the loss of the depth dimension, which is actually of ultimate concern.

In his estrangement, man seeks New Being and can find it only by participation in Jesus the Christ, who was true, essential man under the conditions of existential estrangement. In the biblical picture Jesus is shown to have maintained an uninterrupted unity with the ground of being. He was able to do this because he sacrificed not only his life but also "everything in him and of him which could bring people to him as an 'overwhelming personality' instead of bringing them to that in him which is greater than he and they."[12] Thus, the Christian is freed from Jesusology. Indeed, no doctrine, ethic, polity, Scripture, or law is finally binding on the Christian. The law of love is the single exception—because it is the negation of law.

Let us now raise the issue of freedom and its relation to divine authority. Jesus as the Christ was essential God-manhood. Therefore, his freedom was true, essential freedom. He was tempted by desire for food, for acknowledgment, and for unlimited power, but in each case the desire was taken into his unbroken unity with God. If, however, Jesus really desired these things (and unless he did, he was not actually tempted), he desired to sin. Even so, he remained obedient. But, as Tillich himself argues, obedience presupposes a separation of will from will; it presupposes estrangement.[13] The upshot is that freedom, as genuine choice between God and "the devil," must be absent in the essential state, for obedience, as well as disobedience, implies estrangement. Consequently, I do not understand how one can be said to enjoy genuine freedom in the theonomous relationship. As a matter of fact, Tillich declares that "to be outside the divine life means to stand in actualized freedom."[14] He also says, however, that in the essential state (the God-manhood state), freedom and destiny are in balance. Could this mean a balance that is not actual? If not, what does it mean?

To summarize, we may say that, for Tillich, to be in relation to God is not to turn away from the world or defy its structures or contents, but rather to participate in the ground of all things, the ultimate concern and the ultimate authority. Our problem is how such participation leaves room for genuine freedom. At times, it seems that for Tillich the essential relationship of man to God is not unlike the organic relationship of, say, heart to body: the heart does not desire autonomy, nor is it capable of such desire. Though Tillich is more sympathetic toward cultural enterprises (particularly philosophy) than Sohm or Brunner (and certainly more so than Barth), nonetheless he keeps the relation between human and divine authority in the same general perspective as do they. If Sohm attacks "divine church law" and Brunner philosophy, it seems that *in effect* Tillich attacks human freedom itself, though, to be sure, the picture is not unambiguous, a fact due in part to Tillich's insistence that Jesus as the Christ was not only essential man but actual man as well (and therefore possessed actualized freedom).

Reinhold Niebuhr, whose primary contribution is in the field of ethics, also seeks to relate Christ and culture. He holds that they must be neither identified nor divorced, that their relationship is paradoxical. To understand this, it is necessary to take a look at Niebuhr's doctrine of human nature. Man has the peculiar facility of transcending himself without limit. Man is spirit; he is finite freedom. But also, he is part of nature, with its necessities, processes, and simple harmonies. Because man is free and yet involved in nature, he is anxious, and "anxiety is the internal description of the state of temptation."[15] He is tempted to deny his finitude and claim for himself unlimited knowledge, power, and goodness. He inevitably yields to this temptation, though his sinning cannot be called necessary. It would seem that this doctrine is based not so much on the "ideal possibility" of not sinning[16] but on the fact that man is conceived as basically a free creature. Yet, Niebuhr insists that sin posits or presupposes itself. He is referring to the fact of original sin, a defect of will, with unbelief in God at its root. Man, inevitably existing in pride and sensuality, is aware of his true, essential manhood, but he knows it as law which judges him. Divine grace is available to man: it is power which enables man to become what he truly ought to be, but it is also forgiveness for man's continued sin. It releases him from sin only *in principle, not in fact.*

Thus, the true self, the self with freedom directed toward God, really represents an impossible ideal for man. Inevitably he centers his loyalty about some finite object or defends some limited perspective; he always practices idolatry. Human freedom, which Niebuhr seems to hold in such high esteem, turns out to be forever involved in sin. There may, he grants, be approximations to the Christian ideal of *agape,* for man can establish justice and he can exhibit mutual love. But every such approximation is simultaneously a contradiction of the "impossible possibility" of *agape.* Thus, the situation may be called paradoxical.

Niebuhr is among the neo-Reformation theologians, who carefully avoid confusing the things of God and the things of man. Though he asserts that "the highest unity is a harmony of love in which the self relates itself in its freedom to other selves in their freedom under the will of God,"[17] it seems clear enough that on his terms the self cannot relate itself in its freedom to either neighbor or God without sinning and thereby violating the "law of love." Thus, man stands forever under the judgment of the Christian ethic of love, which he is powerless to fulfill. The implication of all this is that man must surrender his freedom if he is ever to be released from sin in fact and not merely in principle. God's ultimacy and authority can tolerate no rivalry from human freedom and creativity. Man can be freed from sin only if he is freed from freedom.

It seems that we are faced with a rather simple alternative in theology respecting human and divine authority: either synthesis, where we are committed almost from the start to making idols of our polity, of our systems and doctrines, of our autonomy; *or* diastasis, where all cultural achievement, all works of man's hand, heart, or mind, and even human freedom itself are forever less than good. It seems, in short, that the choice is between old-fashioned liberalism and neo-Reformation theology.

One of the few theologians who has tried to find a mediating position between these two camps is Daniel D. Williams. He asserts that neither camp has a place for real redemption (transformation) in history. He feels that actual growth in grace is possible, that belief in such growth is part of the Christian tradition, and that this belief is the basis of man's historical hopes. Liberals made no use of the doctrine of redemption, says Williams, because they did not see man as in need of redemption. They conceived him as a co-worker with God, building with him the kingdom on earth. The basic motif was creation rather than redemption. On the other hand, neo-Reformation theologians make no use of the doctrine of redemption because man is regarded as an incurable sinner. Williams grants that sin is far more serious than the liberals realized, and he dismisses the illusion that progress in the moral life is inevitable. On the other hand, he finds neo-Reformation theology inadequate on a number of counts. I should say that his underlying criticism of neo-Reformation theology, put in the most general terms, is that it employs dichotomies which oversimplify the facts. I do not think it would be claiming too much to say that most of these dichotomies can be regarded as species of the dualism between human and divine authority.

One acute criticism which Williams levels at Niebuhr concerns the latter's definition of *agape*. He points out that for

Niebuhr *agape* excludes any concern for the self; it is utterly self-giving. Hence, self-fulfillment is excluded by definition, and *agape* is placed beyond any reasonable possibility of attainment. Williams argues that the love revealed in Christ is a love in which the participants find their own good realized through the giving of themselves to the life of the whole. Thus, for Williams, not all self-assertion contradicts the ideal of Christian love. A second criticism of Niebuhr's position is that he regards all conflict as evil. Williams insists that conflict can and does function in the growth and good of life. He calls attention to the disciplinary coercion of children by parents, to conflict in play and sports, and to the power struggle in the politics of a democracy. Certainly not all conflict is good, but this is not a reason for denying that some types of conflict may be. Against Brunner, Williams argues that it is false to hold that all law contradicts love. For relations of love can grow only in dependence on certain impersonal elements. One need only consider the importance of privacy in personal relations. By application of impersonal principle to all members of a society, law provides one of the conditions of personal freedom. We should not condemn law, institutions, and political structure as essentially alien to the Christian ideal of love; rather, we should seek to discover the sort of laws, institutions, and political structures under which the growth of love can be furthered. Brunner, like Niebuhr, defines the Christian ideal in arbitrary and wholesale terms which place it beyond any possibility of realization within historical conditions.

Williams seeks to reconceive the relation of Christ and culture. He holds that they are not mutually exclusive, that Christian norms can be realized within historical structures and conditions. Williams believes in the possibility of real transformation of human existence in history under the reign of Christ, who must nonetheless be conceived as embattled.

I would say, in general, that the neo-Reformation theologian feels called as a Christian to a way of life or to a relationship which cannot be understood or fulfilled in terms of the structures, processes, and possibilities open to secular, natural man. The kingdom is not of this world. He feels this in part because of his conception of the freedom, sovereignty, absoluteness, and ultimacy of God. For to will, think, or act in terms of those structures, processes, and possibilities open to secular, natural man seems to jeopardize the divine majesty and authority. Given a theology where God is unconditional, where he is the Creator of all things *ex nihilo,* where he is the very power of being, etc., human works and human freedom must be viewed with justifiable suspicion. Only on the basis of some alternative conception of God can man be viewed in a different light and the transformation of his life be conceived as both a possibility and a fact.

NOTES

1. Cf. James Luther Adams, "Rudolf Sohm's Theology of Law and the Spirit," *Religion and Culture: Essays in Honor of Paul Tillich,* ed. Walter Leibrecht (New York: Harper & Brothers, 1959), Pt. VI, chap. 16, pp. 219-235.
2. Cf. *ibid.,* pp. 230, 235.
3. Cf. *ibid.,* p. 222.
4. Cf. *ibid.,* p. 233.
5. Langdon B. Gilkey, "Neo-Orthodoxy," *A Handbook of Christian Theology* (New York: Meridian Books, Inc., 1958), p. 256.
6. Cf. Daniel D. Williams, "Brunner and Barth on Philosophy," *The Journal of Religion,* XXVII (October, 1947), pp. 244-246.
7. Rudolf Sohm, *Kirchenrecht,* trans. J. L. Adams, Vol. I, pp. 162-163.
8. *Ibid.,* p. 227.
9. Williams, *The Journal of Religion,* XXVII, p. 247.
10. Cf. *ibid.,* p. 249.
11. Cf. *ibid.,* p. 245.
12. Paul Tillich, *Systematic Theology* (Chicago: The University of Chicago Press, 1951), Vol. I, p. 136.
13. *Ibid.,* Vol. II, p. 48.
14. *Ibid.,* Vol. I, p. 255.
15. Reinhold Niebuhr, *The Nature and Destiny of Man* (New York: Charles Scribner's Sons, 1953), Vol. I, p. 182.
16. Cf. *ibid.,* pp. 182-183.
17. *Ibid.,* Vol. II, p. 95.

PART THREE

WORD AND SACRAMENTS

〷11〷

Toward a Theology of Preaching

WILLIAM G. WEST

THE Christian Churches (Disciples of Christ) were born in a tradition of antitheology. Our fathers were not friendly to "theology" because they felt that "theology" was responsible for a divided church.

To be sure, some of them were theologically trained and perhaps most of them had done some reading in theological works. Basically, they were not congenial to theology because they felt that it stood in the way of restoring Christian unity. By and large, they felt that theology needed to be stripped from what they conceived to be the simple Christian message. Beyond theology, creeds and doctrines, to the purely primitive New Testament messages was the aroused cry of our founding fathers as they trumpeted their preaching on the American frontier. Somewhere I have read a statement, I believe from Paul Tillich, which our religious forefathers would have approved, to the effect that the final blasphemy is theology and theology is the final blasphemy.

One hardly needs to observe that some of our fathers were better trained in theology than they would have been willing to admit. No one of them was a creative theologian, but Thomas and Alexander Campbell, Walter Scott, and Barton W. Stone had studied some theology. Each of these men made references

241

to theologians to substantiate his beliefs. Often theology of a sort was used to combat theology.

One of the correspondents writing to Barton W. Stone proposed that instead of preaching sermons, the early reformers simply quote the Bible without comment. Stone, in his reply revealed that he sensed the sad humor in the situation when he stated that such a position would undercut both teaching and preaching.

As our students were entered in interdenominational seminaries, they were naturally enrolled in courses of theology. And around the turn of the century The College of the Bible (Lexington, Kentucky) actually used the word "theology" in connection with a biblical course.[1] This is not to imply that theology was not taught by our professors in our colleges and seminaries in various classrooms. But the word "theology" itself, until rather recent times, was more or less taboo. Only in the last fifteen or twenty years has there been very much emphasis on theology in our seminaries.

What I write here on the topic has grown largely out of my experience[2] and is addressed not to a group of theological professors but to my fellow ministers who proclaim the word in these tension-filled years. I shall deal with our present situation and then make some comments on the preacher's message.

The World in Which I Preach

One way to describe our present situation is to use adjectives. As long as I can remember hearing speakers, which dates back to about 1920, they have been using such expressions as "changing world" and "revolutionary age." Today speakers still sprinkle their sermons and speeches with such hackneyed observations as "I traveled from St. Louis to Chicago in the time it took my grandfather to go out to the barn and hitch the horses to a wagon." Most illustrations of the speed in communication and transportation are outdated by the time the speaker writes his speech and mounts the platform. If he has been so unfortunate as to use the same illustration for six months, he is hopelessly relegated, by the rising generation, to prehistoric days. History in the minds of most early teen-agers began in the dim and distant years of 1945.

My own preaching is done in a world where I have had a brief personal encounter with satellite Communism. The first experience came in 1953, a few days after the now-famous workers' strike, originating in the Brandenburg Gate, on June 17, One morning in a remodeled bombed-out factory building, a group of us saw expellees and refugees from East Germany being "processed." We of the Sherwood Eddy Seminar interviewed some of these people and heard their own stories of conditions in East Germany and what they hoped to gain in their flight to freedom. Later, we crossed over into East Berlin, divided into small groups of four or five persons, aided not by the American army, but only by German students and pastors. For four long hours that afternoon, I seemed to have lived years. I never saw anyone physically threatened the whole afternoon. Only in the faces of the people did I see mirrored the silent terror of living under rulers who had sent armed tanks down the Unter Den Linden and against which bare fists, sticks, and stones had proved weak and pathetic weapons. No one talked; no one laughed. The atmosphere was stifling. No play in a theatre could reproduce it; no great writer could re-create it. As long as I live, I shall hear the cry of silence in the streets of East Berlin where people seemed to be walking automatons in a graveyard. The very air one breathed in East Berlin seemed to be different from that in West Berlin.

My preaching is done in a world where Communism is a growing umbrella covering more and more of the earth's surface, and yet America itself has shown peculiar resistance to Marxian Communism.

I preach in a world also where racial strife has engulfed all nations in new dimensions of depth. Race riots in South Africa, New York, Chicago, Detroit, and in most Southern cities have grown in violence and influence. The decision of the U.S. Supreme Court in 1954 has changed the entire world outlook for nonwhite people. In the Southern States it has caused an unrest and a ferment which is slowly unsettling attitudes and ways of life. Perhaps a generation will go by before ugly racial antagonisms will die down enough for the social historian to give the verdict: an adjustment has been made. Strife in the Congo is a parable of the deep disorder occasioned by racial and political tension all over the earth.

I preach in a world where mental illness has made a terrific impact on life. When I audited seminar courses in psychiatry in the early 1940's at Yale, Dr. Kahn, formerly of Vienna, taught a theory of "psychopathic destiny." He offered little hope for people suffering certain illnesses. But now shock treatments and drugs have changed the outlook for thousands of the mentally ill who otherwise might have been condemned to perpetual mental darkness.

Mental illness though, which strikes about one person in every twelve, is still baffling. Many guesses exist regarding its causes but no psychiatric school can be definitive on either the cause of mental illness or why certain cures work. But laymen have all kinds of theories and popular peace-of-mind ministers of the "don't worry" school still persist in giving easy answers on causes and cures which no reputable psychiatrist will endorse as definitive.

I preach in a world of anxiety. Whereas in the Middle Ages the great problem was guilt, today the deepest problem of people is ontological loneliness. Added to this individual sense of loneliness, is the deep feeling of anxiety about the world itself. For the terrifying events of the last fifty years have shaken the easy confidence men once had about progress and the salvation of the world.

In reaction to World War I and World War II, the Korean War, the Russian Revolution, the Chinese Revolution, the horror of Nazi Germany, racial strife all over the world; men have grown discouraged, pessimistic, and cynical. Millions have given up faith in God.

Theologically speaking, in addition to the anxieties we have already mentioned, there are three other anxieties which are universal and timeless. There is the anxiety prompted by fate and death. Man is mortal and must die. He is subject to fate. There is the terror inspired by the feeling of the ultimate meaninglessness of life itself. Albert Camus stated before his death that man's problem is not to launch a satellite around the sun, but to discover if life is worth living. There is the anxiety which comes from the overpowering force of sin. Guilt is deeply imbedded in man.

I preach in a world where science is less rigidly dominating than formerly but is still all powerful in the popular minds as well as educated minds.

God created the heavens and the earth, according to Genesis. But science has done so much with heaven and earth, that modern man, unconsciously perhaps, feels that the scientist created everything. The man of faith must be grateful for the achievements of the scientist in such fields as physics, mathematics, chemistry, and engineering.

Surely, there are scientists who are deep men of faith and whose philosophy of science is congenial to religious belief. Modern science is a potential ally of Christian faith. Modern scientism, however, deifies scientific procedures. "Scientism," as Frederick West pointed out in a chapter in the Interseminary Series, "absolutizes science."[3] Scientism assumes that science is the natural savior of mankind.

One of the most exciting changes in recent years, however, has been the breakdown of the basis for nineteenth-century dogmatism regarding total rigidity in the determination of natural events which involved the implication that a very similar rigidity determined all human events. As recently as fifty years ago science posited the theory that if we know the positions and velocities of particles and if we knew enough about the forces between them, we could predict the future activities of these particles, and even their past histories.

This determinateness of nature has been changed with the quantum theory which says that we are to think not so much in terms of deterministic laws as statistical averages. The quantum theory cannot predict the future position and velocity of an electron from knowledge of its present state because some indeterminateness is involved. One can talk only about statistical probabilities. Similarly, one sees much the same thing in the case of liquid helium. Under certain conditions, it will do extraordinary things, such as defy the law of gravitation. Thus the quantum theory is needed to describe the properties of liquid helium. All of this holds promise that the scientist and the religious man do not have to be condemned to perpetual warfare with each other. One cannot assume, however, that the theologian and the scientist have already come together on the same ground. Scientism is still powerful and the popular mind which worships gadgets and things tends to idolize applied science or technology.

I preach in a religious world which is dominantly conservative, and sectarian, but which shows signs of wanting ecumenicity.

I refer not to the particular geographical part of the world in which my ministry is cast. The conservatism of the "Bible Belt" is well known. But the entire Christian world is basically conservative and in a sense fundamentalistic.

All denominations have creative and progressive religious thinkers and leaders. But the rank and file of all but a very few denominations are conservative, and many of the most powerful denominations are traditional. The historic creedal churches are basically conservative in their religious outlook. My observation is that this is not simply a matter of formal creed; it involves also a matter of the nonofficial religious presuppositions of the people who comprise the denominations.

The world in which I preach is basically sectarian in its approach. We celebrate ecumenicity, but in the matter of evangelism, for example, there is actually a fierce competition to win people to a particular denomination. This competition which is world-wide among Christians, except for a few areas where comity is practiced, cuts through business, commercial, social, and political life. It has its good side. It gives people an active muscular faith. It has its bad side. It creates pride. This competition, however, is sinful because it wastes tremendous reservoirs of resources which are needed to propagate the Christian faith in a world where the Christian faith is losing the battle from a numerical standpoint.

Over against this sectarian competition is a growing concern, especially among top-level leaders, for an ecumenical church. Recently the World Council of Churches' executive committee voted to accept eight new church bodies into its membership which now comprises 178 denominations. Although the ecumenical movement is not yet a grass-roots event, ecumenicity is one of the heartening facts of contemporary church life. One cannot describe all of the primary forces which make up the world in which we preach, such as the labor movement, the new depths of destruction in weapons of warfare, the various spiritual life movements within Protestant churches, and the religion of recreation which even the Soviets with their recently won Olympic Games gold medals seem to espouse.

One other influence upon the world in which I preach must be noted, namely, the rise of existentialism in many forms and areas of life. All one can do in a paper of this kind is to make some general comments about existentialism, and its growing importance for the Christian preacher. A study of existential philosophy focuses attention on the struggle between contemporary Christianity and so-called secularism.

Existentialism protests against the forces which destroy freedom. It calls men away from stifling conformity. It deals with basic problems; such as the meaning of being a self, how to use our freedom and how to find courage to meet death. And it challenges each individual to wrestle with these problems instead of taking answers from others.

Existentialism raises ultimate questions. But it does not answer them. It cannot serve as a self-sufficient philosophy. It may lead one to Christian faith but, when it leads even to atheism, it is important that the Christian thinker understand individuals who stand in "utter loneliness" and stare at "bleak emptiness." These unbelievers are honest enough to voice the sense of despair which is so widespread in our world.

David E. Roberts, before his untimely death, outlined some of the claims existentialism makes upon religious people. He mentioned five important points of contact between existentialism and religious people:

(a) Existentialist ways of thinking can be "salutary" in warning us against idolizing science which leads to the "dehumanization" of Western culture. Once this negative battle is over, Christian theology and philosophy can be more sympathetic to the constructive part which science and objective reason are able to play in serving the spiritual ends of individual and communal living. It is in this direction many feel that Karl Heim is now successfully moving.

(b) This movement has much to offer religious believers by plumbing the depths of human existence. It explores the "terrifying terrain of guilt, anxiety, despair, and nothingness." This preoccupation with somber themes, which has been also the work of depth-psychology, is repelling to the average optimistic church member. One cannot, however, turn away from the irrational and demonic forces of life. The Christian gospel cannot heal unless it comes to grips with the forces of sin, despair, and death. Men like Job, in their suffering, wrestled with God and we, too, cannot be content with easy and neat theories about God.

(c) Existentialism can give us significant understanding of the relationship between faith and reason. According to existentialism, philosophy does not have to engage in "abstract specula-

248

tion about being itself." It may take other "forms than those of rational structure, logical system, or universal meanings." It asserts that metaphysics or ontology may speak inside "the vivid, concrete personal language of drama and poetry." The way thus may be opened "toward a concordat between faith and philosophic reason." This approach, in the opinion of Roberts, may lead to the liberation of "dogmatic and systematic theology." The new approach will almost certainly be shaped by "images and categories which are closer to those of the Bible than to those typically used in contemporary idealisms, naturalisms, and positivisms." Such an enterprise, to quote Pascal, will avoid each of two extremes: "to exclude reason, and to admit reason only."

(d) A review of the existentialist movement will aid the contemporary Christian apologist by offering a penetrating analysis of the conditions of unfaith. Too much Christian theology today "tries to convince modern man that he is already in despair." The true apologist is one whose faith carries him to the "point of self-identification with those to whom, after all, God is not a premise, but a question or a target." Theologians must not count it virtuous "to overlook the degree to which we too are modern men for whom the world is broken and falling apart."

(e) A final point of relevance between existentialism and religious belief lies at the point of human freedom. Atheistic existentialists insist that man's self-realization is attained only as he masters his own destiny apart from an "illusory, invented God." Believing existentialists, on the other hand, maintain that genuine human freedom is achieved only by renouncing this egocentric attempt to run life all by oneself, and through finding highest happiness in communion with the living God.

The hope of David E. Roberts was that existentialism would not be used as a philosophical support for Christian faith, but rather that existential explorations might be made from a Christian base. If this development takes place, then religious belief would transcend existentialism by including it. Those who believe in God then will see that the ultimate nature of faith is a decision between God and nothing, which man must make for himself. And having made it, commitment becomes conviction and conviction comprehends "the strange ways of God, whose absence is a kind of presence and whose silence is a mysterious mode of speaking to us."[4]

Religion and Science

Many theologians in modern times have tried to harmonize religion and science. F. R. Tennent, Henry Nelson Wieman, and D. C. Mackintosh were exponents of such theologies. But they are not likely to be revived. Today such men as Karl Heim, Teilhand de Chardin, and William Pollard of Oak Ridge have written creatively on the relation of Christian faith and the modern, scientific world view.

Before attempting to express an outline of my theology of preaching I must deal briefly with Rudolf Bultmann whose positions on communicating faith are related to modern science. Bultmann's main concern is that the Christian preacher and teacher do not state the faith in out-of-date terms so as to give modern man the opportunity of discussing or rejecting the terms we use, instead of coming to face the challenge of the gospel itself.

The mythological language of the Bible, and largely of Christian tradition, is pretty much out of date according to Bultmann. Our outlook on the world today is scientific even though we may not be scientists. We may not know or understand what men like Einstein say, but we no longer think as biblical writers did of a "three-storied" world where man lives on the ground floor, the devil and his minions in the basement, while God and his allies dwell in the heavens above the firmament.

Christian preaching and the biblical story of our redemption have been couched in terms that use or imply such a three-story view of the world. Consequently, many outside the church think that they can reject it by dismissing the mythological framework in which the gospel is presented to them, while some inside the church think that such or similar mythological elements are substantial parts of the faith. Parenthetically, we may remark that the Russians in launching Sputnik declared the revolving satellite proved that there was no heaven up there.

So Bultmann urges a demythologized presentation of the gospel independent of any particular world-view, whether Semitic, Hellenistic, Newtonian, or Einsteinian. He thinks he has found the way to it in the recognition that our myths make plain to us man's actual situation.

The biblical myth that man is open to invasion from the demons below, or from angelic powers from above, is, for example, one possible mythological way of saying that human life is open to both good and evil influences. By using this sort of methodology in treating myths Bultmann feels that two aims are accomplished: (1) We can state its essential meaning without the ambiguities and inaccuracies inherent in the language of myth as such. (2) Not only do we translate myth into some other verbal form, but we move its acceptance or rejection from the sphere of intellectual speculation into the world of experience where decisions are made. When the preacher states that a divine deliverer once came from heaven to free men from captivity to demons, we could reply that, as there is no such place as heaven, we must discredit the story. But "demythologize" it into the form that divine help is available in every human situation, and we can affirm or deny it by putting it to the test. Knowledge then becomes dependent upon decision or commitment.

Bultmann unquestionably has done the modern preacher a great service. Ancient cosmology and mythological figures need modern existential counterparts. The church did use mythological forms in recounting the gospel story. Mere historical knowledge of Christ, as Luther said long ago, is not enough. Belief in Christ does mean committing oneself to the power and help he brings in the present. Many, however, including myself, cannot divorce the historical Christ from the existential Christ. Part of my confession is that he lived and died and arose again. If mere historical knowledge is inadequate, so is mere existential knowledge equally inadequate.

The Nature of Theology

Two main conceptions of the content of theology have existed in the church. The traditional conception is that the theologian is concerned to interpret the revelation of God to man. Revelation in its simplest definition means disclosure, and this viewpoint is that theological content is provided objectively by an act of God himself. Such divine self-disclosure is seen primarily in the life, death, and resurrection of Jesus Christ. More generally, revelation is to be found in the Bible as a record of the experiences of the Hebrew people and of the words which God spoke to their leaders and prophets; of the events of Jesus' career and the teachings in which he sought to make the nature and will of God manifest to his hearers. This revelation is seen in the growth of the Christian community following the death of Jesus. Still more generally, this viewpoint holds that God makes himself known to man through the whole realm of nature and in the whole sweep of history, as well as in focal points of illumination and vision which help make plain the meaning of life in our human struggle. Here the primary stress is on the initiative of God. The work of the theologian is to observe, describe, and interpret the truth which is given to men by God who reveals himself in these various media.

For centuries this traditional view of revelation was attacked and finally the opposition came to focus in Schleiermacher in the early nineteenth century. Schleiermacher undertook the systematic elaboration of the content of religious experience. In him the emphasis shifted from the objective act of God to the response of man. In religion, stated Schleiermacher, we are aware of the basic unity of all things and of our own ultimate and unconditional dependence upon the ground of that unity.[5] As religious beings, we have a feeling of absolute dependence upon God coupled with a deep sense of inadequacy and sin. To interpret and systematize the observable content of human experience is the task of the theologian. This view has come to be associated with liberal Protestant thought and in recent years has been under heavy attack.

Personally, in view of man's predicament, I feel that the primary emphasis in preaching must be placed on the impact God has made on man. At the same time, man's response to God's initiative is inseparable from God's self-revelation. Theology is concerned with this response as well as with the great reality which confronts man. Theology deals with God who works through nature, history, personal experience and centrally through Jesus Christ.

An Approach to a Theology of Preaching

I cannot outline in this article a complete theology of my preaching. It changes more often than I realize. There are some questions I simply have not been able to resolve as, for example, the question of baptism on which I still seek light. After I have made some comments on the theological base of my preaching, I shall conclude with a modern statement of faith which I hope to introduce to the members of our congregation in Chattanooga.

I. PREACHING A CHRISTIAN DOCTRINE OF MAN

Christianity takes a realistic view of man. In the seventeenth century, Pascal wrote: "Christianity is strange. It bids man recognize that he is vile, even abominable; and bids him desire to be like God. Without such a counterpoise, this dignity would make him horribly vain, or this humiliation would make him terribly abject."[6]

The Christian doctrine of man accepts neither an extremely pessimistic nor an overly optimistic position regarding man. It says that there are two factors in the situation. There is what is, and there is what ought to be. Man stands somewhere in between. Man is an animal, a child of the natural world. He is continually immersed in nature. Man is a restless animal. He is haunted by dreams and memories. His mind reaches back into the past and thrusts itself forward into the future. Man realizes possibilities never seen before. A struggle for fredom perpetually goes on inside him. Man is a critic and a builder. He judges the stream of events. This frees him to some extent. He remakes part of his environment. He remakes an unseen environment. He makes an unseen environment called culture which molds his life.

The Christian theology of man asserts: (1) Man is created according to the image of God. (2) Man is corrupted through sin. (3) Man is restored in Christ. This is the story of man's life according to Christianity as I understand it. Man is not simply a child of nature whose destiny is fulfilled on earth.

(1) Man is not self-originated. He has not always been, but he has come into being. Man is created in the image of God. This does not mean that man looks like God. In what sense is man created in God's image? It means that man is a rational being who can discover truth and determine his conduct by goals he chooses himself. It means more than this. The "image of God" in man consists not only of his rational capacity to find ultimate truth and value but, also, of his capacity for faith and love. Man is capable of responding to the presence of God. Man is a responsible being; he can see truth, beauty, and righteousness. Animals respond to the stimuli of nature. Man can also respond to the claims of consistency, fairness, and justice. Man can respond to claims which do not exert physical force on him. He responds in love and devotion. Man may not do this most of the time, but he is capable of doing so. Man is capable of knowing himself confronted by the presence of God.

Man has evolved slowly over the years as a cooperating neighbor. He is not a Robinson Crusoe. His animal ancestry is always

254

present, but it is always in the context of a social group. Man
has to be freshly evoked into the status of a person. This gives
us a picture of emergence when the selfsame process is repeated
over and over again. Creation is not final.

(2) Christianity sees man as corrupted by sin. He is responsible
in part for sin. Man finds himself in the grip of evil which breaks
down persons so that they are no longer persons at all.

The question may be raised, what is the essence of sin? It is
a violation of the will of God; a violation of what is right. Sin is
also a violation of man's own nature. Man is capable of responding to God if he is fully himself. He, however, often fails to be
the person he ought to be. He does wrong. There are poisons
which ruin the springs of his action. He is a sinner.

Sometimes man willfully does wrong. Perhaps a large share
of destruction arises out of man's ignorance. He makes muddle-
headed decisions; his actions may be impulsively dangerous. Sin
may be a cumulative web of social wrongs which persist to the
third and fourth generations.

When man is thus in alienation from himself and the world,
he no longer promptly responds to God or his social community.
He becomes a stranger. His insensitivity is increased. He sees
light, but does not respond to it. He does not always wish to be
destructive. A great sense of frustration descends upon him.
Inner civil war arises inside him. Christian theology which is
realistic does not flee from man's real and complex predicament.

(3) My own understanding of the Christian doctrine of man
is that there is *little* that man can do for himself. He can be
restored only in Christ. Hope for man lies not in man's goodness, but in God's initiative. Man can be made whole because
God makes him whole. When a man is corrupted by egoism,
pride, and sensuality, his natural capacities become instruments
of self-love rather than the servants of the love of God and love
of neighbor. Modern man who suffers from emptiness of life is
offered the Christian way of reconciliation with God through
Christ.

II. Preaching a Christian Theology of God

(a) What we say regarding God has to be cast in the context of Paul Tillich's statement, that to argue that God exists is to deny him. God does not exist, because he is the ground of existence. The arguments for the existence of God, he states, are really arguments for the reality or the truth of the idea of God. The traditional arguments for the reality of the idea of God are helpful in strengthening faith, but are not conclusive.

The idea of a divine reality which confronts man and evokes the response of worship cannot be proved. Personally, I contemplate with horror the alternatives which open themselves to me if the world is without God. For millions of people, however, I am forced to realize that there is little terror in the idea of a universe without God. Speculative proofs of his existence and goodness have little appeal to me. Somewhere I make the beginning leap of faith in him who is a beginning without a beginning, and an end without an end.

(b) God is our ultimate goal. He is the good beyond which there is no greater good.

(c) Whatever God is, the Christian affirmation is that God in some ways is like a person. Practically all Christians, except the most childlike, recoil from primitive anthropomorphism. Yet, God is not a gaseous vertebrate.

In attributing a "personal" character to God, the Christian is only using an analogy derived from imperfect human beings. God cannot be comprehended fully. Against this misconception Christian thinkers have constantly warred. Christians, however, have said that God is personal in order to express their living relation to him and to safeguard the idea of God against vagueness and subpersonal conceptions.

(d) Christians state that God is near. He is immanent and he is also transcendent, or beyond the world. Do we mean that God is here like oranges in a crate? This concept is too childlike. Or is God like light, as an energy which pervades the whole of life?

Or is God in the world as our thoughts are in the world? If he is alive, he is the ground, or source, of all that goes on. God is cause of origin.

God is also transcendent. He is beyond. We can communicate with each other through signals, but each of us transcends the other. There is much that we do not know about other people.

(e) God is near and God is far. God is as far as you and I are far from one another. He is as near as we are near at the same time.[7] God is not identical with us. His thoughts are not our thoughts; his ways are not our ways. We can think God's thoughts after him, but not at the same time. God is within, yet he is beyond.

(f) Christian thought has found deep meaning in God as trinity. He is Father, Son, and Spirit. He is rich and diverse.

He is Father and Sovereign Lord. We depend upon his being and his forever bringing into being something which is new. God, it seems to me, doesn't push man around. He is not like a magnet attracting iron filings. But his being creates and sustains everything.

Biologists tell us that there is evidence that the earth in its origin at one time had an atmosphere of heavy gases such as methane, ammonia, and hydrogen. Some way a combination of these resulted in the building stones of living materials being formulated in the so-called amino acids. In some unknown process amino acids are supposed to have gathered in more complex organizational states. In time the ability of these organizational states to reproduce themselves occurred and living matter as we know it evolved. Could creation have arisen as a grand accident or was there a directing hand in creation? The Christian believes that God lies back of past and present processes of creation.

We say that he is Almighty, but however it may seem to you, it appears to me that God is limited in some ways. God cannot create anything which contradicts his own nature. Even God cannot violate the demand for consistency. God cannot create

God. Why then do we call him "Almighty"? Because in spite of all the logical difficulties, God is ultimately in control of the world.

God is also the ground of the good. He is God the Redeemer or the Son. He is not indulgent. He confronts man with what is righteous. This is judgment. He cares not only for man, but ". . . God is bound to his creation and to his creatures by the strongest of all ties: God loves the world."[8] In the New Testament, he is encountered as the One who promises "a new heaven and a new earth."

God is also Holy Spirit. He is the lifegiver. He is regenerating Spirit. God is not a blind force. He is a surging tide of energy which underlies all of life. The Holy Spirit of God pervades the Christian community.

We believe that God is one as the Creator who made us, as the Redeemer who calls us to higher levels of life, as the Holy Spirit who is the Lifegiver.

III. Preaching a Christian Theology of Jesus Christ

I cannot escape the fact that one of the distinctive characteristics of Christian theology is that the focal, crucial, decisive revelation of God to man is to be found in Jesus of Nazareth who has been called Messiah, Christos, Savior, and the Lord. Not in a few words or even in a few isolated events, but rather in the total impact of his life upon his own time and upon subsequent history one finds oneself confronted by an event which requires a genuine response. As I preach, I feel that I am under obligation to cast his illumination of life upon life in our day that men may still find in him light for their darkness and life for their destruction.

Early Christian preaching affirmed that the life and death of Jesus are fully understood only when they are seen as manifestations of the redemptive power of God incarnate in a perfect man.

He gave men a new hold on life. Christ brought regenerating power to them in a world of struggle. The early message was about Christ because they felt his power. Paul said, "We preach Christ crucified" (1 Corinthians 1:23a) and "God was in Christ reconciling the world to himself" (2 Corinthians 5:19a).

Jesus had no social prestige. He was a working man. There is no evidence that he studied in the School of the Rabbis; but when he spoke, he spoke as one having authority. He was a prophet, a trail-blazer in the realm of Hebrew religion.[9]

Jesus said that the sovereignty of God would ultimately make the world over. By this he meant that man's sad story must be changed. God's sovereignty must be acknowledged. A day of judgment will arrive when the people who are in trouble and of low degree will be elevated. Jesus had a vivid sense of the presence of God which brought healing to men.

Jesus portrayed his teaching in the duties of the citizens of the kingdom. He made more searching demands on men than had been made before. The inner attitude must be good so that man's acts will be good. Life must be so transparent that it is obvious that it is good.

His followers were sure that he was the Messiah. Some of them thought that he might become a fighting leader and lead revolts against Roman power. He apparently did not think in such terms. As the end drew near, he talked in concepts that were increasingly baffling—about going the second mile, turning the other cheek, of his suffering unto death and taking upon himself a weight of punishment to set others free. The glimpses into his mind are often elusive in the Gospels, but he came to be thought of as a radical Messiah whose teaching was dealt with by crucifixion.

Christian preaching began not as a system of thought, but as a spontaneous and enthusiastic proclamation on the part of the followers of Jesus, "after a transformation in their lives so amazing as to be almost inconceivable." To despondent disciples in whom hope had been quenched, Jesus came back with new power. If we follow Paul's account and the more probable of the two main lines of tradition in the synoptic records, we are informed that to Peter and to James, to the twelve and to a great company, Jesus appeared with great power after his death. The power they derived from the conviction of his resurrection was greater than any they had experienced while he was alive in the flesh. The familiar sovereignty and fatherhood of God was set in the new perspective of the resurrection.

The church from the beginning tried to find words that were adequate to describe Jesus. It gradually developed the idea of the Messiah or the Anointed One. The non-Jewish world, however, did not respond to the idea of the Anointed One. In preaching to Gentiles, another sort of interpretation was used. Jesus was proclaimed as "Lord." To those familiar with mystery religions, this concept meant that Jesus was God, or at least divine, and could give them some of that divine power.

The "Son of God" was another title used. It could be interpreted in two quite different ways. The phrase Son of God might mean generically any human being, or specifically the celestial messianic figures mentioned in the Books of Daniel and Enoch. In the New Testament, Son of God seems to refer, first of all and uniquely, to Jesus Christ, and then secondly, to his followers who through him are empowered to become sons of God. As applied to Jesus, the title left room for diverse conceptions. But more and more, he came to be regarded as the Son of God sent to redeem all men, the Savior of male and female, Jew and Gentile, bond and free.

A high Christology was born in the vivid impression Jesus made during his earthly career. But Christology grew also for men like Paul—out of the consciousness of the profound change wrought in their lives by faith in him and union with his Spirit. Liberation from sin and fear produced love, joy, and peace. In gratitude, the early Christians gave Christ the glory. According to the Fourth Gospel, Jesus was the incarnation of the eternal Word which co-existed with God in the beginning as the source of life and light, finally taking the form of flesh in order to bring eternal life to men. The early Christians, it would seem, exalted Jesus not as a "second God" but as the one in whom God dwelt to reconcile the world to himself.

Unfortunately, the Council of Chalcedon A.D. 451 which sought to safeguard the full human nature of Jesus and his full divine nature was unable to still the controversy. It tried to put into words what cannot be put into words. The biblical assertions that God was in Christ reconciling the world to himself and that he is the "likeness of the unseen God" are more important to me than any doctrine which seeks to explain in literal and dogmatic fashion that which cannot be comprehended fully or expressed in words.

For modern men, we can still say that Jesus was the Son of God and he was the son of man. He was part and parcel of ongoing natural life. He voiced the cultural strain of his people. But he was also the Son of God, coming from beyond the natural order as we know it. He brought redemption and the life-giving energy of God into the historical stream. He was in our own way of living and yet above it. For our own age—for the beaten generation, the generation of despair, the generation of unrealized social, economic, and political dreams—he exemplified these principles: that resurrection comes from suffering, that God reigns, that Herod and Caesar do not have the last word, that the forgotten man will take part in the work of God. In this way, I try to combine some of the elements of the traditional and the liberal approach to Jesus Christ in my own preaching.

"The simple language of Jesus Christ himself," says Richard Niebuhr, "furnishes to most Christians the most intelligible key to his own purpose and to that of the community gathered around him."[10]

Ralph G. Wilburn has said, "Revelatory preaching points away from itself and toward Christ. It is addressed to man, but toward Christ."[11] We point toward Christ as the final revelation because, as Tillich states, (1) he maintained unity with God, and (2) he sacrificed everything he could have gained for himself from this unity.[12]

IV. Preaching a Christian Theology Regarding the Church

The church is not a social club, it is not a political organization, an economic cell, or a forensic society, though in modern Protestantism, it often splinters into atomic debating divisions. "The church," says Julian Hartt, "is the fellowship of those who honor Christ as Lord and are sustained in a new being by the Holy Spirit."[13] Since the church is composed of imperfect human beings, it often competes for position and has the weaknesses of other institutions composed of sinful men. But I agree with Richard Niebuhr that ". . . no substitute can be found for the definition of the goal of the Church as the *increase among men of the love of God and neighbor.*"[14] National origins and race ought not to be a basis or barrier to membership in the church.

(a) The early church was born in the outpouring of the Spirit of God. In time these enthusiastic teachers realized that they had to be marked off from the surrounding world. The church became the new Israel, the true heir to the promises which God had made to Abraham and his progeny centuries before. A foretaste of the full glory to come was already granted to those upon whom the Spirit had come. Sensitive imagination, and power to speak in an extraordinary way, and courage to defy ecclesiastical and political authority, mastery over physical weakness and fears, these gifts came to the early Christian community.

(b) In the early church there were two fundamental sacraments —baptism and the Lord's Supper. Baptism represents a cleansing away of the old life in a ritual washing and a putting on of Christ in a new life. The Lord's Supper represents an eating and drinking together in fellowship—a sacrifice to God. The sacrament was an (1) oath or pledge to be faithful to one's duty.

(2) It was a symbol or sign of divine grace. (3) It was a remembrance or memorial linking one with the past.

When the early Christians came together, the common meal had two phases. On the one hand, Christians came together for a love feast which was apparently preceded by a ritual blessing of wine and broken bread after the pattern of the Last Supper. The Eucharist was regarded as an expression of gratitude for God's favor and an expression of the glory to come.

(c) This church, as Robert L. Calhoun has pointed out, is characterized by five figures or images in Scripture. (1) It is a chosen community of God's people. (2) It is a holy community composed of saints. (3) It is a fellowship of unity. (4) It is a medium of divine action in history. (5) It is an eschatologically oriented community—a vast company of strangers seeking a homeland not of earth.[15]

(d) These are four characteristics which emerged early in the history of the church: (1) Unity, (2) Holiness, (3) Catholicity, and (4) Apostolicity. To conserve these values for present times, Dr. Calhoun urges that we see the church as a genuine historical reality in time but, beyond time, as both human and divine. Another characterization is to see the church as an eschatologically oriented community.

Unity becomes real primarily in God's gracious action in history; in "Jesus Christ our head and the quickener of our faith" and in the Holy Spirit continually giving us life. If we insist on making unity in our own image, "we accentuate our differences." All of our streams come from one fountain. Therefore, no form or order or creed in the church's life represents perfect unity. We can trust God's purpose and power to maintain and to enhance living unity among us and within us. We can look in faith to Jesus Christ as Lord of the church and of mankind and see in him—who is one Lord of us all—the power and wisdom of God making us one.

Dr. Calhoun describes the God-given unity of the church as

wholeness.[16] The unity we seek is holiness and catholicity. It is God's saving gift evoking our response.

The mind of Christ works in the members of the church as norm and motive. It is a "sacramental corporate community" where God and man meet whether in burning bush, or stable, or the place of a skull. But perfection is not found even in the church. The Christian hope is that a transformed church may see and rejoice in God's holiness and reflect it in its common life and "be lighted by it. "

The church must be catholic in the sense of being inclusive and being orthodox, states Calhoun.[17] The church must be inclusive in its evangelism and also in its communion among all Christians, and in the recognition that God can deal with our honest differences.

The church that is catholic must be apostolic, in outreach and also in continuity of message. Unity cannot be self-centered or self-seeking. As it communicates to a world in need, its message is not a possession, but a trust for others. The church fulfills itself in spending itself.

The one, holy, catholic, apostolic church is sent by its Lord "not to be served but to serve."[18]

The unity of the church is present—it also is to come in the mercy of God. And it will come as Christians of all communions grow up together into Christ who is the Lord of life and of his church.

Conclusion

I conclude with the following statement of faith which I have written for experimental use in services of worship in our own church in Chattanooga. I must forego the opportunity of commenting on each article of this declaration of faith, but I trust that most of them are implicit in the preceding outline of a few elements involved in my historical, interpretive, and apologetic theology. I have entitled this "A Modern Statement of Faith for Members of the Christian Churches (Disciples of

Christ) Who Are Opposed to Totalitarian Systems, and Who Accept the Findings of Modern Science, and Love Freedom." This is a proclamation and is not intended to be a rule of faith.

I believe in God the Father-Creator, who eons ago caused the universe and all living things to come into being. I believe that he, in the long process of time, brought forth man after his likeness and endowed him with worth and dignity.

I believe that God inspired ancient man to worship his name and taught the leaders and prophets of Israel to do justly, to love mercy, and to walk humbly before him.

I believe in Jesus Christ, the Son of the living God, who lived, died, and arose again, whose living presence abides with us always. He is King of kings, Lord of lords, and Ruler of all earthly rulers.

I believe in the teachings and spirit of Jesus Christ as a perfect guide for imperfect lives. I believe that God's will should be done on earth as it is done in heaven.

I believe in the one holy, apostolic, universal church, born under the old covenant, coming to full birth on the day of Pentecost, and continuing as a redemptive fellowship among men and nations.

I believe in the invisible church composed of the followers of Christ of every denomination and of every age. I believe that the divided body of Christ should be one, permitting many forms of belief, worship, and church order.

I believe that baptism is a symbol of the death, burial, and resurrection of Jesus Christ our Lord, and that it is a spiritual door into the church universal. I believe in the weekly celebration of the Holy Communion or Lord's Supper. I believe in the guidance of the Holy Spirit in shedding forth new light on the word of God. I believe in the forgiveness of individual and social sins; the fellowship of the great cloud of witnesses who have gone before, the resurrection of the spiritual body and the life everlasting.

NOTES

1. Roscoe Pierson, librarian of The College of the Bible, has discovered this in the seminary records.

2. Now that I have completed this paper, for example, I know that I use the Old Testament more in my preaching than is indicated here. In my preaching I quote Fosdick, Barth, Reinhold Niebuhr, and others who have influenced me but who are scarcely mentioned in this paper.

3. Frederick West, "Christianity and Organized Education," in *The Interseminary Series* Volume I, edited by Randolph Crump Miller (New York: Harper and Brothers, 1946), Book Two, Part II, Chapter 7, p. 159.

4. David E. Roberts, *Existentialism and Religious Belief* (New York: Oxford University Press, 1957), pp. 333-341.

5. Friedrich Schleiermacher, *The Christian Faith*, edited by H. R. Mackintosh and J. S. Stewart (Edinburgh: T. and T. Clark, 1928), pp. 16-17.

6. Blaise Pascal, *Pensées* (London: J. M. Dent and Sons, Ltd., 1932), p. 144.

7. I do not wish to engage in hairsplitting over theological concepts here any more than I do in my sermons. I realize that God is not "far off" in a physical sense, but that the idea of transcendence to the theologians involves perfection of being and power of God. Similarly, immanence has to do, not with a mediating agency, but rather with immediate operation as the mind enjoys an immediate efficacy of operation with the brain.

8. Julian Norris Hartt, *Toward a Theology of Evangelism* (Nashville: Abingdon Press, 1955), p. 23.

9. I am greatly indebted to Robert L. Calhoun's seminary lectures in Christian Doctrine for my Christology. His statements were at times so illuminating they have become my own.

10. H. Richard Niebuhr, *The Purpose of the Church and Its Ministry* (New York: Harper and Row, Publishers, Inc., 1956), p. 31.

11. Ralph G. Wilburn, *The Prophetic Voice in Protestant Christianity* (St. Louis: The Bethany Press, 1956), p. 208.

12. Paul Johannes Tillich, *Systematic Theology* (Chicago: University of Chicago Press, 1951), I, 135.

13. Hartt, *op. cit.*, p. 64.

14. Niebuhr, *op. cit.*, p. 31.

15. Robert L. Calhoun, "Christ and the Church," in *The Nature of the Unity We Seek*, edited by Paul S. Minear (St. Louis: The Bethany Press, 1958), pp. 66-68.

16. *Ibid.*, p. 77.

17. *Ibid.*, p. 77.

18. *Ibid.*, p. 78.

𒀭12𒀭

The Origin and Meaning
of Christian Baptism

J. Philip Hyatt

B APTISM is one of the seven sacraments of the Roman Catholic Church and one of the two ordinances or sacraments recognized by most of the Protestant churches. It is, and has been, practiced in various forms and with varied meanings.

There is renewed interest today in baptism, as there is in the sacraments in general. This interest is partly in the origin and early meaning of the rite, and partly in the meaning it should have for Christians today. New evidence has come to light since 1948 that may have a bearing on the problem of the origin of baptism. The purpose of this chapter is to discuss the origin and meaning of the rite of baptism in New Testament times.

Pre-Christian Baptism

First let us look at five rites, or types of rites, that preceded Christian Baptism.

1. Hebrew-Jewish Lustrations

In very early times water was naturally considered to be cleansing and healing, not only in a physical but also in a religious sense, since the two were closely bound together. The Hebrews considered especially efficacious "living" water—that

267

is, running water such as that in a river or spring. In the Old Testament we find some purification rites in pre-exilic times, but it is likely that these were multiplied and emphasized in postexilic times. Most of the purification rites that we know in detail are described in the Priestly Code. With the rise of Pharisaic Judaism in the first and second centuries B.C., increasing emphasis was placed on these, since the Pharisees believed that many of the rules for priests should be applied to laymen also.

Various objects or actions might cause a person to be unclean or impure, and often one of the things prescribed for purification was the use of water, by washing, immersion, or sprinkling. For example, a person who ate an animal that had died of itself or had been torn by beasts was required to wash his clothes and bathe himself in water (Leviticus 17:15-16). A man was believed to be made unclean by a discharge of semen, and a women by menstruation (Leviticus 15:13-32). In the ritual for the consecration of priests, washing of the body was prescribed (Exodus 29:1ff.); the priests were required to wash their hands and feet before every act of officiating in the ritual (Exodus 30:17-21). The great expansion of these ideas and practices in late times can be seen in the rule laid down in the Mishnah, *Yoma* iii 5: "None may enter the Temple Court for [an act of the Temple] Service, even though he is clean, until he has immersed himself. On this day [of atonement] the High Priest five times immerses himself and ten times he sanctifies [his hands and his feet]. . . ."[1]

These various rites of purification by water had a twofold purpose: negatively, to remove the ritual impurity, and positively, to prepare the person to worship God. In general the principle was, "the pure shall see God." Sometimes an ethical element was involved, sometimes not. Certain natural functions were thought of as causing impurity; even sacred things might make one unclean; sometimes priests had to wash after making sacrifice, and it was believed that sacred books are those which "defile the hands."

2. JEWISH PROSELYTE BAPTISM

In ancient Judaism three requirements were made of a male proselyte: circumcision, baptism, and sacrifice. Circumcision and sacrifice are easy to understand on the basis of Old Testament practice; baptism was something new. In its developed form, as we know it in the Talmud, proselyte baptism involved total immersion of the candidate, probably unaided, in the presence of three witnesses. The witnesses were required to question the proselyte beforehand, to make sure that he understood the full meaning of the step he was about to take, and that he was joining the Jewish faith from good motives; during the ceremony, as the candidate stood partly immersed in water, the witnesses recited to him some of the minor and some of the major requirements of the Law. Since it was important that the proselyte's whole body come into contact with water, the candidate was nude, and running water was preferred.

Children born before their parents became proselytes were circumcised and baptized at the same time as their father, but they had the right to renounce the engagements entered into in their name on attaining maturity (*Ket.* 11a). Children in embryo at the time of the conversion of the mother, but born later, were exempt from the necessity of ceremonial immersion (*Yeb.* 78a).

Proselyte baptism should not be considered as simply a physical rite, without spiritual meaning. It was an act of self-dedication to God. The Jews insisted that a proselyte must act from pure motive; for example, it was said that anyone who embraced Judaism through desire to marry a Jewish woman, or through any motive that was not "for the sake of God," was no genuine proselyte (*Gerim* I, 3). Conversion to Judaism was considered as a rebirth. In the midrash to Genesis 12:5, it is said, "He who makes a proselyte is as though he created him" (*Gen. R.* xxxix, 14). This is not difficult to understand when one reflects that the proselyte was leaving a faith considered to be heathen and pagan, to join the true faith of Israel. Some scholars insist that repentance was as truly a condition of proselyte baptism as it was of John's rite or of Christian baptism.[2] H. H. Rowley, a British Baptist, speaks of it as being "sacramental."

For our purpose, the question regarding the date of origin of Jewish proselyte baptism is important. Most of our information concerning it comes from the Talmud, and other relative late sources. However, there are indications that the rite was practiced before the destruction of the temple A.D. 70, and that it originated before the time of John and Jesus. The Mishnah reports that one of the points of conflict between the Schools of Shammai and Hillel was whether, if a man became a proselyte on the day before Passover, he might immerse himself and consume the Passover offering in the evening (*Pes.* viii 8; *Eduy.* v2). If this dispute goes back to the time of Hillel and Shammai, it was in the period just before the lifetime of Jesus; if it goes back to the Schools of Shammai and Hillel, it was in the period of the lifetime of John and Jesus, the early New Testament period in general. Furthermore, the fact that sacrifice is named as one of the requirements of a proselyte takes us back to the time before the destruction of the temple A.D. 70. Most scholars who have studied the subject seem to be convinced that proselyte baptism originated by the New Testament period, though of course they admit it may not have had at this time just the same form we find in the Talmud. It does not seem at all reasonable to suppose that proselyte baptism was borrowed from Christianity.

3. Pagan Ceremonies of Baptism

Rites involving the use of water were found in ancient times also in non-Jewish, pagan religions. Of special significance were those practiced in the mystery religions which were found in many parts of the Graeco-Roman world at the time of the rise of Christianity. Some of these were doubtless of very ancient Oriental origin, but they became popular in the Hellenistic world as religions promising personal salvation. The mystery

270

religions usually involved elaborate and secret rites, particularly at the time of initiation.

In the Eleusinian mysteries the rites of initiation occupied a long period. On the second day of the week of "the great mysteries," the candidates ran down to the sea and purified themselves in salt water; it was believed that the effect of this rite was enhanced by sprinkling with pigs' blood. Initiation into the Isis-Osiris mystery was described in ancient times by Apuleius. After a period devoted to meditation and prayer, the candidate bathed, and the priest washed and sprinkled him with the purest water, having first implored the pardon of the gods. The Isis-Osiris mystery originated in Egypt, and the waters of baptism were identified with the life-giving waters of the Nile, and these in turn with the waters of the primordial ocean whence all things had been created. In Mithraism, which became very popular in the Roman world (especially among soldiers) in the early Christian era, there were repeated ablutions as a kind of baptism designed to wash away the stains of guilt, involving probably both sprinkling and immersion at various stages. In the taurobolium rite, the candidate went down into a pit and the blood of a slain bull was allowed to pour over him.

The Mandaic religion, which has been especially emphasized by Reitzenstein in connection with the origin of Christian baptism, had elaborate and repeated rites of baptism; however, we do not know whether this religion goes back to pre-Christian or even early Christian times.[3]

4. Rites of the Essenes (including the Qumran Sect)

The Dead Sea Scrolls—or, more properly, the Qumran Scrolls —and the excavations at Khirbet Qumran have revealed the existence, in the period from the second century B.C. down to the fall of Jerusalem A.D. 70, of a sect in which ritualistic lustrations were very important.[4] Not only are these referred to in their literature, but in the community center which was excavated at Khirbet Qumran, there were found several pools or cisterns, some of which must have been used for ritualistic washings. In one of the larger of these constructions may have been cisterns for the holding of water, there can be no doubt that some were for ritualistic purposes.

The literature of the Qumran sect has shown that their beliefs and practices were very similar to those of the Essenes, who are referred to by a few ancient writers, most notably Josephus and Philo. So close are the similarities that many scholars speak of the members of the Qumran sect as Essenes. This is legitimate, if we use "Essene" in a broad sense and allow for the possibility of development and change in Essenian practice, and even for variation in different parts of Palestine.

Josephus makes is clear that rites of purification in water were very important to the Essenes. He says that a candidate for the sect, after a period of probation, was made "a partaker of the waters of purification" (*War*, II, viii, 7). He describes in some detail their daily practice: after the fifth hour they would assemble together and clothe themselves in white veils, and then bathe their bodies in cold water. After this purification they would partake of their common meal, which had certain sacramental features (*ibid.*, 5).

In another passage Josephus says that the Essenses "do not offer sacrifices, because they have more pure lustrations of their own" (*Ant.*, XVIII, i, 5) thus indicating that they considered their lustrations as a substitute for sacrifice in the Jerusalem temple and probably as having a similar purpose and efficacy.

In the Qumran literature there are many references to rites of purification. While the references show clearly that participation in these rites was a highly valued prerogative of members of the sect, there are passages which teach plainly that the rites must be attended by moral uprightness to be effective.[5]

One is not justified while he gives free rein to the stubborness of his heart. . . . He is not purified by ceremonies of atonement, nor made clean by the water-for-impurity; he cannot sanctify himself with seas and rivers, nor be made clean by any water for washing.

Unclean, unclean, will he be as long as he rejects the ordinances of God, not being instructed in communion with Him. . . . By an upright and humble spirit will his sin be atoned, and by the submission of his soul to all the statutes of God will his flesh be cleaned, that he may be sprinkled with water-for-impurity, and sanctify himself with water for cleanness. (1QS iii 3-9) [6]

No one is to go into water in order to attain the purity of holy men, for men are not purified unless they repent of their evil, for impurity is on all who transgress His word. (1QS v 13f)

The Qumran sect believed in a future, eschatological baptism in the spirit—called a holy spirit or spirit of truth—as the following quotation shows:

In his inscrutable and glorious wisdom God has ordained a period for the existence of error, and at the appointed time of visitation he will destroy it forever. Then the truth of the world will emerge victorious, for it has wallowed in the ways of wickedness during the dominion of error until the appointed time of the judgment that has been decreed. Then God will purify by his truth all the works of man and refine for himself the structure of man, bringing to an end every spirit of error within his flesh and cleansing him by a holy spirit from all evil doings. He will sprinkle on him a spirit of truth, like water-for-impurity, cleansing him from all abominations of falsehood and from wallowing in a spirit of impurity, so as to make the upright understand the knowledge of the Most High and the wisdom of the sons of heaven, and to instruct those whose way is blameless. (1QS iv 18-22)

The baptismal rites of this sect were repeated often. We do not know whether they had a special baptismal rite as initiation into the sect. In any event, however, the privilege of participating in these baptismal rites was considered one of the most significant privileges of a member, and it may be that they did have a "first baptism" that served as an initiation ceremony.

5. THE RITE OF JOHN THE BAPTIST

In the period immediately preceding the public ministry of Jesus, there appeared on the scene in the lower Jordan valley a man named John. He proclaimed a message which summoned men to prepare for the coming kingdom of God, and he performed a rite which caused him to be given the title "the Baptist" or "the Baptizer." John looked forward to the coming of a messianic figure, one who would be mightier than himself. His rite was "a baptism of repentance for the forgiveness of sins" (Mark 1:4; Luke 3:3). John's message had a strong element of the ethical, for he gave specific ethical injunctions to various groups who came to hear him preach.

John the Baptist started a movement, or founded a community, that was probably more important and longer lasting than we are accustomed to think. He had disciples whom he taught to pray and to fast. Some of his disciples joined the Christian movement, but apparently not all. Even after the death of John some of his disciples continued to believe in him, some perhaps even considering him as the Messiah rather than as simply the forerunner of the Messiah.

John's baptism was a rite which was intended in some manner to help prepare those who received it to enter the kingdom, to be ready for the new Age-to-come. In reporting on John's baptism, Josephus says that John thought that his rite would be acceptable "if it were used not to beg off from sins committed, but for the purification of the body when the soul had previously been cleansed by righteous conduct" (*Ant.*, xviii, 5, 2).

In assessing the significance of John's rite we should not think that the rite itself induced repentance or secured forgiveness for the candidate. It was an outward manifestation of his repentance, one of the "fruits that befit repentance" to which John summoned men (Luke 3:8).

John's baptism is usually considered to have been an administered rite, but there is a little evidence to the effect that it was self-baptism like proselyte baptism. In Luke 3:77 Codex Bezae and the Old Latin read "to be baptized in his presence" *(enopion autou)* rather than "to be baptized by him." Some scholars believe that the middle voice of *baptizo* when used in connection with John's rite (and the early Christian rite) indicates self-baptism. On this point, however, we cannot reach certainty.

Early Christian Baptism

Now that we have surveyed these five types of pre-Christian rites, what can we say of the origin of Christian baptism?

We must indicate first what we mean by "Christian baptism." It is well known, of course, that about three thousand were baptized on Pentecost, and that baptism was the usual rite of entrance into the nascent Christian church thereafter. Several specific cases of baptism are described by Acts, and Paul refers to baptism in several passages. There are a few references to baptism in other books.

We must not overlook, however, the baptism of Jesus by John, and the information which is contained in John 3:22 and 4:1f. Jesus was baptized by John and then, according to the Fourth Gospel, he and his disciples baptized in the land of Judea, while John was still baptizing at Aenon near Salim, though John 4:1 specifically states that Jesus himself did not baptize. This ministry of Jesus paralleling that of John is not recorded in the Synoptics, and the historicity of it has been denied by some in view of the general character of the Fourth Gospel, and its absence in the Synoptics. Yet it seems likely that the report is historical. An increasing number of scholars are willing to accept an early date for John (particularly in view of the Qumran discoveries) and a large element of historical veracity in the Gospel. The author of this gospel is apparently embarrassed by the fact that Jesus and his disciples baptized along with John, and his statement that Jesus himself did not baptize may have in it an apologetic note. It appears likely that Jesus did in fact "join the movement" initiated by John, and thus carried out a ministry for a time paralleling John's, marked by the rite of baptism.

In seeking the origin of baptism, we must therefore keep in mind its close association with John's baptism. If we call this baptism which is reported in the Fourth Gospel "early Christian baptism," then we must say that it is hardly distinguishable from John's baptism. Perhaps those to whom it was administered were believed to have the gift of the Holy Spirit as was the case with Jesus, but we do not know this.

The baptism of Pentecost and subsequent times had new features: it was baptism "in the name of Jesus" (later in the name of the Trinity); it was accompanied by the gift of the Holy Spirit; and it was interpreted in the light of the death and resurrection of Jesus. As Paul interpreted it, Christian baptism symbolized the death and resurrection of Jesus, and the death of the candidate to sin and his resurrection to a new life in Christ. (Perhaps we should not use the word "symbolized" here; perhaps baptism was conceived to be the agency by which the candidate entered into a mystical union with Christ in his death and resurrection, but more of this later.)

It is this post-Pentecost baptism that we ought to call "Christian baptism." It was similar to the baptism of John in being a "baptism of repentance for the forgiveness of sins," and a preparation for the new Age-to-come; it was accompanied by a very strong ethical element. It went beyond John's baptism in that it was administered in the light of the closing events of Jesus' earthly life—that is, his death and his resurrection.

The new features in Christian baptism are explainable in terms of the life of Jesus, as understood and interpreted by his disciples. We do not need to seek their origin elsewhere. But since this baptism was to a degree "borrowed" from John, we have to ask the question: Where did John derive his baptism?

Many answers have been given to this question, and there is not space here to discuss all of them. Carl H. Kraeling in a recent book, *John the Baptist*[7] emphasizes the fact that John spoke of two baptisms—his own baptism by water, and baptism by the one coming after him in the Holy Spirit and in fire. Kraeling thinks the original emphasis in the second was upon fire. This he traces back to the old Iranian idea that at the day

276

of judgment there would be a great refining fire to destroy the evil and purify the good. Kraeling then suggests that

the water of baptism represents and symbolizes the fiery torrent of judgment, and . . . the individual by voluntarily immersing himself in the water enacts in advance before God his willing submission to the divine judgment which the river of fire will perform. John's baptism would, therefore, be a rite symbolic of the acceptance of the judgment which he proclaimed.[8]

While this is an interesting suggestion, it has apparently met with little acceptance. It is indeed difficult to see how water could serve as a substitute for fire in the judgment process. Kraeling wrote before the Qumran finds had been carefully studied. We have seen that the Qumran sect practiced ritual lustrations and expected a future baptism by the Holy Spirit. There are in addition passages which indicate that they expected an eschatological judgment by fire.[9]

In seeking the origin of John's baptism we may safely leave out of consideration the pagan rites of baptism, and the ordinary Hebrew-Jewish purification rites, at least so far as *direct* influence is concerned. It is very doubtful that John was influenced by the pagan mysteries, although it is possible that they did influence Paul in his interpretation of baptism, and likewise some of the early Christian fathers, particularly when they referred to baptism as a "seal" or "illumination." We cannot show that these were known to John and to Jesus in Palestine; furthermore, it does not seem that their baptism was sacramental in the sense in which the rites of the mysteries were.

It is more fruitful to think of the probable influence of the rites of the Essenes and of proselyte baptism on John.

It is a striking fact that John and the Essenes of Qumran lived and worked in the same general region. John preached in the wilderness of Judaea; the Fourth Gospel gives the place-names Bethany (or Bethabara) and Aenon. These sites were a little north and east of the Wadi Qumran.

Scholars have long conjectured that John may have been associated with, or at least influenced by, the Essenes. This is made much more probable by the new discoveries at Qumran. Both John and the Qumran Essenes had a strong eschatological emphasis. Both made use of the verse from Isaiah 40:3.

> In the wilderness prepare the way of the LORD,
>   make straight in the desert a highway for our God.

In the Manual of Discipline this verse is explained as meaning the study of the Torah (IQS viii 12-16). In the larger sense the Essenes sought to prepare a community for the coming of the Messiah, a community that was to a degree ascetic. John's purpose was similar, but did not envisage so rigid and tight-knit an organization as that of the Essenes. In both there was a very strong ethical note.

W. H. Brownlee has suggested that John was adopted by the Essenes of Qumran and brought up by them, and subsequently he withdrew from them, wishing to preach a somewhat different message.[10] This is, of course only speculation. While we cannot deny that this is a possibility, it is not necessary to suppose that John was at one time actually a member of the Essenes. He could have been influenced by them in outlook and practice without being a member.

The baptism of John differs from the purification rites of the Essenes in that it was a once-for-all rite, whereas theirs was repeated daily. Yet, we have seen that the Essenes may have had an initiatory baptism; in any case they had a "first baptism." Also, though John's characteristic baptismal rite apparently was not repeated by any given individual, we must suppose that the Jews who followed him carried out the usual purification rites, at least so long as they participated in the temple worship and sought to keep the Jewish law. (Christians likewise may have continued to participate in those rites so long as they kept the Jewish Law and worshiped in the Jerusalem temple, as we know many of them did for a time.)

In adopting a rite that was a rite of initiation and a once-for-all act, John probably was influenced by proselyte baptism. His rite differed from proselyte baptism in that the latter was administered to gentiles who adopted Judaism, whereas John baptized those who were already Jews, and probably also some gentiles, for we hear of his having a special message for soldiers, who may have been Romans. In both cases, those who submitted to the rite believed they were coming into the "true Israel." Those gentiles who had submitted to the rite of proselyte baptism would no doubt have observed the purification rites of the law if they wished to live as good Jews.

Back of the proselyte baptism lie the various purification rites. If they did not directly influence the baptism of John or of Jesus, they probably did influence proselyte bastism. The usual explanation of the origin of that rite is that gentiles who had lived in impurity and had not observed the law were required to undergo an initiatory bath before they could be considered as full proselytes.

The Meaning of Early Christian Baptism

We may turn now to consider briefly the meaning of early Christian baptism, that is, of the rite observed after Pentecost. The meaning of the rite must be determined on the basis of careful exegesis of all the New Testament passages, but the origin of the rite has some bearing upon its meaning.

(1) Baptism was a rite of initiation into a community—at first an eschatological community, later the church as the body of Christ. Both Jesus and John had the basic message: "Repent, for the kingdom of heaven is at hand" (Matthew 3:2; 4:7). Whatever the precise messianic ideas and beliefs of both, they sought to prepare men to receive or enter the kingdom. Later, as the expectation of the *parousia* became less vivid and the Christian church took form, baptism was initiation into membership in the church.

(2) Baptism was connected with repentance and forgiveness. John's baptism is called "a baptism of repentance for the forgiveness of sins" (Mark 1:4). We are told that people "were baptized by him in the Jordan, confessing their sins" (1:5). Similar ideas are connected with Christian baptism—most notably, of course, in Acts 2:38.

(3) The most characteristic feature of Christian baptism, especially as interpreted by Paul (but he certainly was not alone in this), was that it somehow stood for death-and-resurrection, both of Christ and of the believer (Romans 6:3-5; Galatians 3:27; Colossians 2:12).

(4) Christian baptism had associated with it the gift of the Holy Spirit. This was apparently one of the main features of Christian baptism as distinguished from John's (see the incident at Ephesus recorded in Acts 19:2-6).

Symbol or Sacrament

When we have said these things, we still have to ask certain questions: Was Christian baptism in New Testament times *only* a symbol or was it considered to have some efficacy within itself? Was it a sacrament? Was it counted "necessary for salvation"? These are difficult questions to answer, and it may be that there is no uniform answer that fits all of the New Testament.

When we try to let the New Testament speak for itself, it seems that we must say that in some instances, and certainly to some people in New Testament times, baptism was not merely a symbol, but had some efficacy within itself. Three facts stand out here as being specially worthy of notice.

(1) The incidental reference in 1 Corinthians 15:29 to "baptism for the dead" must, on any plain interpretation, mean baptism on behalf of the dead (the Greek is *hyper*). Whatever the exact meaning, it must have been a rite observed by certain living people on behalf of the deceased, with the thought that it had some efficacy for them. Of course this is referred to only

in passing by Paul, but it must indicate that some people in Corinth practiced it. Perhaps they were influenced by their pagan background.

(2) Paul's interpretation of baptism may have been influenced by the mystery religions. When he spoke of baptism as death and resurrection, he may have been thinking not simply of a symbol or a re-enactment, but that the burial into water and resurrection from water somehow effected the believer's mystical union with Christ. Scholars are quite divided on this point. Even if we do think of baptism as being in some sense a "sacrament," that is not the same thing as magic, and it is not the same thing as saying that Christianity was only another mystery religion. The earthly life and teaching of Jesus were too important and real for that to be possible.

(3) It is later books of the New Testament that seem to speak most clearly of baptism as having efficacy in itself—phrases such as "washing of regeneration" of Titus 3:5, or 1 Peter 3:21, "Baptism . . . now saves you, not as a removal of dirt from the body but as an appeal to God for a clear conscience, through the resurrection of Christ."

Concepts of Efficacy

Perhaps we can understand how even Christians of thoroughly Jewish background could think of baptism as having efficacy within itself, without being magic, if we keep in mind two facts:

(1) Hebrew-Jewish thought was not dualistic, making a sharp distinction between matter and spirit. If they had ever defined it, the Hebrews probably would have said that spirit is highly refined matter. Thus they could think of a physical act as having spiritual efficacy. They did not make the careful distinctions we attempt to make between the physical or material on the one hand, and the spiritual or religious on the other.

(2) For the ancient Jew there was always a close relationship between word and deed. The most natural thing for a Jew to

ask was, "What must I *do* to be saved?" rather than "What must I *believe* to be saved? Belief was indeed important and fundamental, but belief was expressed in deeds.

In the Old Testament we frequently read of the prophets performing symbolic or dramatic acts, such as Hosea's naming of his children (1:4-9); Isaiah's walking naked and barefoot for three years (20:2-3); Jeremiah's going around with a yoke on his neck to indicate to the Jews they ought to submit to the yoke of Babylonia (27:2-7). These were to some extent symbolic actions, but many interpreters see them as being more than symbolical: in line with the dynamic nature of Hebrew thought, these actions were believed to set in motion forces that would help to accomplish that which they symbolized. The act of baptism may be considered as an "acted parable," like these prophetic actions.

Thus a Jew who submitted to the baptism of John or to early Christian baptism could have believed that it had some efficacy within itself, but this is not to say that it was in any sense *magic*, or that the efficacy of the act was independent of the faith of the candidate.

Suggestions on the Meaning of Baptism Today

Churches and denominations that practice baptism of believers only, and by immersion, are in a strong position. This should not be a matter for pride; the fact that they are correct at this point does not make them correct in all matters of faith and life. They too need to reconsider the theology of baptism.

They are in a strong position for the following reasons:

(1) Many New Testament scholars who attempt to be objective—perhaps even a majority—agree that the normal practice in New Testament times was believers' baptism by immersion, if not exclusively so. This is not based simply on a study of the words *baptizo* and *bapto,* but the exegesis of all the passages in the New Testament. We must admit that there is a

possibility that in the few household and family baptisms mentioned in the New Testament (Acts 16:15, 33; cf. 18:8), some children and/or slaves were baptized who did not express personal faith. Also, the *Didache,* the origin of which may go back to late New Testament times, allows for the practice of pouring of water when immersion in running water is not feasible (ch. 7).

(2) There is much discussion in theological circles today of the meaning of baptism. Karl Barth has published a remarkable little book in which he pleads strongly for baptism of believers only, and by immersion. The English translation is entitled *The Teaching of the Church Regarding Baptism.*[11] Barth says that the chief actor in baptism is Jesus Christ. The second actor is the baptized person. He should be one who comes voluntarily to baptism, not one who is brought; only as he comes under his own free decision and with faith can baptism be a responsible act. The person being baptized must participate actively in his baptism, and not be merely passive.

Neither by exegesis nor from the nature of the case can it be established that the baptized person can be a merely passive instrument *(Behandelter).* Rather it may be shown, by exegesis and from the nature of the case, that in this action the baptized is an active partner *(Handelnder),* and that at whatever stage of life he may be, plainly no *infans* can be such a person.[12]

Barth examines the New Testament to prove his case, and he criticizes the Reformers for championing infant baptism.

Though he does not discuss it very fully, Barth favors immersion, and writes:

Is the last word on the matter to be that facility of administration, health, and propriety are important reasons for doing otherwise? Or will a Christianity return whose more vigorous imagination will be satisfied no longer with the innocuous form of present-day baptism any more than with certain other inoffensive features of modern Christianity?[13]

He considers his own baptism incorrect, but valid. He does not advocate rebaptism, which he considers blasphemy against God.

Karl Barth's son, Markus Barth, who now teaches at the University of Chicago, has written a large volume on baptism.[14] It is reported that he refused to have his children baptized in Germany, and thus forfeited the possibility of a professorship in that land.

(3) The central and most characteristic figure in Christian baptism is that of death and resurrection. Only immersion can properly symbolize, portray, or re-enact that figure.

Areas of Caution

As we consider the meaning of baptism for the Christian and for the Christian Church today, we must say certain negative and certain positive things. On the negative side are the following:

(1) We should not interpret baptism as being in any sense a rite that conforms to the principle of *ex opere operato*. It is not magic. Such is wholly foreign to the outlook of the Bible. Baptism is not "necessary for salvation." We cannot say too strongly that it is God who saves us and forgives us when we respond to his grace by faith in Jesus Christ. We should not believe that a rite such as baptism is necessary before God will save us. Thus we should reject any literal interpretation of the New Testament that would say the contrary.

(2) We should also reject all legalism. Often it has been said that one must be baptized in order to obey the command of Christ. While it is true that the Christian owes to Christ loving and faithful obedience, mere obedience to Christ is not the highest possible motive for baptism. Baptism is not a law, but a privilege.

(3) Baptism is not a mere symbol which can be taken lightly and be easily dispensed with.

Some Positive Meanings

On the positive side we would say the following:

(1) In baptism the believer gives a sign of the commitment of himself to Jesus Christ and to the Christian way. He says by means of a deed that which has already been spoken in his heart.

(2) In baptism the church receives the believer into the covenant community, to surround him with its warm fellowship and to give him instruction in the Christian faith and the Christian life. Both the church and the believer should be aware of the nature of the covenant into which he is entering.

(3) In baptism the believer and the church both witness to Christ—to what he has done in his death and resurrection, and to the hope of a new life in him for the believer. Alexander Campbell spoke of baptism as "the gospel in water," and Luther said it was "God's Word in water." Karl Barth has written: "The efficacy of baptism consists in this, that the baptized person is placed once and for all under the sign of hope."[15]

(4) Properly understood and received, baptism may indeed be a sacrament—that is, a means or channel of God's grace. In true baptism there are both objective and subjective elements; the objective element cannot be present unless the subjective element is first present.

(5) If the rite of baptism is to be meaningful to the Christian and to the Christian church, the church should practice much more often than it does the early church policy of giving instruction before baptism, instruction both in the Christian faith and life and in the meaning of baptism. In the *Didache,* it is said that instruction in the way, and also fasting, were to precede baptism. While there is no guarantee that instruction will make baptism meaningful, the act of baptism can hardly have genuine significance unless the believer attempts to understand its meaning and the church attempts to make it a meaningful and important rite.

NOTES

1. Quotations from The Mishnah are from the translation by Herbert Danby, Oxford, 1933.

2. H. H. Rowley, "Jewish Proselyte Baptism and the Baptism of John." *Hebrew Union College Annual,* XV (1940), 313-334; I, Abrahams, "Pharisaic Baptism," in *Studies in Pharisaism and the Gospels,* First Series (Cambridge: University Press, 1917), 36-46. On Jewish proselytism, in general, see William G. Braude, *Jewish Proselyting in the First Five Centuries of the Common Era, The Age of the Tannaim and Amoriam* (Brown University Studies. Vol. VI; Providence, R. I.: Brown University, 1940); and Bernard J. Bamberger, *Proselytism in the Talmudic Period* (Cincinnati: Hebrew Union College Press, 1939).

3. R. Reitzenstein, *Die Vorgeschichte der Christlichen Taufe* (Leipzig and Berlin: B. G. Teubner, 1929).

4. On the Qumran discoveries in general, the best books in English are Millar Burrows, *The Dead Sea Scrolls* (New York: Viking Press, 1955) and *More Light on the Dead Sea Scrolls* (New York: Viking Press, 1958). For the present writer's views see his article, "The Dead Sea Discoveries: Retrospect and Challenge," *Journal of Biblical Literature,* 76 (1957), 1-12.

5. Cf. J. R. Mantey, "Baptism in the Dead Sea Manual of Discipline," *The Review and Expositor,* 51 (1954), 522-527.

6. The Manual of Discipline (IQS) is published in Millar Burrows, ed., *The Dead Sea Scrolls of St. Mark's Monastery,* Vol. II, Fasc. 2 (New Haven: American Schools of Oriental Research, 1951). For English translation and study see P. Wernberg-Moller, *The Manual of Discipline* (Leiden: Brill, 1957). Translations in this paper are my own.

7. *John the Baptist* (New York: Charles Scribner's Sons, 1951).

8. *Ibid.,* pp. 117-118.

9. See, *e.g.,* IQH iii 29-36.

10. "John the Baptist in the Light of Ancient Scrolls," in *The Scrolls and the New Testament,* ed. by Krister Stendahl (New York: Harper and Row, Inc., Publishers, 1957), pp. 33-53. Cf. John A. T. Robinson, "The Baptism of John and the Qumran Community," *Harvard Theological Review,* 50 (1957), 175-191.

11. Transl. by E. A. Payne (London: SCM Press, 1948; distributed by Alec R. Allenson, Naperville).

12. *Ibid.,* p. 41.

13. *Ibid.,* p. 10.

14. *Die Taufe—ein Sakrament?* (Zurich: Zollikon, 1951). It is reported that he is preparing an English edition on the subject.

15. *Op. cit.,* p. 55.

❦13❧

The Place of Jesus Christ
in the Lord's Supper

JAMES G. CLAGUE

F ROM the earliest days of the Christian church the rite of the Lord's Supper has been a central part of worship. The brief description of the corporate activity of the original community[1] refers to *koinonia* and the breaking of the bread. Whether or not the second phrase is placed by the author in apposition to and describes the first, it is still in the early period when the two terms become synonomous. *Koinonia* is seen as actualized by and focused in the Lord's Supper. Even if we reject the authenticity of the command: "Do this in remembrance of me," reasons for the repetition of the rite are not far to seek. It took place at the most poignant time in the relationships between Jesus and his followers, and was for them the last occasion when the fellowship met as a group. It easily became the means whereby the memory of Jesus was prolonged among them. But more than this, it is impossible to doubt the historical core of the event, and it is obvious that Jesus himself invested this last meal with special significance. The incident was thus pregnant with theological possibilities as the developing faith of the church was posed the task of unifying its present experience of its living Lord with the historical finality of his life and death.

These two aspects of the Lord's Supper illustrate the two most widely held and, at the present, irreconcilable views of the rite.

287

There are those who claim that it is a purely memorial feast, that its celebration has no other intention or effect than to call to mind the reality for which it stands. That is to say, the elements of the Lord's Supper are emblematic, mere signs which in the mind of any given individual are associated with the whole pattern of the original event in such a way that it is called up in idea when they are used. On the other hand, there are those who insist that the Lord's Supper is a "sacrament" and not a mere sign. That is to say, the elements are symbolic; they partake of the reality which they symbolize, and are therefore vehicles of spiritual grace, the very life of Jesus Christ. Within this second view there is a further division which stems from the question whether the Lord's Supper conveys in a special way the life and grace of Christ, or whether it is to be understood in exactly the same way as the "sacrament" of preaching, which is also the vehicle of saving power.

It is, I think, germane to our purpose briefly to consider the stated positions of the various churches in this regard, both as illustrations of the previously mentioned differences and also as pointing up two further difficulties which must be faced in any attempts to say something constructively about the place of Jesus Christ in the Lord's Supper. The theological positions which follow are distilled from *The Ministry and Sacraments*[2] and can therefore be taken as official.

Baptist churches hold that the rite of the Supper is purely memorial. It is a sacred privilege in which is brought vividly to mind the life, death, and resurrection of our Lord and in which we renew our allegiance to him. With them stands the *Dutch Reformed* church which denies any absolute necessity of sacraments. Where sacraments are celebrated, their aim is to strengthen the faith of believers and assure them, by a parable in action, that "Jesus Christ is meant for us." *The Scottish Reformed, Lutheran, and Congregational* churches all insist that the sacraments are a means or method by which the central message of the gospel is brought close to individual lives. They do nothing that this message may not conceivably do without their intervention; they do not add anything to the message of the Word, they but movingly reiterate it. Yet each of these churches also insists that the sacrament is a means of grace. The Lutheran position assures those who receive the sacrament of the forgiving and sanctifying grace of God in Christ, and thus *it is a means* whereby men may receive "forgiveness of sins, life, and salvation." The Congregationalist declares that the sacrament is more than a mere sign; it illustrates spiritual realities with so moving an actuality that it *verily conveys them. The Church of Scotland* insists that the sacrament is a means of grace; the outward elements duly set apart have such a relation to Christ crucified that truly, yet sacramentally only, they are called by the name of things they represent: the body and blood of Christ. *They mediate a real grace. The Methodist Church* makes no comparison between the sacraments of the Lord's Supper and preaching, but declares that the Supper is the act in which the risen Lord grants and renews that personal communion with himself to the believing soul for which the soul was made: where Christ is really present and imparting new life.

Those churches which are regularly called "Catholic" agree in giving to the sacrament a special place as vehicles of the grace of God. Not that they are the only means of grace, but they are necessary for salvation and for the continuation of the saving work of Christ. The *Episcopal* church affirms that the celebration is not only for remembrance of the sacrifice of the death of Christ but also for the benefits we receive thereby. The body and blood of Christ are "verily and indeed taken and received by the faithful; our souls are refreshed and strengthened by it as our bodies by bread and wine." But whereas there is no attempt to explore or explain the phrase "verily indeed taken and received," the *Roman Catholic* and *Eastern Orthodox* churches take this same declaration to its logical conclusion. In the one case it is in the well-known dogma of transubstantiation; in the other the doctrine of μεταβολή by which is apparently meant a change in function as regards the bread and the wine, rather than μετουσίωσις a change in substance or essence.

It seems to me that two difficulties which are inherent in all these positions must be considered. The first is in the nature of a dilemma. On the one hand, it is possible to pursue a view to its logical conclusion, in which case one holds either the purely memorial doctrine of the Lord's Supper, or the full doctrine of transubstantiation or μεταβοή. But as regards the words of Jesus the memorial view does not do justice to the historical core of the originating event, and the quasi-materialist explanation of physical change of the elements is philosophically and theologically untenable. On the other hand, those churches which attempt to avoid both the "low" and the "high" doctrine of communion end by affirming two quite irreconcilable statements. They at once affirm that there is no special grace attached to the rite of the Lord's Supper; it is an assurance to the faithful, adding nothing to the word of preaching. Yet they also declare that it is the *means* of salvation and forgiveness. God became visible under an earthly veil, the illustration of spiritual realities with so moving an actuality that they verily convey them. The dilemma arises in the desire to emphasize the real presence of Christ in the act. How does one move from a merely subjective memorial conception to an objective conception of the presence of the living Christ? The trouble may be, and I think is, in the emphasis on the presence of Christ as something to be mediated in terms of elements rather than in terms of action.

The second difficulty noted is in the comparison of the Supper with the act of preaching. In whatever sense one speaks of the sacrament of the Word, it remains true that we measure the efficacy of preaching by our feeling or response, for it depends upon the mediation of human thought and activity. This is not the case with the Lord's Supper. It is not merely an inward and individual approach to God, nor does any kind of mediation stand between its direct action and the worshiper. It is worship which publicly acknowledges God and his gifts and represents those gifts in direct symbolic action. Moreover, the basic form of the act is unchangeably given and stands in a direct relationship to Jesus Christ, apart from all explanation and interpretation.

Because of their total rejection of creeds, Disciples of Christ have never clarified their view of the Lord's Supper. On the other hand, because of their restorationist emphasis they have, in practice, tended to one, or other, or both of the two attitudes. By many communions is looked upon as a purely memorial feast, an ordinance of the Lord to be repeated because of the command. By others it has taken its significance from its function as an expression of Christian unity and as a means whereby a greater unity could be experienced and achieved. Perhaps the greatest number of Disciples hold both these views together. Despite the lack of a common theological position, these emphases have tended towards stressing the objectivity of the sacrament. If we are to come to some deeper theological understanding of ourselves, it is necessary for us to re-examine the nature of the Lord's Supper and the place Jesus Christ takes within it.

So far as the text of Scripture is concerned, the institution of the Lord's Supper is recorded in four books of the New Testament: Matthew 26:26-29; Mark 14:22-25; Luke 22:15-20; 1 Corinthians 11:23-26. The earliest of these narratives are Paul and Mark, and as they are obviously independent of each other they are the primary sources. It can easily be shown that the Matthean and Lucan versions are derivative. The variations in Matthew are simply due to verbal choice and they are all explicable by what we know of the characteristics of that Gospel. Luke contains a longer and a shorter version: longer in *Sin. Alex. Vat.;* shorter in the Western text, the Old Latin versions, and the Syriac versions. In the longer versions there appears an extra cup (cup, bread, cup); in the shorter versions the order is, in the Western Text: cup, bread; in Syriac: bread, cup. The shorter form is identical with Mark's version except it omits "and they all drank of it" as well as "this is my blood of the

291

covenant shed on behalf of many." The longer form, however, is almost verbally identical with that of Paul except that it omits "shed on your behalf." From this evidence it is obvious that Luke's version is derived from Paul and Mark. The question resolves itself, then, into the significance of the extra cup in the longer version of Luke and the inversion of the cup and bread in the shorter version. This question is not weighty, however; as it concerns variations in a derived version, it is not independent evidence. It is a textual and not a historical problem, and we can accept with confidence the account of the institution given us in Mark and Paul. The core of the rite is then the following: taking bread, blessing, the words "This is my body broken for you," taking a cup, blessing, the words "This is the new covenant in my blood shed for you (many)" or "This is my blood of a new covenant."

With this as its basis, I think we can discount the idea that the Last Supper was a normal Jewish *Chaburah* or fellowship meal and that its continuation was merely a memorial act. If, as even the most radical form critics admit, there is reason to believe that an *ipse dixit,* though short and out of context, lies behind many of the Gospel incidents, it is unlikely that the words of Jesus here reported must be rejected. Though the *Chaburah* may have been the basis of the meal, this particular meal contained its special significance. Moreover, the Passion narrative is thought to have emerged as a unit very early in the tradition, leaving little scope for community creativity. In the Emmaus incident[3] we have a strong suggestion that there was a special significance about the breaking of the bread by Jesus. It was in this action that they recognized his presence among them. The supper was seen to have interpreted in advance the significance of the Passion; it was not merely a fellowship feast of reunion with the risen Jesus but an identification with his sacrifice, a communion of the Lord's body and blood.

This is the way the Apostle Paul understands the matter. He does indeed call the rite a memorial,[4] but he also speaks of it as participation or communion.[5] Moreover, this latter passage occurs as an incidental reference within a different discussion and therefore presupposes a view universally accepted. When speaking specifically to the nature and meaning of the rite, Paul solemnly declares[6] that he has delivered to the Corinthian Christians the tradition he himself received. Although he affirms that he received it "from the Lord," the word ἀπό used here and elsewhere[7] indicates that it came by way of tradition rather than by revelation, for in the latter case the word (according to Paul's own usage) would have been παρά or ὑπὸ τοῦ κυρίον. If, then, Paul received this tradition on his Jerusalem visit,[8] it would be only about six years after Christ's death—a very short period for changes in the *form* of the rite to take place under the so-called influence of the mysteries, or under any general theologizing tendency. This is true even as regards interpretation when we remember that it was Paul who really opened the church to the Gentiles, and when we remember the strong reaction to Gnosticism displayed both by Paul and other writers of those early days. When one thinks of the furor caused by the very entrance of the Gentiles into the church, the reflection of which is in all the Apostle's work, we may be reasonably certain that there would have been strong opposition to the insertion of Hellenistic ideas into the communion, not as a means of interpreting an established attitude but as changing and corrupting the whole rite. There would have been polemic and didactic passages diffused throughout the epistles. Paul says "Know you not"—and there was no church without its Judaizers and watchdogs for heresy. This means, then, that we must think of the Lord's Supper as an act wherein the gathered church really meets its Lord and in dedication receives his life in the common partaking of bread and wine.

This would appear to be the witness of the worship of the early church. Its devotional life centered in the Lord's Supper, both as the concrete symbol of the earthly life and sacrificial death of its Lord and the place where its own life was renewed.

It is not without significance that the Apostle Paul could warn the Corinthians to "discriminate"[9] between common bread and the eucharistic loaf which in accordance with the common tradition and experience he had declared (and they had accepted) to be, in a spiritual sense, the Lord's body. "Discrimination" means that this loaf and wine must be seen to be different from ordinary bread and wine. The unworthy partakers were not those who were short on moral virtue but those who looked on this bread and wine as mere food and on the act itself as mere rite. But there are twin dangers in the very reality of the experience itself. One of these dangers is to forget the necessary relationship between the common *act* and the individual *experience* with the result that the *experience* becomes an end in itself, and the means and inducement are forsaken. If there is any sacramental significance in the 6th chapter of the Gospel of John, it is that the writer, starting from the eucharistic rite as the agreed basis of discourse, rejects any theosophic mysticism or spiritism as the ground of the Christian's new life, and insists on the centrality of the Lord's Supper as the continuing source of "everlasting life." It is for this reason that the writer almost delights in the material *act*—Τρώγω—to gnaw the flesh of Christ, without which action "you have no life in you" (John 6:53). The second danger is that of materializing and defining the elements within the act itself in an attempt to particularize for dogmatic purposes the moment of the communicated life. If one takes the elements and the terms "body" and "blood" as specifically significant, one immediately faces the problem: what is the relation between this body and the earthly body? Clement of Alexandria, Jerome, and Ratramnus of Corbie declared it to be the very same, though now received spiritually—not in material particles but in spiritual virtue. Irenaeus, Tertullian, Cyril of Jerusalem, and Gregory of Nyassa emphasized the material nature of *this* body, given to nourish for immortality the perishing flesh; hence the phrase "the medicine of immortality." This is the beginning of theories of transubstantiation and consubstantiation: the belief in a physical change in the elements whereby mortals receive immortality.

The proper understanding of the place of Jesus Christ in the Lord's Supper depends upon a proper understanding of the relationship between the elements of the rite and the action of the rite. These two aspects are inseparable, and most of the difficulties arising in theological understanding have been due to the perennial tendency in the church to divide them. The church itself has a dual nature. It is a visible sign in this world of a reality which, like Christ, belongs to another world. So also the Christian: he is dead to the flesh, yet living in the flesh; born again of the Spirit, yet possessing only the promise of the full spiritual life. The reality of the church is due to the presence of Christ in the midst of the assembly of the faithful who meet in his name. This existential fact was experienced and declared in the Lord's Supper, and the undivided church lived a rich sacramental life without formulating any sacramental dogma. But as the church developed, it found itself performing two functions, one devotional and the other apologetic. For both, the Lord's Supper was the central fact; but the clamant need for definition and stability led to an apologetic use of the sacrament which depreciated and finally overcame the devotional. Thus Athanasius in his attempt to vindicate the true godhead of Christ and the unity of his person claims that we become partakers of the divine nature (are "deified") by partaking of the body of Christ because what we receive is not "the body of some man, but the body of the Lord himself."[10] Cyril of Alexandria,[11] Hilary,[12] and Augustine[13] reiterate the same points for the same reasons. Emphasizing the counter aspect of this truth—the permanence and reality of Christ's manhood—Leo uses the same argument:

Can they (his opponents) lie in such depths of ignorance as not even to have heard of what is so familiar in every one's mouth in the Church of God, that not even infant's lips are silent about the truth of the body and blood of Christ in the sacraments of communion? For this is what is given, this is what is taken . . . . receiving the virtue of the heavenly food, we should pass into His flesh who was made our flesh.[14]

So also Ignatius, repelling false teaching which denied the reality of Christ's manhood, declared: "[They] abstain from eucharist and prayer because they do not acknowledge that the eucharist is the flesh of our Saviour Jesus Christ, which suffered for our sins, which by His goodness the Father raised up"[15] "Take care then to frequent but one eucharist, for there is one flesh of our Lord Jesus Christ and one cup for unity in His blood."[16] It was, therefore, in the struggle for unity and self-definition that the church, seizing upon the act in which was found the essence and expression of unity, made use of its universally accepted devotional content in illicit ways. The spiritual unity which was threatened was protected by claims of a material unity which perverted the meaning of the sacrament.

We must not ignore, however, the continuing emphasis that was laid on the life-giving function of the Lord's Supper as the place where the church met its Lord. The early liturgies all bear witness to this expectation. The prayer of consecration was that bread and wine might, by the power of God, be made Christ's body and blood—but not as a magical expression of a static unity and deification; rather "those receiving them may be confirmed to holiness, may obtain remission of sins and . . . eternal life."[17] In other words, the life of Christ given and received in the sacrament was to the end that his risen activity might continue and extend the work begun in the flesh.

How are we to understand the meaning of the sacrament in this way? It is fundamentally the declaration that, though we meet the benevolence of God in nature in many ways, we do not so meet his grace. Grace does something for us that we cannot do for ourselves. The gift of God is God himself who is received in faith, in the act of communion which commemorates the once-for-all act of God's giving, and at the same time is the means of that gift being continually received anew. If we deny that this means the elements of the Lord's Supper are, by some magical means, material vehicles of God's grace, how can we make intelligible the devotional content of the rite and its objective meaning? Would a "metatelic" view suffice: that is, not a change of nature, but of end or purpose? The elements serve to concentrate and focus Christ's activity toward us for a special purpose. Thus the nourishing "end" of bread and wine disappears and another "end" takes its place, namely, to mediate Christ to the believer. Bread is no longer bread, or wine wine; in faith they are heavenly food by the action of God in Christ, and this "end" demands the consent of all for its event: of the minister, the believer, and the whole body of the church.

This "metatelic" idea has proved attractive to many, but its fundamental weakness is in its continued emphasis on a change wrought in the elements. So long as bread and wine have somehow to change into something other, either in nature or function, the presence of Jesus Christ is linked with subpersonal and magical phenomena. In fact, this is true of any attempted doctrinal explanation which concentrates on the elements, and thus focuses attention on a specific section of the whole activity. We do not escape this difficulty in terms of a symbolic explanation if the symbolism is narrowly related to the elements. If we review a symbolic explanation, it will be obvious that it falls into the same magico-material pitfall as a theory of metaphysical or metabolic change.

The typical symbolic approach insists that the reality revealed in the religion, worship, and life of the Christian is not the absolute essence of God, but the power of God insofar as it is directed towards the soul of man and its salvation. The counterpart of worship is a real God; corresponding on the human side to this transcendent reality is faith, also a gift from God, the outcome of this immanent activity. The process is thus a circle proceeding from God and returning to him. The spiritual weakness of our physical nature demands, and is given, *forms* of worship—words, things, gestures—which become symbols by God incarnating himself in them. The faith of the worshiper, aspiring to communion with God, is also turned towards the forms of worship which, by pointing the way, transport the soul into the sphere of the Spirit. This mediation also imparts a symbolic character into the forms of worship which must be both metaphysical (transmitting the grace of God) and psychical (concentrating and directing the aspirations of human faith). The symbol therefore is permeable. The grace of God guides the faith of the worshiper past the concrete symbol to his own spiritual reality. The symbol loses its contingent reality and becomes part of the higher reality to which everything on earth owes its life. The corporeal is never brought completely into the sphere of the spiritual. The symbol is real not by denying its empirical elements, but by emphasizing its giveness and its intentional tendencies. The divine spirituality penetrating time and space through the medium of the symbol is not to be identified with the sacramental object, liturgical formula, or person of the celebrant; nor is the symbol's material form important. It is invested with a kind of hyper-realism by the double spirituality of its function-directive of faith and medium of the Spirit of God. Thus an organic relationship is established between divine grace and the symbol through which it passes, and also between human faith and the symbol which enables it to rise to God. The symbol secures the continuity of the divine current and the circuit of the religious life.

In such a view there is great effort put forward to avoid any suspicion of material change in the symbol. It retains its giveness and empirical quality, but in order that it may function as the medium of spiritual reality it must be invested with a hyperreality, and indeed demands a further activity of God "incarnating himself" in it and directing the faith of the worshiper beyond it. In the end, it acts as a kind of cut-in switch between the transcendent power-circuit of God and our dependent series. And this will always be so if particular elements of the sacramental act are singled out as the focus of its reality. So long as the conception of the place of Jesus Chirst is bound up with the conception of his metaphysical or real presence, this is inevitable. For the Lord's Supper is more than memorial and more than symbol.

The Lord's Supper is an act, an act of the church and not of the individual. It is an act created by the eternal act of Christ which made, and which makes, the church. However much the Eucharist may be a specific reminder of a particular event, it must never be considered as self-subsistent, that is, not of the frame of reference of the whole churchly act of worship as an intrinsic part of the common life of the church. As the action of Jesus initiated the Lord's Supper, even so the action of the church alone reconstitutes it. Bread and wine, prayer and participation outside the *koinonia* of the church and apart from its nature as a people created and redeemed in the death and resurrection of Jesus Christ, are mere forms bereft of any reality. They are even mere parody of true eucharistic worship. Christ is alive in his church. He acts through its action in preaching, sacrament, and daily witness. But he acts through its action, not through particular, even if inevitable, media or material instruments of its action. The elements of communion are not and cannot be the presence or activity of Christ any more than the words of a sermon are the preacher, or the preached word can be the Bible. They are all the witness of the Christian soul to its Redeemer who created both Bible and church.

If the elements are symbolic, they are only so in pointing to, without including, the reality to which they witness. It is the action which is symbolic in a deeper sense: it contains and conveys the reality. The elements are only materials to enable the symbolic act to be carried out—like the sounds in language. It was thus the breaking, not the bread, that was symbolical, the pouring, not the wine. "This is my body broken," "This is my blood shed." This is why it was a covenant—a mutual act—a giving and partaking. For the disciples received it in that first Supper, and this is the real significance of the words *"Do this in remembrance of me."* What they received was his person, his will, and perfect obedience for them. This was communicated in the act objectively and in reality. We do not enact a private mystery in the Lord's Supper—a picture of Christ's sacrifice—but in the act of his church Christ gives himself anew to us and we give ourselves anew in responsible faith. And it is to us Christ gives himself, not to God. His saving act is repeated within us. The emphasis is not on flesh, but on body or person, not on blood but on covenant. The place of Jesus Christ in the Lord's Supper depends upon our experience of salvation—our Christology. The symbol is in the eating. Bread and wine are not purveyors of magic, but food to be consumed. In the act we receive the benefits of his death. As P. T. Forsyth finely says, "We live on the holy person and grace of Christ, about Whose substantial Being or cryptic virtue we know nothing, as their is no sign that He knew anything. Our communion is not with Christ's body except as that image stands for the person; and it is not with His person except as that person in its consummate and eternal Act is our Redeemer."[18] The church is new, created life in Christ. As we perform the act of Christ, Christ performs his act in us. Bread and wine do not signify his absence and become the means of his presence only by mysterious and theosophic change. They signify his presence, and the whole act of which they are the elements is forgiveness, communion, and covenant.

Disciples of Christ have always declared that the gospel or the Christian faith is good news about God's action as Holy Energy personally directed and morally conditioned. The emphasis has been on real action rather than real presence. It is time that Disciples made their witness theologically intelligible. I close with a quotation from Walter Scott. Scott wrote: "What, then, are Baptism and the Lord's Supper? I answer that they are the crucifixion, or death, burial, and resurrection of Christ, repeating themselves in the life and profession of the disciples, and proclaiming to the ages that he, that was to come, is come."[19]

NOTES

1. Acts 2:42.
2. *The Ministry and Sacraments,* ed. Roderie Dunkerley (London: S.C.M. Press, 1937).
3. Luke 24.
4. 1 Corinthians 11:24-25.
5. 1 Corinthians 10:16-21.
6. 1 Corinthians 11:23.
7. Cf. 1 Corinthians 15:3.
8. Galatians 1:18.
9. 1 Corinthians 11:29.
10. Ep. *Ad. Serapion* 61:2.
11. *Luc.* 72:19.
12. *de. Trin.* 8:14.
13. *Evang. Tract.* 27:5.
14. *Ep.* 59:2.
15. *Ad. Smyr.* 7.
16. *Ad. Philad.* 4.
17. J. M. Neale (ed.), *Primitive Greek Liturgies* (London: 1896), p. 25. Trans. J.G.C.
18. P. T. Forsyth, *The Church and the Sacraments* (London: Independent Press, Ltd., 1947), p. 302.
19. Walter Scott, *The Messiahship* (Cincinnati: H. S. Bosworth, 1859), p. 284.

301

CONCLUSION

❈14❈

Disciple Thought in
Protestant Perspective: an Interpretation

Ralph G. Wilburn

THE theology of Discipledom has, from the beginning, been a growing, progressive quantity. One has but to compare tendencies in present-day Disciple thought with positions held by the founding fathers to realize that the progressive spirit is part of the very life-blood of Discipledom.

For example, Disciples have assimilated the insights of biblical criticism, and have adjusted their understanding of the Bible and the nature of its authority accordingly. They have appropriated the modern historical understanding of human existence, with its emphasis on the relativity of all human thought, and have thereby seen the fallacies in the early plea for the restoration of "the ancient order of things." Many similar developments have taken place in the Disciple mind.

My aim in this concluding chapter is to describe, in broad outline, what seems to me to be a kind of synthesis toward which Disciple thought has been, and still is, moving. To indicate the historical significance of this synthesis, I have designated numerous points of correlation with the general, theological perspective of Protestant theology.

Throughout, I am endeavoring to describe what Disciples believe. The reader doubtless does not need to be reminded that the statement represents the author's understanding of what is best in present-day Disciple thought. Many of those in the "Church of Christ" wing, and many of the "Independents" will doubtless express dissent. However, after considerable consultation with a number of leading Disciple thinkers, who have already read this statement, the author believes that he is fairly articulating, in broad outline, the main theological current of contemporary Disciple thought.

In the main, Disciples of Christ are resolved to avoid the "idol of the cave" of one-sidedness, and to maintain the proper balance in the reception and expression of the Christian gospel. Ignoring peripheral impulses and fringe movements, the character of the Disciple mind can perhaps best be sketched briefly, by describing it in terms of the following eight pairs of concepts.

Freedom and Community

A basic aspect of the genius of Disciples of Christ is the concern to restore "the liberty of the Christian man," which makes the Christian "the most free lord of all and subject to none," as Luther expressed it. Even as Luther dedicated his life to liberate the Christian conscience of his day from external church authority (pope and church councils), so Disciples of Christ have sought to remain true to this Protestant principle of liberty, and to free the Christian conscience also from the external authority of the creeds developed by Protestant orthodoxy. As Thomas Campbell expressed it, "Resume that precious . . . liberty, wherewith Christ has made his people free; a liberty from subjection to any authority but his own, in matters of religion."[1]

Disciples of Christ believe that Protestant orthodoxy lost the spirit of reform and consequently developed in a way which falsified the true, prophetic nature of Protestantism; freedom of biblical interpretation was once again being curbed, this time by Protestants themselves. Disciples of Christ are a group dedicated to the task of recovering and safeguarding the prophetic spirit of liberty in classical Protestantism. They have steadily resolved to keep the fires of freedom burning brightly.

To this very day, Disciples of Christ have no "creed," in the historic sense of this term. One of their early slogans, still deeply cherished, is the watchword: "No creed but Christ!" This is their only confessional requirement for church membership: the simple confession of faith in the lordship of Christ.

This emphasis on liberty, however, must not be confused with individualism. Christian freedom is not the self-will of a stalwart individualist. From the beginning, Disciples of Christ have been aware of the need to hold this principle of individual freedom in creative balance with the principle of community, as did Luther in his treatise "On Christian Liberty." With the Apostle Paul, Disciples of Christ know that Christians are "called to freedom," but that the only *Christian* use of this freedom is "through love [to] be servants of one another" (Galatians 5:13). The individual finds true fulfillment of his freedom only in community, *in* Christian fellowship. The independence of individual freedom can find *Christian* fulfillment only in the responsible dependence of community, for in the Christian perspective man's freedom is inseparable from his destiny: the community of Christlike men.

Throughout the history of the Disciple movement, the emphasis on liberty has been held in inseparable connection with responsibility in cooperative fellowship. Hence, Disciples have attempted to avoid *that kind* of liberty fostered by radical individualists and enthusiastic spiritualists; they have also avoided *that kind* of community which becomes distorted into what Emil Brunner calls "objectivism," a community which is overinstitutionalized and fails to nurture the values of individual liberty.

Disciples insist that these two—libery and love—must be held together, and that a relation of mutual reciprocity can and must be maintained between the insights of the individual and the corporate mind of the Christian community.

Unity and Diversity

This second pair of concepts represents a tension-filled unity which lies deep in the theology of Disciples of Christ. No historic statement of the Disciple movement is quoted more frequently by Disciples than that in which Thomas Campbell affirmed "that the church of Christ upon earth is essentially, intentionally, and constitutionally one."[2]

From the beginning, however, Disciples have insisted that the "essential" unity of the church cannot be realized by a theology which holds the basis of unity to consist in unanimous agreement on a confessional foundation. The confessional pathway to unity is difficult, if not impossible to follow, for the simple reason that there never has been, nor is there now, any one confession which is acceptable to all Christians. Nor does it seem likely that there ever will be such doctrinal unanimity, inasmuch as the Christian knowledge of God in Jesus Christ is always, or should always be, in process of vigorous development, and is always being shaped, in part, by historically and culturally determined (finite) perspectives.

The confessional road to unity is, in principle, the pathway which Roman Catholicism has followed down through the centuries. All Protestants are aware of the evils which this kind of unity promoted: a stifling of individual liberty, an absolutizing of church dogmas and institutions, a spirit of sectarian exclusiveness, failure in Christian charity, un-Christian religious bigotry and the like. Disciples have continually reminded their brethren throughout Christendom of these and similar perils which beset the confessional pathway to unity. A study of Christian history shows undeniably that such evils have been the end product of the confessional pathway to unity.

The basis of Christian unity must therefore lie at a deeper level than doctrinal congruency. It must be the kind of basis which provides for a unity that comprehends diversity. The world of God's creation is infinitely variegated. Its variety and diversity are essential parts of its beauty, its harmony of contrasts. Similarly, the church of God's creation is glorious, in part, by virtue of its diversity in cultural and ideational forms of expression.

The Apostle Paul himself made use of a particular analogy from creation in describing Christian unity, when he used the illustration of the organism of the human body.[3] The various members of the human body have different functions to perform, Paul argued; yet nothing is more truly one than the human body, with its multiplicity of parts all performing their several functions, yet helping and supplementing one another. The unity of the church, says Paul, is like this: it is a corporate unity. This means that the more each individual becomes *his own true self,* under Christ, and makes his own unique contribution to the common life of the church, the more the church as a whole will attain unto its true oneness.

Part of the glory of Christ's church lies in the fact that there is a unity in it which *comprehends* all of its diverse forms of historical fulfillment, a unity which binds together, in Christ the Lord, a Francis of Assisi and a Walter Rauschenbusch, an Origen and a Karl Barth, a Gregory the Great and a John Calvin, a Tertullian and a Schleiermacher.

Genuine Christian unity includes diversity of historical forms of expression, for the Christ, in whom we become one, remains always what he is: the transcendent source of the life of his historically diversified body, whose Spirit cannot therefore be *identified* with any of its historical forms of expression, even though it finds fulfillment in a diversity of such forms.

If the confessional pathway to unity is fallacious, so also is the pathway advocated by the *Religionsgeschichtlicheschule.* The approach of this school of thought preserved (although in a distorted way) the values of individual liberty, but at the expense of *genuinely Christian* unity. It fostered, to be sure, a unity in the spiritual values of humanism, in general, but it proved itself to be lacking in evangelical depth. It was more a unity in moral, human values and good citizenship; it was a kind of religious version of political democracy. To be sure, political democracy is a praiseworthy political ideal; but is political democracy adequate to supply us with a basis for *genuinely Chris-*

tian togetherness? Surely Christian community is something more than political community, for the former rests upon the evangelical ground of the gospel of God. As Professor Edmund Schlink of the University of Heidelberg puts it, the unity fostered by the *Religionsgeschichtlicheschule* was not yet unity in evangelical faith.

Against the authoritarian tendency of the creedalistic pathway to unity, Disciples have stressed the ecumenical plea of Thomas Campbell, arguing that "until you associate, consult, and advise together; and *in a friendly and Christian manner* explore the subject, nothing can be done."[4] Or as expressed in *The Last Will and Testament of the Springfield Presbytery* of Kentucky (June 28, 1804), "we *will,* that preachers and people cultivate a spirit of mutual forbearance; pray more and dispute less."[5]

Against the spirit of Renaissance culture, which threatened to reduce Christian unity to *nothing but* the unity of *humanism,* Disciples of Christ have pointed to the supreme act of God's revelation in Jesus Christ, as the center and bond of unity. The constitutive principle of the life of the church is the living Word of God, mediated through Jesus Christ. The oneness of the church is therefore correctly understood and realized only when it is seen in organic relation to this dynamic center of faith. As Thomas Campbell expressed it, "A manifest attachment to our Lord Jesus Christ in faith, holiness, and charity, was . . . the foundation and cement of Christian unity."[6] Or as Luther expressed it in one of his sermons, "Since we are one with Christ, the result is that we become one with another. . . ."[7]

True Christian unity thus can only be realized by maintaining this field of tension between unity and diversity. In Christ's church there should be both unity and diversity, but neither without the other. Unity at the expense of diversity leads to a dogmatism or absolutism which destroys the spirit of Christian charity; and diversity without unity cuts the vital bond of the church's life with the lordship of Christ. But unity *in* diversity is historically realistic and makes it possible for our fragmentary perspectives on the truth of the gospel to be complemented and corrected by cross-fertilization with the perspectives of other Christian individuals and groups. Such unity in diversity constitutes a dynamic fellowship which promotes growth "in the grace and knowledge of our Lord and Savior Jesus Christ" (2 Peter 3:18).

Disciples of Christ, therefore, claim their rightful liberty to express and fulfill their own understanding of the gospel, in freedom. But with equal boldness they claim unity and fraternity with all other Christians, with whose theology they differ. Disciples of Christ insist upon a frank and forthright mutual recognition among all Christian groups. They plead that we must believe in the validity of the different historic forms of the faith, their ministries and their sacraments. Disciples plead vigorously for a recognition of the fact that the truly catholic body of Christ is big enough to embrace all of us, even those who are reluctant to be thus embraced.

From the principles delineated above, it will be evident that Disciples of Christ find themselves thoroughly at home, theologically, as a member body of the World Council of Churches, although all, of course, recognize that we have not yet attained the full realization of the unity of Christ's church.

Scripture and Experience

One may say that the emergence of the Disciple movement in Protestantism represents a recovery of the principle of *sola scriptura,* as construed in the classic period of the Reformation. Luther used the principle of *sola scriptura* to liberate the Christian conscience from external church authority. Furthermore, Luther did not intend that Scripture should be distorted into any similar external authority, for he insisted that *sola scriptura* was a correlative of *sola fide.* Luther's central norm of justification by faith made possible a free and creative use of Scripture. Scripture was, for him, an authority only insofar as it "drove Christ into the heart"; that is, Scripture was an authority only in its correlation with faith. To some extent also Calvin's doctrine of the inner witness of the Holy Spirit prevented him from reducing Scripture to an objective, external authority.

Protestant orthodoxy, however, distorted this principle of Scripture into a wholly external, infallible authority, *independent of the realm of faith*. And it proceeded to support the authority of Scripture, so construed, by developing a rigid theory of mechanical inspiration. But since it is absurd to hold that every Christian must actually know all the multitude of infallible truths in Scripture, orthodoxy proceeded to draw a distinction between those truths of Scripture, a knowledge of which is *essential* to salvation, and those which are *unessential*. And here the authority of the creed became a necessity to define explicitly what the essentials are. Creed and Scripture are logically inseparable in orthodoxy.

At this point Disciples effected a loosening up of the external authority of orthodoxy by repudiating the authority of the creed, thereby making possible, once again, a correlation of *sola scriptura* with *sola fide*. So it is, in the main, correct to say that the founders of the Disciple movement once again made use of the apostolic principle of reform, in its original Protestant sense.[8]

Thomas Campbell expressed this reformation principle aptly when he wrote:

Although inferences and deductions from Scripture premises, when fairly inferred may be truly called the doctrine of God's holy word: yet are they not formally binding upon the consciences of Christians farther than they perceive the connection, and evidently see that they are so; for their faith must not stand in the wisdom of men, but in the power and veracity of God.[9]

This "power and veracity of God" clearly points in the direction of the Reformation understanding of scripture in the classic period. Campbell was attempting to liberate the Christian conscience from external church authority and to direct absolute religious devotion once again to the lordship of Christ, the Christ pre-eminently of Scripture. Therefore, said Campbell, "no such deductions or inferential truths ought to have any place in the church's confession."[10]

This Disciple use of the principle of *sola scriptura* also represents one of the earlier ecumenical impulses in Protestant Christianity. Subsequently, a large number of Protestant groups similarly effected a loosening of the authority of the creeds and, at the same time, developed a renewed interest in Scripture. Out of this impulse has grown a veritable renaissance of biblical theology during the past two decades, which supplies the ecumenical movement with a common, objective basis upon which significant progress is being made toward greater unity.

Three influences, however, which have been dominant in shaping Disciple theology, have helped to prevent the *sola scriptura* principle from being distorted into an irrational biblicism. These influences are (1) the appeal to experience, derived from the philosophy of Lockean empiricism, (2) the rationalism of the Enlightenment, and (3) the historico-critical approach to the study of the Scripture, another expression of the empirical method of science. From the beginning, these influences have been major, positive factors in shaping Disciple theology. Alexander Campbell was a leading exponent of the method of historical criticism, and his thought was shaped by the philosophy of John Locke perhaps more than by any other philosophical system. Indeed, all of the leaders of the Disciple movement labored under the dominant influence of the Enlightenment, in general.

These three forces, combined with the original insight of Luther's principle of justification by faith, in which the authority of Scripture was joined inseparably with the experience of justification, have created the field of tension between Scripture and experience, within which Disciples have sought to understand the meaning of religious authority.

On the one hand, therefore, Disciples have attempted to avoid the erroneous view of Roman Catholic and Protestant orthodoxy which regards the truth of Scripture as a given objective datum, an infallible deposit of truth, although they have had no small religious struggle to liberate their communion, as a whole, from this theological fallacy of orthodoxy. Disciples have remained aware, however, that the truth of Scripture is the truth of experience. Indeed, Scripture is, first of all, an expression of the early Christians' experience of God in the fact of Jesus Christ. Like all truth, the truth of Scripture also is truth tested in experience. The truth of the gospel is truth known and tested in actual experience of reality. To distort Scripture therefore into a pseudotruth, not grounded and tested in experience, is to engender a biblicism foreign to the essential nature of biblical truth and to the genius of Protestant Christianity.

On the other hand, Disciples have maintained a firm belief in God's unique self-manifestation in Jesus Christ, through Scripture, and in abandoning the objectivistic authority of orthodoxy, they have not permitted their religion to be watered down to *nothing but* universal, natural religion, as did many during the Enlightenment. Like all Protestants, Disciples have struggled to gain a clearer understanding of the meaning of revelation as personal encounter. In this struggle they, too, have come to abandon the notion of the infallibility of the Bible, and have come to view Scripture as a historical, human witness to the gospel of God in Jesus Christ. As such, Scripture serves as a medium of Chirstian revelation.

We are led thus to the final authority to which this human biblical witness points: God's self-revelation in Jesus Christ. A dominant emphasis on the actual experience of the lordship of Christ has, after a lengthy struggle, rescued the Disciple movement from literalistic biblicism and supplied a norm in the light of which to judge all things, including the word of Scripture. The emphasis on an experience-centered grasp of Christ has finally saved the Disciple communion, as a whole, from the erroneous view in which one regards something historically objective (in this instance the biblical writings) as the actual *object* of faith.

314

Faith and Reason

A fourth pair of concepts which Disciples of Christ have sought to maintain in proper theological balance is that of faith and reason. The main current of Disciple thought has never been satisfied with the irrational approach of fundamentalism, for the Disciple movement has operated under the demand for rational integrity generated by the Enlightenment, in general, and by the philosophy of common sense Scottish realism, in particular. Yet neither have Disciples been willing to abandon the biblical grasp of truth through faith, and settle for the pure rationalism of humanism or speculative philosophy.

Like most Protestant groups, there has been an ambiguity among Disciples in regard to the nature of faith. Two concepts of faith have struggled for the mastery of the Protestant mind. One view, stemming from Protestant orthodoxy, regards faith as belief in the divine truth written in holy Scripture. This conception interprets faith as a doctrinaire affair and generates a rationalistic and/or legalistic understanding of the religious relationship. The other concept, derived from the classic period of the Reformation, is theologically more sound. In this view, faith is understood as a relation between persons; faith is the relation of one's personal affirmative response to the call and claim of God in Christ.

The combination, in Disciple thought, of a critical approach to the study of the Bible, and a Christ-centered religious orientation have made possible a liberation of Disciples of Christ from the doctrinaire view of faith and led them to adopt the personalistic view.

In the Disciple synthesis of faith and reason, it is recognized (1) that faith is more inclusive than reason, for "faith" is a word which characterizes the primal life-relationship between man and God; faith is the dynamic, whole response of personality to the call and claim of God in Christ; it is the response of one's whole being, in absolute trust and commitment; (2) that only in such total commitment to the claim of God does

315

one receive the power of God's Spirit to heal the cleavages which characterize human reason apart from faith, and to make one whole; (3) that only in such total commitment to the leading of God is the mind of man redeemed from that sinful self-centeredness of personality which blurs and distorts man's vision of the good and leads him to view the world of his fellow men, sinfully, as material to be manipulated and exploited for selfish advantage; only the commitment of faith can generate the vision which looks out upon the world in the spirit of service and Christlike love.

Yet reason also has its part to play in the total religious relationship: (1) reason plays a kind of John the Baptist role, in so far as it prepares the way for the coming of faith by analyzing the problem of man's existence, exposing his basic contradictions, and pointing out the urgency of his need for redemption; (2) reason also plays an integral part in the total response of faith, for part of this response is intellectual in nature; the response of faith is intellectual as well as volitional and emotional; there is a seeing and a knowing which is a part of the experience of faith; (3) most Disciples would also insist that reason has an apologetical function to perform; not only must reason operate in explicating the meaning and content of faith (thus bringing faith into significant relation with culture), but it must also show the revelance of the gospel of redemption to man's actual situation. Without this latter function, faith resolves itself into a pietistic mouthing of traditional shibboleths or a letting off of sentimental steam. And if the gospel is revelant to our human situation, then in some basic sense, it must be continuous with reason or the general intelligible structure of human existence.

For these reasons, Disciples of Christ have insisted on holding faith and reason together. Faith without reason is blind; but reason without faith is impotent, divided, and distorted, and its knowledge is naught but the soliloquy of subjectivism. Faith provides the wider framework of community in which the dialogue of worship finds fulfillment.

Grace and Free Will

There are three major interpretations of Christian experience in terms of the pair of concepts of grace and free will which Disciples of Christ have rejected as erroneous.

First, Disciples of Christ have always rejected *that kind* of predestinarian view of grace which nullifies man's moral freedom and interprets election as a streamlined, atomistic divine decree that operates with mechanistic rigidity. Disciples have consistently maintained that a true understanding of grace (God's limitless graciousness) is one that is compatible with belief in man's moral responsibility in freedom. Hence, grace cannot be irresistible, in any absolute sense. God has created us as persons. In so doing, he has defined the manner of dealing with us in redemption. His grace approaches us in a personal way; it is the power of his loving persuasive concern, which calls to the spirit of man for his response. A working of grace which fails to deal with the subject in a personal way could not be truly redemptive of human personality. Hence, Disciples have always vigorously rejected the traditional idea of a *double predestination,* for such a doctrine implies that the divine decree of election operates in arbitrary fashion, and that it rides roughshod over man's freedom.

Second, Disciples of Christ have remained aware that Christianity is pre-eminently a religion of grace, that God's gracious and utterly free act of forgiveness in Jesus Christ is wholly without man's merit, and that nothing but his grace can "heal the wounded will" (Augustine) and make man truly free. Hence, Disciples are opposed to the Erasmian and Thomistic understanding of free will, which says that man must *first* do what is within his own power, *and then* whatever grace is needed will be added. Luther was correct when, in *The Bondage of the Will,* he contended (against Erasmus) that the will of man is under the servitude of sin and is not free to do the good until *freed* by God's grace and empowered by his Spirit. Disciples agree with Luther in rejecting the autonomous view of free will

317

in humanism, for, in the final analysis, such autonomy cuts the nerve of the doctrine of redemption.

A third inadequate understanding of grace and freedom is to be found in the view which regards them as correlates, for if grace and free will are genuine correlates, then either grace or free will can initiate the process of salvation. Disciples believe that man's freedom is not a coordinate, alongside God's grace. The religious relation is not one of teamwork involving equals, for such a conception runs counter to the biblical truth of the creature's dependence upon the Creator. Rather, freedom must be viewed as the action of man *under, and in response to,* God's grace. Man's freedom of spirit is not, as the Greeks mistakenly thought, something which he possesses independent of his relation to the divine. Man's freedom, like his very being, he holds as a gift from his Creator. Man's freedom is the *answer* of finite spirit to the creative call of the infinite Spirit.

There is, therefore, a basic threefold truth in the traditional, evangelical doctrine of predestination. When construed properly, this doctrine aims to express and secure three basic aspects of grace. It says (1) that it is God, not man, who takes the initiative in the work of redemption, (2) that salvation is by grace alone *(sola gratia),* wholly eliminating the notion of human merit, and (3) that "our salvation is then sure to us when we find the cause of it in the breast of God," as Calvin expressed it.[11] Or, as the Apostle Paul put it, "If God is for us, who is against us?" (Romans 8:31).

The divine promise, received through the gospel of Jesus Christ, imparts to him who responds in faith an inner stability of personality. Through this gracious promise, one taps something of the infiniteness of God's power "to save those who draw near" (Hebrews 7:25). To live under the sky of grace means that one is enabled to face the horizon of the future with an absolute openness, for it is God's horizon. It means that one is enabled to achieve a spiritual victory in any crisis whatever, including the ultimate crisis of one's own physical dissolution. It means that the Christian lives life with death at his back, instead of in his face. The victory is won by the power of him who makes all things new—to men of faith.

The grace of God is thus the power which redeems us from the unbelief and anxiety that grow out of our finitude; it is the power which gives us the courage to be, whatever the tragedies that befall us in the historical realm of existence. Grace and freedom are thus wholly compatible, for it is God's grace that makes us truly free, free from guilt, from unbelief, from anxiety, from self-centeredness, free to fulfill our destiny of becoming Christlike men. Grace does not nullify the freedom of man's decision; it challenges and inspires man's freedom to such decision.

Spirit and Sacrament

A sixth pair of concepts which is also crucial in grasping the character of Christianity is that of Spirit and sacrament. In reference to these concepts, Disciples of Christ have always rejected two extreme theological points of view: (1) the mystical view, which so emphasizes the inner reality of Spirit that the external aspect of the sacraments (the sign) loses all vital significance, a view which in principle would, in the final analysis, break the continuity of the church as a historical community, and (2) the institutional position, which Emil Brunner calls "objectivism," the view, namely, which crystallizes and hardens the formal aspect of the sacraments, with the result that little room is found for the free, inner working of God's Spirit and the personal encounter of faith.

Thomas Münzer and the reformation radicals (whom Luther called the *Schwärmerei*) represent a clear historic expression of the first error. The Roman Catholic dogma that the grace of the sacraments works objectively and with a kind of mechanical precision is a valid expression of the second fallacy. In the Catholic sacrament of penance, for example, genuine contrition is not an absolute necessity to valid sacramental action, according to Catholic dogma;[12] mere attrition (fear of punishment) suffices to fulfill the first requirement of penance. The sacrament works *ex opere operato;* it works by working, objectively, with little or no relevance to faith and repentance. Similarly, it is difficult to see what *faith* has to do with the miracle of transubstantiation; the consecrated host is the "medicine of immortality." What does such idolatrous objectivism have to do with faith, the Spirit, and the grace of God's forgiving favor?

Alexander Campbell stated the Disciple position on this problem succinctly when he affirmed that " 'the word alone' system is as far from the . . . truth as 'the Spirit alone' theory."[13] The Disciple position on this problem of the relation of Spirit and sacrament is, first of all, one which holds the vertical and the horizontal dimensions of Christian experience together. Without sacrament, there is no sharing in the holy Spirit; but without the presence and working of God's Spirit, the sacrament is no longer a sacrament. Our relation to God is bound inseparably to our historic relation to our fellow men. This union of the vertical and the horizontal dimensions of Christian experience gives a sacramental significance to the institutions and forms which serve to make the church a cohesive, historic community with a definite character.

It is interesting to note that even as Luther and Melanchthon were obliged to deal with radical prophets of the Spirit, such as Münzer and Karlstadt, in the initial phases of the sixteenth-century Reformation, the early founders of the Disciple movement were forced to deal with similar leaders who sponsored highly emotional revivals, in which religious experience flamed up and went beyond rational control. And even as Luther did battle with the *Schwärmerei* by emphasizing the indispensable role of Scripture in Christian experience, so Alexander Campbell constantly emphasized the Bible as a *sine qua non* of sharing in the working of God's Spirit.

Disciples of Christ thus find themselves in hearty agreement with Luther when in his treatise *Against the Heavenly Prophets* he wrote,

Since God has sent forth his holy gospel, he deals with us in a two-fold way; first outwardly, secondly, inwardly. Outwardly, He deals with us through the word of the gospel and through physical signs, namely baptism and sacrament. . . . So then he has decreed that he will give no man the inner reality except through the outward. For he will give the Spirit and faith to nobody except through the external word and signs which he has instituted.[14]

In a similar passage in his longer catechism Luther wrote:

These wise birds, the new spirits (Karlstadt *et. al.*) contend that *faith alone* saves us, and that works and external things add nothing of value. We reply that of course nothing works inwardly but faith. . . . But these leaders of the blind will not see that faith must have something in which it believes, to which it clings, and on which it can firmly plant its feet. Thus faith depends on water. It believes that real salvation and life are in baptism, not in the water, as such, but because it is bound up with God's Word and with His name.[15]

Said Luther,

we have the Apostle Paul to thank that Christianity was long ago delivered from such factious spirits as these fanatics. Otherwise we would be sitting quietly throughout the Sabbath day, gazing blankly into empty space, like they do, holding our head in our hands, waiting for the heavenly voice of the spirit.[16]

In a highly similar vein, Alexander Campbell wrote,

the word of God is but a specific embodiment of the Holy Spirit. It is veiled spirit, or . . . grace; and hence, the Spirit works only through the word upon the understanding, the conscience, and the heart. . . . We speak to God in words, and he speaks to us by his word.[17]

In addition to the evangelical principle of Scripture, the rationalistic temperament of the Enlightenment made Disciples of Christ suspicious of the doctrine of the Spirit, so much so that they have developed a doctrine of the holy Spirit slowly and with considerable caution. They have done so, however, and thereby saved their movement from pure rationalism.

The empirical strand of Disciple thought has led them to develop a concrete concept of God as "Spirit," in contrast to the abstract notion of "Spirit" in the theology of mysticism. Disciples believe that God is to be found and known in concrete empirical experience, not in speculative theology nor in the ethereal notions of the mystics. Here again, there is a strong affinity between Disciples of Christ and Luther's idea of God of "Spirit," immanent in history and the world, not transcendent in the sense of being separate and apart from the world.

Disciples of Christ have thus been led to emphasize the sacramental character of the word of Scripture as a form in which the Spirit of God is historically present and through which God's Spirit speaks to man. Disciples also hold the belief in the *actual presence* of the Spirit in the sacraments of baptism and the Lord's Supper. Yet there is no crystallization of any one theology of the sacraments which prevails among Disciples of Christ.

The sacraments have been given a central and dominant position in the theology and practice of Disciples of Christ. Disciples have always made the Lord's Supper the central feature of their weekly, corporate worship. Their celebration of the Supper, furthermore, has always been genuinely ecumenical in spirit. Except for a short period in their early history, Disciples in America have never practiced "close communion." On the contrary, they have shared this most sacred Christian experience with all who consider themselves to be Christians. The Disciple celebration of the Supper has, therefore, been a unifying, ecumenical force rather than an instrument of exclusion. Disciples believe that in the fellowship of communion Christians ought to stretch their minds to appropriate their identity with the fullness of the truly catholic body of Christ.

The Disciple movement actually began because Thomas Campbell, originally a minister of the anti-Burgher Seceder Presbyterian church, felt deeply the sinfulness of division in his own communion. Consequently, he began inviting all his Presbyterian brethren on the Pennsylvania frontier, of whatever party, to share in the communion service. This ecumenical practice eventually led to Campbell's deposition from the Presbyterian ministry.

Disciples of Christ have never entertained the idea of transubstantiation or consubstantiation in their understanding of the Eucharistic act. Indeed, they have been so staunchly opposed to such notions that they have been reluctant to use the term "sacrament" (preferring the word "ordinance"), due to its historic associations. Yet neither has the Disciple understanding been restricted to the early Zwinglian view of the Supper as a bare memorial ritual. In the main, Disciples find themselves in agreement with Calvin's view of Christ's real, but spiritual, presence in the Eucharistic act. With Schleiermacher also. Disciples believe that the act of corporate communion is central in the life of the church, because in it two dimensions of fellowship are merged: fellowship with Jesus Christ, and fellowship with one another. As Alexander Campbell expressed it,

Ties that spring from eternal love, revealed in blood and addressed to his senses in symbols adapted to the whole of man, draws forth all that is within him of complacent affection and feeling to those joint heirs with him of the grace of eternal life.[18]

Disciples believe that the holy Spirit is active as the unseen Presence in the fellowship at the Lord's table, for the holy Spirit (the Spirit of the living Christ) is the fellowship-forming power which calls the people of Christ's church together out of the life of the world. As Christ himself said, "Where two or three are gathered in my name, there am I in the midst of them" (Matthew 18:20). The holy Spirit is therefore the corporate mind of the Christian community, in which individual Christians share. This sharing is especially vivid in corporate study and worship, and in the act of communion. Such visible signs and symbols are thus indispensable means for the historic actualization of Christ's church.

Disciples of Christ have stressed the symbolic significance of the bread and wine of the Eucharist. In principle, the Spirit of Christ is present in these symbols in the same way that it is present in the linguistic symbols of scripture. Even as the Bible is no holy thing, but a historical, human book, through which God acts and speaks, so also the elements of the Supper are not holy things; they are (and remain) simple bread and wine, yet also symbols through which the presence of Christ's Spirit is realized and appropriated, through faith.

As for baptism, Disciples of Christ have always practiced the mode of immersion (1) because they believe that this mode is in agreement with the practice of the rite in the New Testament, (2) because it symbolizes better than any other mode the central meaning of the rite, namely, the crucifixion of the old self and the resurrection of the new being in Christ (Romans 6), and (3) because it is universally accepted by the church as a valid form of Christian baptism, and can therefore exercise a unifying influence in the life of the church.

This emphasis on the immersionistic mode of baptism, however, is not such that it prevents Disciples from recognizing the full validity of the Christian experience of those whose baptism has been of another mode, and the full liberty of each Christian body to follow the light of the gospel as God gives them to see the light. As Barton W. Stone aptly put it, "none of us are disposed to make our notions of baptism, however well founded, a Bar of Christian fellowship."[19] Stone wisely warned all "reforming Baptists" that should they make their own peculiar views of immersion a test of fellowship, "it will be impossible for them to repel, successfully, the imputation of being sectarians, and of having an authoritative creed. . . ."[20]

From the beginning, Disciples have boldly rejected the traditional, Augustinian idea of original guilt, which constituted one of the strongest historic bases of infant baptism. Consequently, Disciples have never practiced infant baptism. In keeping with the New Testament, they understand the meaning of baptism to be a voluntary act of obedience to the lordship of

Christ, on the part of a responsible subject. Hence, they have regarded baptism as an act which is significant only for one who is capable of faith. Disciples are aware, however, that there are positive values in the traditional rite of infant baptism which should and can be preserved by a church ceremony of dedication for parents and infant.

Baptism is regarded by Disciples as possesing a saving significance, because it is an act of faith whereby one submits himself to the lordship of Jesus Christ. It is an act by which one seals his dedication to Christ, publicly, and thereby takes the reign of Christ his Lord upon his total personality, in all of its aspects. Also, baptism is an act whereby one is initiated into the Christian fellowship, an act whereby one is incorporated into that realm where Christ exercises his lordship; and, as such, baptism possesses a saving value. Like the Lord's Supper, baptism also is basically social in significance; there is no such thing as valid Christian baptism, separate and apart from the body of Christ.

It should be added also that since the Disciple concept of the church is thoroughly in accord with the Protestant doctrine of the "priesthood of all believers," Disciples of Christ have never developed any ministerial exclusiveness in connection with the administration of the sacraments. So far as theological validity is concerned, they believe that it does not matter who officiates in the administration of the sacraments, so long as he is a member of Christ's body. Hence, Disciples heartily recognize the validity of the ministries and the sacraments of other Christian groups. No doctrine of "apostolic succession" blocks the way of Disciples of Christ to ecumenical action and cooperation.

Congregationalism and Catholicity

The church polity of Disciples of Christ falls into the traditional classification of congregationalism. The congregational type of church structure developed among Disciples of Christ, partly due to the fact that the Disciple movement represented an attempt to recover congregational freedom from an overhead structure of religious authority, partly as an expression of the individualism which obtained on the American frontier in the early nineteenth century, and partly also due to the Disciple plea for a "restoration of New Testament Christianity." The Disciples found no warrant in the New Testament for overhead religious authorities dictating to congregations in ways which ride roughshod over congregational liberty.

A weakness to which congregational church polity is sometimes subject is a *kind* of congregational individualism which loses the values of catholicity and distorts the nature of the church, even as American democracy has not always avoided the evil of a disintegrating individualism which loses the values of creative community in an ideal democracy.

Disciples of Christ have experienced considerable difficulty arising out of this weakness. From the beginning of the Disciple movement, however, their leaders have been aware of this danger, and they sought to guard against it, while yet cherishing their newly won freedom. Alexander Campbell, for example, fought valiantly to maintain the values of catholicity, alongside those of liberty. Campbell believed that the church is "the congregation of God, a great community of communities."[21] No one of these communities is under the jurisdiction of any other; each is to all other communities as "an individual disciple is to every other individual disciple in any one particular community meeting in any given place."[22] This means that when any one of these particular communities withdraws itself from, or deliberately refuses to cooperate and identify itself with the larger (catholic) community, the "great community of communities," it thereby forfeits its right to be regarded as a part of the body of Christ.

The experience of most church groups has led them to realize that it is not always an easy matter to maintain the proper balance between these two aspects of the structure of the church. Yet most Protestant bodies would agree with Disciples that true ecclesiastical polity demands such a balance.

It is true, as Bishop Angus Dun warns, that with congregationalism "there can readily come a spirit of local independence that loses a feeling for the organic quality of the church as indeed 'one body.' "[23] Yet Disciples would add also the reciprocal warning that it is equally true, as the long and eloquent record of Christian history bears out, that catholicity can easily be distorted into *that kind* of universal togetherness which breeds the perils and evils of external church authority, the demonic distortion of catholicity which made the Protestant reform necessary in the first place.

These, then, are two evils in church polity to be avoided: (1) *the kind* of congregationalism which loses the values of organic oneness is true catholicity, and (2) *the kind* of catholicity which eradicates the evangelical principle of "the free congregation of the free Word of God,"[24] as Karl Barth expresses it. Both evils represent distortions in the historical actualization of the church.

Similarly, there are two ecclesiastical truths to be preserved and realized: (1) a vigorous kind of congregational liberty which is keenly aware that its congregation is, first of all, an organic part of the church universal, and that its basic task is that of making its own life and practice, in its particular historical situation, a significant expression of the church universal; as Nathaniel Micklem of Great Britain contends, true independency means responsibility, not separation; and (2) the kind of worldwide oneness which not only does not stifle congregational liberty, but which undergirds and supports it. The immediate task confronting us in ecumenical growth is that of developing an inclusive structure of the worldwide church which will more adequately bring the unity of the church into a practical, visible reality, but which will also be wholly compatible with the ideal of Christian liberty.

As Disciples of Christ understand it, the current ecumenical movement represents a noble attempt to avoid these two basic evils and to secure and promote these two vital ecclesiastical principles, in the emerging structure of the Great Church. Disciples of Christ are therefore ardent promoters of the ecumenical effort toward greater organic unity. Their church polity is not at all a frozen one. So long as the values of liberty are preserved, they would submit that the particular nature of the structure of the church to be developed is a purely functional matter. They would happily adjust to that kind of structure which best promotes the growth of Christlike community and which preserves the true values of congregational liberty and catholicity. But Disciples insist that nothing short of organic unity will fulfill the demand of the truly catholic nature of the body of Christ.

Christocentrism and Liberalism

Finally, Disciples of Christ have sought to work out a balance in which the evangelical values of a Christ-centered theology are combined with a realistic understanding of the relative, historical character of all of man's spiritual achievements.

From the beginning, the Disciple movement has developed under the strong positive influence of the forces operative in liberal Protestantism. As a result, most Disciples have come to cherish the positive values wrought out in the liberal phase of Christianity's historical development, such as an antidogmatic way of holding religious convictions, a receptive attitude toward new ideas and toward change which promotes genuine growth, a positive appreciation of modern science and an awareness of the need for a creative synthesis between science and religion, a broad humanism, an emphasis on liberty, and on the historical relativism which determines and shapes the whole of human life and thought.

Yet Disciples have remained aware of the fact that modern liberalism has been too closely allied with the humanistic philosophy of renaissance culture, and that this has tended toward a restoration of ancient Greek naturalism, an understanding of reality which runs counter to the God-centeredness of the ancient Hebraic-Christian outlook.

At its prophetic center, therefore, the Disciple movement has developed under the power of a vigorous and dominant Christ-centered life and message. Disciples have thereby saved their movement from the floodtide of *that kind* of relativism which washes them away from the shores of the Eternal. Disciples have remained aware that religion needs to be anchored to the absolute, and that Christianity must be anchored to the supreme disclosure of God in Jesus Christ.

It is equally true, however, that liberalism has helped to prevent Disciples from falling prey to that fatal metamorphosis in which the emphasis on Christ is corrupted and distorted into dogmatism, a fate which has been the bane of orthodoxy, both Protestant and "Catholic." Disciples have vigorously maintained the distinction between Jesus Christ our Lord, on the one hand, and our human response to him, on the other. The lordship of God in Christ is the reality to which Christians are committed with absolute religious devotion; but their human response to this reality remains, at best, relative, both in terms of righteousness of life and understanding of truth. Try as they may, no Christian group can *possess* the truth, in any absolute sense. Angels in heaven may possess such intellectual ability, but we are human beings on earth, shaped and fashioned in manifold ways, throughout the whole of our beings, by the relative forces of historical existence. As Christians, it is our privilege, therefore to know the absolute, but not absolutely. By the grace of God it is given to us to have a knowledge of the absolute, but we have no absolute knowledge.

The two deadly evils in this theological area to be avoided, therefore, are (1) the frozen stalemate of doctrinal and ecclesiatical absolutism, on the one hand, and (2) the tragic loneliness and lostness of radical relativism, on the other. A happy combination of Christocentrism and liberalism has, in the main, enabled Disciples of Christ to develop a liberal, evangelical perspective which has avoided the absolutism of dogmatism and the humanistic self-sufficiency of radical liberalism.

This is the reason why Disciples of Christ refuse to allow any particular interpretation of Jesus Christ and his redemptive work to be placed in the confessional requirement of church membership. Disciples believe that we are redeemed by God acting in Jesus Christ, not merely by our human ideas about this divine activity. So long as this intellectual freedom does not become an occasion for theological obscurantism (which it sometimes has among Disciples of Christ), Disciples believe that it is a wholesome and stimulating aspect of Christian freedom. There is, therefore, considerable diversity in the Christologies which are found among Disciples of Christ.

There are several aspects about a Christian understanding of Christ on which all Disciples are agreed. They agree that the *figure* of Jesus stands at the vital center of Christianity, and that Jesus is "Lord and Savior," which means, primarily, that God has revealed himself to man in a unique and supreme way through the total event summed up by the phrase "Jesus Christ." Disciples believe also that nothing short of the idea of incarnation is adequate to describe this unique act of God in history.

In regard to the redemptive work of Christ, Disciples would submit that we are saved by the *whole* Christ, not merely by any one aspect of the total Christ event. There are several basic aspects of this redemptive act of God in Christ which all Disciples believe:

(1) The illuminating influence of Jesus as a teacher, and the uniqueness of his disclosure of the nature of the kingdom of God.

(2) The matchless beauty of his own incarnation of the principles of the kingdom which he proclaimed, the living portrayal, on the canvas of human flesh, of God's ideal of perfect love (sinlessness).

(3) The saving value of Jesus' death on the cross. The cross represents the consummation (in crisis) of the spirit of creative love, of which his entire life was an inspiring example.

Disciples have no crystallized theory of atonement, but for the most part, they are in agreement in rejecting the substitutionary view of Anselm, for this theory breaks the continuity between God's love toward us and Christ's death for us. All Disciples would agree that part of the saving value of Christ's death is to be found (a) in the supreme disclosure of the forgiving love of God in the cross of Christ, (b) in the moral influence which such love exercises on our hearts, leading us to faith and repentance, (c) in the assurance and trust generated in our hearts by one who has suffered as we suffer, "who in every respect has been tempted as we are, yet without sinning" (Hebrews 4:15), (d) in the release (through the resurrection) of the victorious power of Christlike love to conquer the forces which hold the human heart in the bondage of sin, and (e) in the supreme example of what God's love means, in the context of human existence.

Many Disciples would also insist that the cross means that God himself suffers and has taken into his own heart the burden of man's guilt, and by bearing it, in patient, longsuffering love, has overcome the judgment under which sinful man stands. But they would insist that commercial or political or economic analogies (which have been used in the history of the idea of the atonement) are inadequate to explain this act of God, and that only personal analogies can, with any adequacy, explain the meaning of the act of God in the cross of Christ. As a person who loves very deeply finds it in his power to respond in forgiving good will to all who have deliberately harmed him, so God who is the infinite source and fullness of such love, finds it in the power of his loving will to forgive his sinful children, to redeem the situation, and to effect reconciliation. This is the deepest meaning of the cross; it says that when man sins, God suffers, and that the suffering love of God is the only ultimate ground of man's salvation.

(4) The *reality* of the resurrection of Christ, without which Christ's death would indeed be incomplete. Like most Christians, Disciples are questing for a more adequate understanding of this

331

supreme event. The notion of a physical resusciation is obviously inadequate to describe what happened in the resurrection of Christ. Christ's resurrection is something vastly more than mere physical resuscitation, for it reaches out *beyond history,* into the eschatological realm. The resurrection of Christ is indeed our *entree* into eternal life.

(5) The universal lordship of the living Christ, who through the church, his body, "must reign until he has put all his enemies under his feet" (1 Corinthians 15:25).

(6) The divine-human nature of the church which is indeed the "body of Christ." Disciples find themselves in agreement with the current, realistic interpretation of this magnificent truth.

(7) The doctrine of the second coming of Christ as containing an important truth. Few, if any, Disciples would wish to maintain the truth of this doctrine in any literal sense, such as premillenniarian groups do. The doctrine does, however, point to an important aspect of the Christian hope, namely, to the final consummation of God's work of redemption. Since this consummation lies in the future and is yet to come, it can be regarded as a kind of "second coming" of Christ. But it is a second coming which is in continuous process of realization. Christ is *always* coming into our world; he is continuously exercising his lordship effectively, through his body, the church, so as to bring the process of the redemption of the world to completion.

Convictions of Ecumenical Value

It seems appropriate to conclude this statement with a brief list of fundamental convictions that Disciples of Christ hold which they believe to be of vital significance, in the formation of the Great Church, beyond our denominational and confessional groupings.

Disciple Thought in Protestant Perspective

I. The Principle of Free Discussion

The lifeblood of Discipledom flows from the heart of sincere and free theological inquiry and discussion. Disciples stand opposed to the principle of religious authoritarianism (creedalism and all other forms) root and branch, for such external authority not only fails to nurture, but actually stifles, the growth of authentic individuality, in freedom.

Disciples therefore believe that the only legitimate pathway to greater unity is for those who hold faith in Christ to think together, work together, worship together, and pray together, *within* the fellowship of Christian love; by so doing, we can all think our way more deeply into a truer understanding of the gospel of God in Christ, and thereby achieve, by God's grace, an increasingly greater unity in freedom. Disciples believe that any desirable plan of union must make provision for the maintenance of this principle of free discussion.

II. The Developmental Character of Christian Truth

Disciples believe that Christian understanding of the truth of the gospel will always be in process of vigorous growth, if it is as God intends it. It is a fundamental betrayal of the lure of truth in the call of God in the gospel ever to think that we have arrived at the fullness of knowledge of God's truth. Growth in a knowledge of the truth and in righteousness of life is normative in Christian experience.

This awareness of the developmental character of our human grasp of Christian truth is of vital significance for the further success of ecumenical Christianity. It will clothe all of us with intellectual as well as moral humility, and thereby save us from the sin of absolutizing our human interpretations of the gospel and placing the stumblingblock of dogmatism in the pathway to greater unity.

III. The Principle of Congregational Liberty

Disciples believe that the principle of "the free congregation of the free Word of God," when correctly understood, holds lasting value, and that any plan for church merger which fails to provide a significant place in its constitution for this liberty is, to this extent, not wholly desirable. Disciples will gladly submit to revision of their church structure, for the sake of achieving greater unity and catholicity; but they would insist that a truly catholic structuring of the life of the church will be one which (unlike traditional Catholicism) does make a secure place for the principle of congregational liberty so that no overhead church authority shall ride roughshod over the life and mind of the congregation of believers.

IV. God's Call to Greater Unity

Disciples of Christ are convinced that the Spirit of God is leading the followers of Christ into a greater unity than ever before known in Christian history. Disciples therefore desire to keep the witness to this ideal unity vitally alive, in all ecumenical endeavor and church mergers. It would be tragic, indeed, if the success of church mergers here and there (vitally important as they are) should eventuate in a kind of joy and complacency which might cause God's continuous call to perfect unity to grow, once again, feeble and weak. Disciples of Christ wish to keep this call of God vital and alive until the gladsome day of the perfect fullfillment of the beloved community.

V. The Transcendent Lordship of Christ

Disciples believe that Christ remains forever Lord of the household of the faithful, and that although it is imperative that we continually work our way toward greater confessional agreement, in ecumenical endeavor, such confessional agreement must never be permitted to blind our eyes to the *deeper* dimension of oneness which is already ours by our common acknowledgement of and commitment to Jesus Christ as Lord, however diversified our various responses to God's call in Christ may be. Important, therefore, as our Christologies are, they must never be permitted to replace, decentralize, or idolatrize Christ, who will always stand above us and over us, in judgment and in mercy. It will always be primarily because we are one with Christ that we are therefore bound in unity to one another.

NOTES

1. Thomas Campbell, *Declaration and Address* (Indianapolis: International Convention of Disciples of Chirst, 1949), p. 14.
2. Campbell, *op. cit.*, p. 16.
3. 1 Corinthians 12:12-31.
4. Campbell, *op. cit.*, p. 14.
5. *Ibid.*, p. 57.
6. *Ibid.*, p. 36.
7. *D. Martin Luthers Werke*, Bearbeitet von G. Buchwald, G. Kawerau, P. Pietsch (Weimar: Hermann Bohlaus, 1891), XII, 488.
8. Cf. *The Christian System*, p. 87.
9. Campbell, *op. cit.*, p. 17.
10. *Ibid.*
11. *Calvin's Calvinism*, trans. Henry Cole (London: Wertheim & Mackintosh, 1856), p. 11.
12. See "The Canons and Decrees of The Council of Trent," Session XIV, Nov. 25, 1551, Ch. 4.
13. *The Millennial Harbinger*, 1836, p. 232.
14. Martin Luther, *Ausgewählte Werke*, herausgegeben von H. H. Borcherdt & Georg Merz, dritte Auflage (München: Chr. Kaiser Verlag, 1957), IV, 207.
15. Luther, *op. cit.*, 1950, III, 269-70.
16. Luther, *op. cit.*, IV, 111.
17. *The Millenial Harbinger*, 1851, pp. 483-4.
18. *The Christian Baptist*, p. 175.
19. *The Christian Messenger*, V., p. 109.
20. *Ibid.*
21. *The Christian System*, p. 55.
22. *Ibid.*, p. 56.
23. Angus Dun, *Prospecting for a United Church* (New York: Harper & Brothers, 1948), p. 28.
24. In *Men's Disorder and God's Design*, I, 75.

INDEX OF SUBJECTS

INDEX OF SUBJECTS

INDEX OF SUBJECTS

INDEX OF SUBJECTS

INDEX OF NAMES

INDEX OF NAMES